DO NOT REMOVE FORMS FROM POCKET

Published under the auspices of
THE CENTER FOR JAPANESE AND KOREAN STUDIES
University of California, Berkeley

JAPANESE
RADICALS
REVISITED

JAPANESE RADICALS REVISITED

Student Protest in Postwar Japan

ELLIS S. KRAUSS

001

UNIVERSITY OF CALIFORNIA PRESS

Berkeley, Los Angeles, London

University of California Press
Berkeley and Los Angeles, California

University of California Press, Ltd.
London, England

Copyright © 1974 by
The Regents of the University of California

ISBN: 0-520-02467-2
Library of Congress Catalog Card Number: 73-78546

Designed by Jim Mennick
Printed in the United States of America

To Carol

CONTENTS

TABLES

. . . although the young today do have reasons for distrusting the older generation, anything that is worth doing involves their having to get old. What they are now is not so important as what they will be ten years from now. And if ten years from now they have become their own idea of what it is to be old, then what they are fighting for now will have come to nothing.

—STEPHEN SPENDER

. . . nearly every country has a version of the saying: 'He who is not a radical at twenty does not have a heart; he who still is one at forty does not have a head.'

—JEROME SKOLNIK,
citing S. M. Lipset

PREFACE

THE RESEARCH and writing of a book, especially one based on a Ph.D. dissertation, is in itself a "socialization process." Like all socialization processes it takes place in a social context and many individuals and institutions contribute to the final product. The process by which this book reached "adulthood" is no exception.

Professor Tsurumi Kazuko [1] of Sophia University made the research possible by generously providing me with the data that allowed me to conduct this follow-up study, and also aided me in many ways throughout the field research. Professors Nobutaka Ike, Kurt Steiner, and George Spindler, of Stanford University made numerous helpful suggestions that vastly improved the original draft. Professor Ike, my mentor in Japanese politics throughout my graduate career, gave unstintingly of his advice during the entire research and writing process. Professor Steiner made many suggestions and criticisms that strengthened the study's theoretical and methodological basis, and Professor Spindler made several useful comments as to its organization and applicability. I am extremely grateful to these individuals, not only for assistance in this endeavor, but for providing me with models of scholarship, integrity, and graciousness.

To the fifty-three respondents in my sample, especially to those who sat through the long depth-interviews, go my thanks for giving their valuable time to answer my questions patiently, sharing with me their beliefs and life-stories.

Many individuals and organizations also helped in the technical

---

[1] In the text, Japanese names are written with family name first, as is the custom in Japan. In the footnotes, the Japanese order is also followed except in cases where the author has published in English and the publisher followed the Western convention (thus, for her book in English Professor Tsurumi would be cited in the notes as Kazuko Tsurumi, but for her articles in Japanese as Tsurumi Kazuko). Because some English language journals follow the Japanese custom and others the Western, readers in doubt should refer to the bibliography where all the authors are listed family name first .

aspects of researching and preparing this book. The director, faculty, and staff of the Inter-University Center for Japanese Language Studies in Tokyo spent an entire year (1968–1969) trying to improve a slow student's command of the Japanese language prior to the beginning of the field research. During the following year, some of the Center's faculty, Mizutani Osamu and Otsubo Kazuo, and staff, Messrs. Noto and Nakazawa and Miss Kawamura, voluntarily gave of their own free time to help me in various ways to prepare, administer, or interpret the questionnaires and interviews. The Institute of International Relations, Sophia University, honored me with the title of "Visiting Scholar," and thus provided me with a base from which to conduct my field research.

Kondo Junko, Matsushita Chikaku, and Hirota Yukiko were conscientious interviewers, and the latter two assistants were also immensely helpful in the translation of the questionnaire and interview responses. My thanks also go to our dear friends Tetsuo and Kazuko Hisamori for introducing me to these two ladies and for helping me to locate some of the respondents.

Financial aid during the year spent in conducting field research was provided by a National Defense Foreign Language Fellowship and a grant from the Committee on International Studies, Stanford University. The Bureau for Faculty Research, Western Washington State College, provided manuscript-typing services, and Mr. Richard Adloff and Ms. Susan Peters of the University of California Press guided a novice through the process of turning a manuscript into a book.

Finally, my wife, Carol Draper Krauss, to whom this book is dedicated, not only shared with me the heights and depths of the years of research and writing, but also performed yeoman service as my editor in charge of the English language. I can think of no one to whom I'd rather give my love and rough drafts.

My heartfelt thanks to all these individuals and institutions for their aid. As with any socialization process, the final product is ultimately the individual's own: all errors of commission and omission are entirely my responsibility.

E.S.K.

Bellingham, Washington

INTRODUCTION: PROTEST
AND THE TREATY CRISES

ON THE night of June 18, 1960, hundreds of thousands of demonstrators, protesting the Japanese Diet's approval of the United States–Japan security treaty, surrounded the Diet building in the center of Tokyo. Radical students battled police, as they had on June 15 when a Tokyo University coed, Miss Kamba Michiko, was killed in a particularly bloody clash inside the Diet compound. The day after her death, Prime Minister Kishi Nobusuke was forced to cancel the planned state visit of President Eisenhower to Japan. Kishi himself, under pressure over his handling of the crisis from both the left wing demonstrating outside the Diet and from his own party, announced his resignation on the morning of June 23.[1]

A decade later, on June 23, 1970, Tokyo's streets again teemed with antitreaty protestors, as nationwide demonstrations involving three-quarters of a million people continued late into the night. Once again police and students clashed as the face of Kamba Michiko stared out of mourning portraits carried by some of the hundred thousand who attended 35 memorial rallies in Tokyo marking the tenth anniversary of her death.[2] In the Prime Minister's chair sat Satō Eisaku, younger brother of Kishi Nobusuke. An observer present at both "Ampo" (security treaty) crises might well note the similarities.

Probably even more striking, however, were the differences. Al-

---

[1] The most comprehensive account and analysis in English, as well as complete English and Japanese bibliography, on the 1960 crisis appears in George R. Packard, III, *Protest in Tokyo*. See also Robert A. Scalapino and Junnosuke Masumi, *Parties and Politics in Contemporary Japan*, ch. 5, and Teiji Yabe, "Background of Recent Mass Demonstrations."

[2] *Asahi Shimbun* (hereafter cited as *Asahi*), June 15, 1970, p. 3. The figure of 740,000 demonstrators in one day is cited by *The Japan Times*, June 24, 1970, p. 1. The *Asahi* of the same day (p. 1) gives 770,000 as the number participating.

though the numbers demonstrating on one particular day in 1970 exceeded those at the largest demonstration in 1960, the demonstrations were generally orderly and had little of the salience or intensity of ten years before: the press noted the lack of a "feeling of urgency" (*seppakukan*) on the part of the demonstrators.[3] Labor strikes throughout the month of June, 1960, involved a record number of workers; ten years later only half as many unions participated in brief walkouts.[4] Furthermore, many of the faces seen in the crowds of enthusiastic demonstrators ten years before were missing now. Shimizu Ikutarō, leader of the Japanese peace movement and the 1960 campaign against the security treaty, had long since separated himself from the movement and announced his disaffection. Interviews with leaders and citizens affiliated with the Koe Naki Koe no Kai (Voiceless Voices Society), a citizens' group active in the 1960 struggle and a forerunner of the Japanese new left, brought out the fact that 1970 participants tended not to be those who had participated in 1960.[5] Despite the larger crowds, Oda Makoto, a leader of the antiwar new-left organization Beiheiren, voiced the disappointment of some individuals and groups over their inability to mobilize their fellow demonstrators of 1960:

> Anyway, why are the people so immobile today compared with 10 years ago? . . .
>
> Ten years ago . . . an 'Ampo' storm was raging in Japan, if I may use a bit of exaggeration. For instance, various individuals and organizations issued statements against Ampo, met in gatherings and demonstrated.
>
> Where are they now? What are they doing? I sometimes wonder. . . .[6]

The 1960 Ampo struggle can validly be called a "crisis," an overt challenge to governmental legitimacy, "in which passions are aroused

---

[3] *Asahi*, June 22, 1970, p. 11. Another article on the demonstrations of June 23 had a subheadline, "Lack the Suffocating Air of 10 Years Ago" (*Jūnenmae no Ikigurushisa Naku*), and described the relaxed atmosphere of the demos; *Ashai*, June 24, 1970, p. 3. Takashi Oka in the *New York Times*, June 16, 1970, also noted that the demonstrations were "relatively quiet" despite the throwing of gasoline bombs at the police by students. Many of the reasons for the differences are analyzed in Ōmori Shigeo, "June, 1970."

[4] On the 1960 strikes, see Packard, pp. 258–261. *The Japan Times*, June 24, 1970, p. 5, says that of the industrial unions in the left-wing Sōhyō labor federation, 47 and 57 participated, respectively, in the two major strikes of 1960. In 1970, only 26 participated and some of the walkouts were as brief as an hour.

[5] *Asahi* (evening edition), June 17, 1970, p. 8. On Shimizu's disaffection, see *Asahi*, June 11, 1970, p. 10, and "Notes by the Editor" to part III, *Journal of Social and Political Ideas in Japan*, II, 1, April 1964, p. 85. On other 1960 participants who did not participate in 1970, and their reasons, see *The Japan Times*, June 23, 1970, p. 12.

[6] *The Japan Times*, June 23, 1970, p. 12. This statement originally appeared in an article written by Oda.

and the very survival of the system is often at stake." [7] In 1970, the survival of the political system was never in question, nor did the leadership change. Prime Minister Satō and his cabinet calmly ignored the demonstrations, controlled the demonstrators, and remained in office. The 1960 Ampo struggle has been described rather dramatically by one scholar as the greatest movement in Japan's political history,[8] an event that marked the high tide of the left wing in Japanese politics. The 1970 one seemed merely the ritualized tenth-anniversary observance of that crucial crisis in the postwar Japanese political system.

The 1960 Ampo crisis was the most intense confrontation between the two political communities that emerged in Japanese society after the Second World War. Japan's political culture has been seen by some scholars to have polarized into left and right in the late 1940s. Although distinguishable social and political groups tended to cluster at each pole—intellectuals, students, labor unions, and the Socialist and Communist parties in the "progressive" (kakushin) camp, and business, shopkeepers, farmers, and the ruling Liberal Democratic Party in the "conservative" (hoshu) camp—as Watanuki Joji has pointed out, the basic conflict between the camps rested primarily on differences in fundamental values rather than on differences in occupation or status. This characteristic led Watanuki to refer to Japan's "cultural politics." [9]

The magnitude of this split in the political culture did not solely result from the extent of the differences dividing the two subcultures. The fundamental nature of the values upon which they diverged, as well as the perception of these values as being interrelated, contributed to the polarization. The two subcultures differed in regard to crucial political beliefs: the nature and extent of political authority, the political process and the individual's relationship to it, and the need for military forces. The beliefs of each side regarding these fundamental political questions were perceived as parts of an interconnected whole.[10]

The conservative subculture, through its superiority in numbers and power, maintained an electoral dominance, and in the process

---

[7] Sidney Verba, "Comparative Political Culture," p. 555.

[8] Scalapino and Masumi, p. 125.

[9] Joji Watanuki, "Patterns of Politics in Present-Day Japan," pp. 456–460. Watanuki also discusses the polarization of Japanese political culture in his Gendai Seiji To Shakai Hendō (Contemporary Politics and Social Change), pp. 230–231. Herbert Passin, "The Sources of Protest in Japan," contains an excellent historical and sociological analysis of the origins of the two subcultures.

[10] Passim, p. 393. Watanuki sums up the most basic fissure as the lack of agreement over the "basic principle of rights and duties, the relationship between ruler and ruled. . . ." in Gendai Seiji To Shakai Hendō, p. 231.

contributed to a fundamental stability in the system. However, issues in any way relating to the basic value differences separating the two subcultures—issues concerning foreign affairs and defense, public safety and police, and the revival of prewar traditional ideology,[11] issues which together are summed up as the problem of "reverse course" or turning the clock back to prewar days—were easily generalized beyond the specific issue involved and mobilized the progressives to extra-parliamentary opposition to the government, bringing the two sub-cultures into intense and open battle. In the 1950s, Japan witnessed a series of large and sometimes violent clashes between the two political camps: "Bloody May Day" of 1952, the Subversive Activities Prevention Law and Police Duties Performance Law controversies, and the Sunakawa Incident.[12] This decade of struggle culminated in the 1960 crisis. Its greater magnitude and intensity can be explained by the range of issues and value differences it evoked. The treaty itself involved questions of rearmament and alliance with the U.S., and Kishi's "snap vote" (police had entered the Diet building and carried off Socialist Diet members who were sitting in, in an attempt to block the treaty's passage, and a rump session of the Diet composed solely of LDP members then proceeded to extend the session and pass the treaty) turned the treaty issue into a "crisis of democracy" over the decision-making process and governmental responsiveness to the people. Throughout the crisis, the use of the police and Kishi's background and record brought back memories of prewar days to the left.[13]

In all of the left-right confrontations, but especially in 1960, the Japanese student movement played a key role in the "progressive" subculture. Always the "shock troops" of the left, adding tension and escalating incidents with their active demonstrations and battles with the police, the student radicals of Zengakuren both originated and catalyzed incidents at key points in the Ampo struggle. At every crucial juncture, Zengakuren students were in the forefront of the crisis, often changing its nature by their actions. Student radicals broke into the Diet compound on November 27, 1959, setting the stage for the later escalation of the conflict. Zengakuren activists attempted

---

11 Kyōgoku Jun-ichi, *Gendai Minshusei To Seijigaku* (Contemporary Democracy and Political Science), pp. 225–226. On the ability of the conservatives to maintain their dominance, given the polarized political culture and the nature of Japanese society, see Scott C. Flanagan, "The Japanese Party System in Transition."

12 On "Bloody May Day" of 1952, see Rōyama Masamichi, *Yomigaeru Nihon* (Japan Revived), pp. 160–162, and Packard, p. 25; on the Subversive Activities Prevention Law, see Rōyama, pp. 158–160; the Police Duties Performance Law controversy is discussed in D. C. S. Sissons, "The Dispute over Japan's Police Law," and in Packard, pp. 101–105; and see Packard, pp. 131–134, also on the Sunakawa Incident and case.

13 Packard, pp. 47–54, 242–251, and ch. 10.

to prevent Prime Minister Kishi from leaving Haneda airport for the United States to sign the treaty in January 1960, and kept the issues of the ratification of the treaty and government repression constantly alive with demonstrations and clashes with the police from April to June 1960. At the height of the crisis, it was the students who surrounded Press Secretary Hagerty's car when he came to prepare the way for Eisenhower's visit and who clashed with police in the battle in which Kamba Michiko died, causing both the cancellation of Eisenhower's visit and a resurgence of opposition to the treaty and the Kishi government.[14]

Four years before the Free Speech Movement at Berkeley portended the waves of student protest in the United States, Japanese students had proved the potential power of students and student movements in opposition politics. In Japan itself, the experience of the 1960 treaty crisis was so salient as to create a generation of students who, to this day, are referred to as the "Ampo generation" and whose leaders' names became household words in Japan.

What has become of these student activists of 1960? Have they continued their militant and aggressive role as "professional revolutionaries," exhorting a new generation of students to duplicate their own efforts? Are they now among the thousands still expressing their opposition to the treaty and their political alienation, albeit through peaceful and nonviolent protest? Or, entering adult society and careers, did they undergo a transformation of political belief and behavior and observe the second Ampo struggle, as did those whom Oda Makoto bewailed, with indifference or inactivity? Do they still hold beliefs about the ends and means of political action that place them in a subculture of the left? The study that follows seeks to provide answers to these questions and others concerning the background and fate of the 1960 Ampo generation of students. Its method consists of a report of the results of research on a sample of former Japanese students, most of whom took some part in the 1960 antitreaty struggle and a few of whom played important roles in that crisis. The importance of such research lies in its value as a case study of the process of political socialization and as a study of the relationship between society and polity in Japan.

---

14 *Ibid.*, pp. 94–101, 156–167, 173–178, 226–228, 262–270, and 285–302; Harada Hisato, "The Anti-Ampo Struggle"; Nobushige Ukai, "Whither Students of Today"; Scott C. Flanagan, "Zengakuren and the Postwar Japanese Student Movement," pp. 236–242.

1
STUDENTS, POLITICS, AND ADULTHOOD

THE QUESTION of what Japanese student activists become after graduation, particularly the fate of the 1960 Ampo generation of students after assuming adult roles in society, has been widely discussed by scholars and journalists in the United States and Japan. In Japan, radiobroadcasts, books, and magazine articles have traced many of the leaders and followers of Zengakuren at the time of the 1960 Ampo crisis and described their postgraduation occupations, thoughts, and behavior. Although most of the articles present examples of former activists who have not abandoned their ideals even after joining large companies, and depict others who are still revolutionary in thought and deed, many have also described dramatic and complete changes in political belief and behavior in the intervening years since Ampo. The most famous case, and one frequently cited, is that of Karoji Kentarō, Zengakuren chairman during the 1960 crisis, who became associated with a right-wing businessman after graduation, abandoned his radical beliefs, and now runs a "Let's Go Sailing Club" in Tokyo.[1]

The cases of Karoji and other noted examples of the lapsing or turnabout of former activists' beliefs and activity after graduation have come to be subsumed under the label of *"tenkō." Tenkō* is the

---

[1] See, for example, Mainichi Shimbun Shakaibu (Ampo Gakusei Han) (ed.), *Ampo: Gekidō no Kono Jūnen* (The Security Treaty: These Ten Years of Upheaval), 9–23; Tachibana Takashi, "Rokujūnen Ampo Eiyū no Eikō to Hisan" (The Glory and the Tragedy of the 1960 Ampo Heroes); Ino Kenji, *Zengakuren*, pp. 163–188; Mainichi Shimbunsha (ed.), *Suchūdento Pawā* (Student Power), pp. 66–75. The last-mentioned source describes a TBS broadcast concerning former leaders three years after Ampo. The most recent articles on the subject that have appeared are in the series "Gakusei Kaikyū, Sono Konnichiteki Kōzō: Katsudōka no Kiseki" (The Student Class, Its Present Structure: The Tracks of the Activists), which contains less extreme accounts of the postgraduate experiences of both the 1960 generation and more recent graduates.

general phenomenon of "ideological change" or "ideological transformation," the study of which has a long tradition in Japan. The term became widely used before the war, perhaps somewhat euphemistically, to refer to the recanting of Marxists under the threat and actuality of government pressure—arrest, imprisonment, and even torture. Through the work of the Science of Thought Study Group (Shisō no Kagaku Kenkyūkai), composed of influential postwar Japanese intellectuals and scholars, the study of *tenkō* was broadened to include many types of change in beliefs in both prewar and postwar Japan.[2] The turnabout of former student activists in the postwar period has occasionally been called *"shūshoku tenkō,"* [3] or "employment conversion." This term can refer to changes in belief and behavior after graduation and employment, or to the frequently noted tendency of many Japanese student radicals to stop demonstrating in their senior year in college so as not to jeopardize their employment chances and then quietly to take jobs in business and the professions.

Conventional folk wisdom that student radicalism is merely a passing phase of youth, and the publicity given the dramatic *tenkō* of some former Zengakuren leaders, have together given rise to a widespread belief in Japan about the inevitable fate of the Ampo student activists. One American journalist in Japan has noted what I myself became aware of in conversations in Japan: many Japanese believe that "the leaders of that youthful rebellion have now largely taken their ordained places in the middle ranks of the Mitsubishi or Mitsui empires, or are working their way up in the prestige [sic] Finance or Foreign Ministries." [4]

American scholars who have studied the Japanese student movement have by no means challenged this belief. Robert Lifton in his famous psychohistorical study of Japanese youth's search for "selfhood" and "social commitment" (*shutaisei*),[5] describes in detail the extreme and frequent role changes of one former student after graduation. He finds that Japanese youth must face two great problems, first "totalism" (or psychological extremism) and, later, postgraduation loss of beliefs: "The second great problem, that of 'moral backsliding,' involves giving up one's ideals in order to make one's peace with organized society. . . . In this sense, every youth is expected to have,

2 Shisō no Kagaku Kenkyūkai, *Tenkō* (Ideological Transformation). In English, see Shunsuke Tsurumi, "Cooperative Research on Ideological Transformation"; Kazuko Tsurumi, *Social Change and the Individual,* ch. 1; Patricia Golden Steinhoff, "Ideology and Societal Integration in Prewar Japan."

3 Mainichi Shimbun Shakaibu, p. 15.

4 Donald H. Shannon, "The Student Revolution in Japan," p. 5.

5 Robert Lifton, "Youth and History: Individual Change in Postwar Japan," pp. 260–290.

and every youth expects to have, an experience of *tenkō* on graduating from his university and 'entering society. . . .' " [6]

In his book on student movements, Lewis Feuer ends his chapter on the Zengakuren by citing a *Japan Times* article on the present occupations of former student leaders of 1960. He observes that "political action founded on obscure emotions of generational rebellion tends to terminate with the end of that generational phase." [7] The article to which Feuer refers is based on a Japanese magazine item that quotes security officials, discussing the number of former leaders of the 1960 anti-security-treaty students who remained revolutionaries, as saying, "You don't need five fingers to count them." [8]

In his 1963 article, "Japanese Students and Japanese Politics," Philip Altbach also observes, first, the tendency of many students involved in student demonstrations to "make their peace with the system and become cogs in the corporate wheels. . . ," and second, that Zengakuren activists have not continued to be active within established political parties after graduation but rather have "confined themselves to academic writing or withdrawn from political life altogether." [9]

The amount of attention devoted to the *shūshoku tenkō* of former student activists in Japan is remarkable when compared with the attention accorded the equivalent problem in other countries. Despite a burgeoning comparative literature on student movements in Western nations and developing countries during the last decade, hardly anyone has considered the postgraduate experiences of student activists. A few newspaper articles on the subject have recently appeared in the United States, the most thorough being a follow-up by a free-lance writer of some of the leaders and organizers of the Free Speech Movement at Berkeley in 1964. In this article, which appeared in the *New York Times Magazine*,[10] the writer notes the hope, or fear, of many that since student radicalism springs from youthful energy and free time, it will give way after graduation to an acceptance of the social order. Surprisingly, he finds that this expectation was not fulfilled in the case of the former FSM members whom he interviewed:

> I was surprised to find that none of the rank-and-file members or the lower-echelon organizers I talked to were radicals turned bourgeois. This pattern was more pronounced, if somewhat less surprising, among the former Free Speech leaders I talked to, all members of the steering committee. Not

    [6] *Ibid.*, p. 285.
    [7] Lewis S. Feuer, *The Conflict of Generations*, p. 214.
    [8] *The Japan Times*, December 16, 1967, p. 5.
    [9] Philip Altbach, "Japanese Students and Japanese Politics," pp. 183 and 187, respectively.
    [10] Wade Greene, "Where are the Savios of Yesteryear?."

only have they remained as radical as ever in their political perspectives, but some would appear to have become considerably more radical and all are still very active politically.[11]

Related articles, based on interviews with former students involved in the 1968 Democratic Convention protests and battles [12] and with former students at the University of Washington,[13] disclose similar results. Of the radicals, although some had become disenchanted with political action, a few had become less radical, and many were now trying to work through more established political channels, most remained as politically concerned and left-wing as during their student days.

The articles referred to above that have appeared in Japan and the United States concerning the problem of student activists after graduation share common limitations, however, which make any conclusions or genuine comparisons about the maintenance or change in belief and behavior of former student radicals extremely tenuous. Whether by scholars or journalists, these articles have been based either on impressionistic evidence or on interviews with only a few individuals, and in the latter case the criteria for selection of the interviewees are not usually clear. Furthermore, because of the varying length of time after graduation at which the interviews took place and the lack of distinction made between types of students—leaders, organizers, or even bystanders—it is difficult to compare reports or make cross-national generalizations. Finally, almost all the reports have been descriptive, making no attempt to explain the conditions under which a change in beliefs and behavior after graduation has occurred and those under which it has not.

The only scholarly, systematic, empirical research on this topic of which I am aware is the work, now in progress, of James N. Fendrich and his associates.[14] In a follow-up study of former civil-rights activists and other students at American universities in the South in the early 1960s, he found that the former activists were heavily concentrated in professional and human-service occupations, seeming to

---

11 *Ibid.*, p. 36.

12 Daniel St. Albin Greene, "Chicago Epilog: What 'The Kids' Think, Three Years Later."

13 Grant Fjermedal, "The Movement . . . on the Wane, but Not Forgotten," and Ross Anderson, "Missing Marchers: Still Concerned but No Longer Active in Demonstrations."

14 James M. Fendrich, Alison T. Tarleau and Ronald J. Simons, "Marching to a Different Drummer: The Occupational and Political Orientations of Former Student Activists." My thanks to Prof. Fendrich for a copy of this paper and a revised and updated version with the same title, as well as for personal communications concerning his research.

reject occupations offering status or financial reward in favor of those that promised autonomy, humanistic service, and creativity. Most identified themselves as radicals or liberals, followed political events in the media, voted, did political-organization work, and were members of leftist, antiwar, civil-liberties, political-party, and environmental groups. Many were still participating in demonstrations or illegal political activities. In short, the former civil-rights activists had maintained their political commitments but were now attempting to reconcile them with the pressure of making a living.

No systematic research has been conducted in other countries that can be compared with the Fendrich data. These data and the reports from the infrequent newspaper articles about American student activists after graduation make the often-cited conversions in Japan all the more intriguing. The importance of doing cross-national research on this topic far outweighs the dubious rewards of confirming or denying popular belief or delving into a fascinating human-interest story. The problem of whether, and under what conditions, student radicals change upon entering adult society is integrally connected with two related theoretical concerns of social and political science: the origins and meaning of youthful protest and the explanation of the process by which political identities are formed.

YOUTHFUL PROTEST: MATURATION VS. GENERATION

When do protest groups of young people arise? What is the social significance of student movements and the generational conflict they reflect? Do political groupings based on age persist in adulthood, or do the youthful protesters upon entering adult society adapt themselves to the values and norms of the previous generations? A number of scholars [15] have recently pointed out that in attempting to answer questions such as these, social theorists have advanced two opposing general hypotheses: one I will call the "maturational" model, and the other the "generational" model.

The "maturational" model is represented by the work of functionalists like S. N. Eisenstadt, whose theory of the origins of youth groups in modern society is probably the most highly developed in the literature.[16] We shall be referring often to his theory in this study. Eisenstadt sees in the rise of self-conscious youth groups and oppositional movements a response to social change. In modern society, they

---

[15] See Ted Goertzel, "Generational Conflict and Social Change," and Seymour Martin Lipset and Everett Carll Ladd, Jr., "The Political Future of Activist Generations."

[16] S. N. Eisenstadt, *From Generation to Generation.*

result from industrialization or cultural contact in which a discontinuity comes to exist between the values and norms of adulthood and those of the family. The chief discontinuity is between universalistic criteria for allocating roles in the adult sphere of modern society and the particularistic norms of the family. These terms, of course, constitute one set of Parsons' pattern variables in which universalistic criteria refer to general role expectations for behavior applicable to all persons with whom the individual interacts without regard to membership in specific groups or familial or other personal ties; particularist criteria refer to expectations that the proper way to behave is "in a special way towards other people according to their *particular* relation to the individual." [17] Citizenship in modern society or the doctor's treatment of his patients would be examples of universalistic role expectations, whereas relations between relatives would be an example of particularistic role relations. Other pattern variables, such as the specificity or diffuseness of roles or the criteria of achievement or ascription, are also brought into Eisenstadt's analysis, but only as they relate to the universalistic-particularistic focus of the study. The pattern variables are of course dichotomous "ideal types," and all societies contain elements of both universalistic and particularistic expectations. However, in modern societies, universalistic criteria will be the "principles of overall integration of societies," and "the criteria which organize the membership in a total society and the overall interrelations between the various subsectors of the society. . . ." [18] In industrial-bureaucratic societies, for example, the universalistic, achievement norms of the workplace contrast sharply with the particularistic and ascriptive norms of the family, causing strains in youth. The transition to adulthood requires youth to learn the universalistic standards of action characteristic of relationships beyond the family, and yet this very transition may threaten emotional security.[19] Relationships with age-mates in youth groups or youth movements provide emotional security and, at the same time, relations of wider scope than the family. The youth group is both a defense against the anticipated new roles of adult society and a preparation for them. In the two types of politically rebellious youth groups that he analyzes, Eisenstadt indeed finds a discrepancy between the family, identified with the reactionary, conservative, authoritarian, or traditional old order, and the values of adult institutions in societies undergoing change. The German youth movement, for instance, arose in a context of

---

17 *Ibid.*, pp. 22–23, note; see also pp. 116–117, where the universalistic-particularistic distinction is further described.
18 *Ibid.*, p. 118.   19 *Ibid.*, p. 45.

industrial development where the family was still "based internally on a relatively strong authoritarian and ascriptive value, and strongly oriented towards the old traditional collectivity images." [20]

Other functionalists have applied Eisenstadt's theory to the United States. Parsons, in an analysis of youth in American society in the 1950s, accepts Eisenstadt's model and sees youth peer groups as the vehicle for expressing both conformity to, and alienation from, the strains arising from the transition from the family to modern adult society.[21] Although Eisenstadt is ambiguous when it comes to "deviant" or rebellious youth movements, generally he and the other functionalists see the youth group or movement as a bridge between family and the adult world, a bridge performing integrative functions for modern, industrial society. Youth groups and movements provide temporary but necessary means by which youth can later adjust themselves to adult society. Thus, while Parsons admitted there were strains in the American society of the 1950s, he considered that these were relatively minimal and that such youthful protest and alienation as did exist was not a basic opposition but a preparation for acceptance of the system as institutionalized.[22]

Karl Mannheim's classic discussion of generational conflict [23] may be contrasted with the functionalists' view of the ephemeral nature of protest in youth. Mannheim, like the functionalists, sees generations and youth movements as a product of social change. This change may bring about a common generational perspective among those influenced by the same intellectual and social trends. Within the same generation, there may exist different generational units: youth who share common experiences but respond to them in different ways. Thus a liberal and a conservative generational unit may exist within the same generation and even be antagonistic toward one another precisely *because* they are oriented toward each other and are responding differently to the same common historical and social situation. In opposition to the functionalists, however, Mannheim sees generational differences and the impressions of youth as long-lasting and persisting into adulthood. The later development of human consciousness is shaped by the early experiences of youth, the "primary stratum of experiences from which all others receive their meaning." [24] To Mannheim, therefore, the basic worldview acquired in one's youth persists into adulthood, as do differences between generations. The identifications formed by

---

20 *Ibid.*, p. 318.
21 Talcott Parsons, "Youth in the Context of American Society," especially, pp. 129–140.
22 *Ibid.*, pp. 139–140.
23 Karl Mannheim, "The Problem of Generations."
24 *Ibid.*, pp. 298–299.

historical and cultural conditions prior to entrance into adulthood or into new adult roles have a formative influence generally resistant to adaptation to specific adult environments.

We may also classify as "generationalists" some of those who have studied student movements in the United States and Western Europe. In this category, Frank Pinner's work is explicitly a criticism of the "maturational" view that the political activity of youth necessarily represents transitional adaptation to adult society.[25] Pinner studied student organizations in Western European countries and concluded that those organizations cannot be considered as merely agents of anticipatory socialization to adult roles. The transition from childhood or adolescence to adulthood may be characterized by acting out roles as a student in preparation for adult roles, but

> . . . this process can operate only if role models are available, and if the available models are acceptable to the young person. Anticipatory socialization is, thus, the "normal" process in societies and among social strata undergoing little change. But in changing societies, role models may become unavailable or their images may become blurred. Moreover, since economic change is usually accompanied by changes in value patterns and behavior forms such role models as are available to the student may become unacceptable to him.[26]

Richard Flacks's attempt to update Eisenstadt to account for the rise of student protest in the United States in the 1960s leads him to a conclusion similar to Pinner's, but with the added twist that the roles students seek in opposition to adult society may be patterned on those in their own families. Flacks, like Eisenstadt, finds a "sharp disjunction between the values and expectations prevailing in the occupational sphere and those embodied in the family." [27] He sees the discrepancy in the United States as resulting, however, not from traditional, authoritarian, or conservative family values, but from *new* patterns of relationships in the middle-class American family—egalitarian, permissive, non-achievement-oriented relationships—which contrast with the rationalized, hierarchical, competitive relations in the "multiversity" and in modern corporate and governmental bureaucracies. Hence, student activists seek through protest to fulfill the values of their parents rather than to rebel against them. Although Pinner and Flacks, like Eisenstadt, see social change as causing discontinuities and strains in the transition to adulthood, they reject the

---

25 Frank A. Pinner, "Student Trade Unionism in France, Belgium, and Holland: Anticipatory Socialization and Role-Seeking."

26 *Ibid.*, p. 194; emphasis in the original.

27 Richard Flacks, "The Revolt of the Advantaged: Exploration of the Roots of Student Protest."

assumption that such a transition period must necessarily be integrative. Rather, they see the possibility of ideological protest and "role-seeking" during the university years. These involve rejecting and attempting to supplant or change the adult role structure that exists, rather than adopting its values and norms.

It is possible that the beliefs of youth persist into adulthood at least in part because students select adult environments compatible with those beliefs. Theodore Newcomb interviewed a sample of students at Bennington College between 1935 and 1939. In 1960 and 1961 he reinterviewed most of them, and compared their political attitudes (conservative versus liberal) then and now. The purpose of the study was to test the hypothesis, which he found confirmed, that those who had changed their attitudes in college (becoming more or less liberal or conservative) tended to seek out environments after graduation that would provide reinforcement for that changed attitude.[28]

The "maturational" and "generational" models thus contain basic differences in their interpretations of youth, protest, and the prospect of change in adulthood. The "maturational" model sees (1) youthful protest as a passing phase which aids the transition to adult society, and (2) entrance into adult roles as influential in bringing about changes in belief and behavior, usually into conformity with dominant adult roles. The "generational" model sees youthful belief and behavior as resulting from historical and social trends in a formative pre-adult period, during which basic patterns are set that persist through adulthood, in part because adult roles and environments are selected which support the earlier patterns. The "generational" approach does not completely preclude the possibility of change in adulthood. However, it views such change as not affecting basic orientations and resulting from the development of general historical and social trends, not from conformity to specific adult roles.

Ironically, some of the very scholars who have recently made us aware of these differing approaches to the problem of students and youth movements and their implications have merely added to the "debate" rather than resolved it. Goertzel has compared the differences between such functionalists as Eisenstadt and such generationalists as Mannheim and argues that Mannheim's approach, which does not expect youth to adjust to existing institutions, is more useful for explaining the political role of youth today because youth seems to reject the values associated with adult technological society.[29] Lipset and Ladd, on the other hand, basing their argument on surveys of college graduates of varying ages in the United States, conclude that

---

[28] Theodore Newcomb, "The Persistence and Regression of Changed Attitudes."
[29] Goertzel, pp. 345–347.

the effects of postgraduate experience and aging seem stronger than the radicalizing impact of the college environment in youth.[30]

A similar divergence of views about the relative impact of early versus adult experience exists in the literature on political socialization, the more general process of which the study of students and youthful protest is a part.

POLITICAL SOCIALIZATION AND ADULTHOOD

The study of political socialization is as old as the study of society and politics: witness the premise of Plato's *Republic* that a particular type of polity requires a particular type of training for its citizens. What is new is the systematic study of political socialization as part of the postwar political-science "revolution"—employing formal concepts, attempting to isolate and relate variables, and verifying hypotheses through replicable empirical methods. The study of political socialization in this sense began with the seminal work of Herbert Hyman.[31] But it was Gabriel Almond who placed political socialization into both a comparative perspective and a more general theoretical framework. Almond identified political socialization as one of the seven functions performed in all political systems, and one "basic to the whole field of political analysis," because it produces fundamental orientations in society toward the political system, its roles, and policy.[32]

The importance of political socialization to an understanding of the operation of the political system has been indicated in the intervening years since Hyman's and Almond's early work by the voluminous literature, of ever-increasing methodological sophistication, on the subject.[33] Political socialization has become one of the major subfields of political science. Although most political scientists would agree that political socialization is the process in which orientations

---

[30] Lipset and Ladd, pp. 82–84; they do, however, concede that committed activists may be an exception to this generalization.

[31] Herbert Hyman, *Political Socialization.*

[32] Gabriel A. Almond and James S. Coleman (ed.), *The Politics of the Developing Areas,* p. 31.

[33] Reference to this large body of work must of necessity be selective. Richard E. Dawson and Kenneth Prewitt, *Political Socialization;* Fred I. Greenstein, *Children and Politics;* Robert D. Hess and Judith V. Torney, *The Development of Political Attitudes in Children;* and Kenneth P. Langton, *Political Socialization,* are the major single-volume works of a general nature. Richard E. Dawson did yeoman service with his concise summary of concepts, hypotheses, and research in the field that appeared in "Political Socialization." Recently, three excellent anthologies of more specific research have appeared: Roberta S. Sigel (ed.), *Learning About Politics,* Edward S. Greenberg (ed.), *Political Socialization,* and Norman Adler and Charles Harrington, *The Learning of Political Behavior.*

toward politics are developed, no commonly agreed upon definition of
the term has been accepted in the field despite its extensive literature.
Various definitions of political socialization have emphasized cultural
transmission, role-learning, or the development of personality; many
scholars have stressed system consequences; still others have preferred
the perspective of individual learning. The intentional inculcation of
beliefs and values has been seen as the core of the process in some
cases, whereas others view unintentional learning as the key.[34]

My own definition of political socialization is intentionally broad:
the process by which political beliefs and behavior are acquired, maintained, and changed throughout the life cycle.[35] This definition is
broad in three senses. First, it does not identify one particular conceptual or methodological approach as the essence of the socialization
process. In other words, given the diverse perspectives—cultural, psychological, and sociological—and emphases that have been brought to
bear in political-socialization research, and the potential contributions
of each to our understanding of the process, it seems to me extremely
unwise at this stage in the development of the field to force political-
socialization research by definition into one narrow channel. We thus
also leave open the possibility that certain emphases and approaches
may be more or less useful for studying different aspects, or even stages,
of the political-socialization process.

Second, the definition is wider than most in that it specifically
includes *both* subjective orientations *and* behavior as legitimate end
products of the political-socialization process. Most definitions of
political socialization have emphasized only beliefs, values, and orientations and have assumed a close correspondence between these and
behavior. This type of analysis is deficient on a number of grounds.
To begin with, as is argued in a recent case study of directed political
change in Cuba, such an approach excludes from consideration cases
where the goal of the elite is the directed transformation of behavior,
conflicts with most anthropological research, and fails to provide for
"a dynamic relation between behavioral change and attitudinal
change." [36] Moreover, the actual correspondence between subjective
orientations and behavior is an empirical question. One of the most
neglected areas of political science is the study of the actual conditions
under which subjective orientations and specific types of behavior do

[34] Dawson, and Langton, contain cogent summaries of the differences in definition and approach and the issues involved.

[35] For another broad definition and interesting discussion of the political socialization literature, see David Easton and Jack Dennis, *Children in the Political
System*, chs. 2 and 3. Some of my ideas concerning political socialization are strongly
in accord with those of Easton and Dennis, although I did not discover their work
until after completing the original draft of this chapter.

[36] Richard R. Fagen, *The Transformation of Political Culture in Cuba*, p. 10,
pp. 4–6, and footnotes 4–7 and 9, pp. 230–231.

or do not coincide. Political socialization should therefore include as a subject of study the origins of political behavior as well as of political beliefs.

The third and most important sense in which my definition is broad concerns the time span covered by the political-socialization process. Most studies of political socialization have concentrated on the process of the acquisition and development of political beliefs in children and adolescents rather than in adults, although usually with the caveat that the process is life-long. I included the phrase "acquired, maintained, and changed throughout the life cycle" to emphasize that political socialization is also a process whereby new belief and behavior patterns may be acquired and earlier belief and behavior patterns may be reinforced, modified, or changed, in adulthood.

Indeed, basic to the goals of this study is the assumption that political scientists should do more than include adulthood in their definitions: they should also conduct empirical studies of adult political socialization. In a recent critical review of the field and some of its major works, William R. Schonfeld [37] has pointed out the disparity between the way the concept of political socialization has been conventionally used (its denotative definition) and statements as to what ought to be the proper focus of inquiry in the field (connotative definition): whereas "almost all empirical work in the field has been done on children," [38] practically all theorists agree that the focus of theoretical research should not be limited to children.

There are good reasons to account for the belated recognition by political scientists, though more in their words than in their practice, of the need for greater attention to adult political socialization. These same reasons demonstrate the theoretical significance of a case study of the postgraduate experiences of activist students. The payoff in political-socialization research is to explain the pattern of political beliefs and behavior of adults, not children. Unlike the child psychologist, the political scientist does not study the beliefs and behavior of children for their own sake. Rather, "the political scientist is concerned with developmental processes only insofar as they are antecedents of the individual's later behavior—and, in particular, those aspects of his behavior that affect the functioning of political systems and subsystems." [39] The child's political world may be interesting, but

---

[37] William R. Schonfeld, "The Focus of Political Socialization Research: An Evaluation." Many of the problems dealt with by Schonfeld were a prime motivation for my undertaking the present study before the publication of his article; however, my thinking on the subject subsequently, and the discussion that follows, have been influenced by his lucid arguments.

[38] *Ibid.*, p. 551.

[39] Fred I. Greenstein, "A Note on the Ambiguity of 'Political Socialization': Definitions, Criticisms, and Strategies of Inquiry," p. 975.

if there is no relationship between it and belief and activity as an adult, it is largely irrelevant. As Schonfeld has put it:

In other words, does the child acquire behavior and/or attitudes that persist in later life and influence (or determine) the nature and style of his relation with the polity? This question is obviously of basic and crucial significance: unless there is some linkage between what a child learns and his future political behavior and attitudes, there is little reason for political scientists to study children. Complementing and supplementing an inquiry of this sort would be analyses of the types of childhood attitudes and behavioral patterns that persist, and investigations into the conditions under which they become operative or inoperative in adulthood.[40]

The linkage between childhood and adult patterns has always been a crucial assumption of political-socialization research but has never been demonstrated convincingly.

By restricting our inquiry primarily to childhood, we have failed to make use of the more dynamic theories of our sister social-science disciplines concerning youth, generations, and social change, some of which have been described above. Political scientists have looked at only one segment of the political-socialization process at a time without considering the connections between stages. Studying the continuities and discontinuities between stages might well have more explanatory potential than studying the content of any one particular stage, and would add a dynamic element to our hitherto static models of an on-going process.

The investigation of the linkages between childhood socialization, adult experiences, and adult political patterns of belief and behavior is also essential because the sparse theory and research concerning the relative importance of adult political socialization have been inconclusive and contradictory, much like the literature on student protest. Those who have studied children have tended to emphasize the continuity of early learning and therefore its importance. On the other hand, some have argued that political socialization, like other socialization in modern industrial society, must of necessity be incomplete and its effects somewhat limited, given the rapidity of social change, the possibilities for geographic and social mobility, and the nature of early socializing agencies.[41]

The rare data we do have that have been collected explicitly to study adult political socialization tend to support the assertion that

---

40 Schonfeld, p. 552.

41 Dawson and Prewitt, pp. 52–54. They cite Arnold Rose's discussion of "Incomplete Socialization" in this regard. The entire problem of discontinuities between stages of socialization is taken up by Dawson and Prewitt in ch. 6 of their volume.

it may be an important variable to consider in the development of the products of the overall political-socialization process. Almond and Verba in their cross-national study found that participation in decisions on the job was more closely related to the development of a belief that an individual can influence his government than was participation in family and school decisions. Furthermore, although such job participation cannot replace family and school participation, it can reinforce it in the development of such beliefs. Almond and Verba interpret their findings as indicating the larger role of social experiences closer in time and structure to the political system in the formation of political attitudes.[42] Eulau also concluded, on the basis of his data on the socialization of American legislators and councilmen, that early political-socialization experiences were not related to orientations toward their official role. He goes on to suggest that intervening political experiences, those more closely associated with the entrance into and performance of the adult political role itself, were probably more formative.[43]

We find, then, a "maturational" versus a "generational" approach not only in the literature on students, youth, and protest, but also in studies concerned with the more general process of political socialization.[44] It should be noted, however, that Dawson and Prewitt have made one of the few attempts to reconcile the seemingly contradictory hypotheses and data of those who stress the formative influence of earlier learning and those who stress adult socialization experience. Dawson and Prewitt hypothesize that learning is cumulative and that in adulthood "new orientations are acquired, but in most instances they occur within the bounds established by the deep and persistent orientations acquired during childhood." [45] Although change in certain dimensions of political belief and behavior does occur, "the identifications and attachments acquired early are persistently held." [46] They go on also to hypothesize that the impact of adult experiences may vary with the type of belief and behavior pattern in question. Basic identifications and loyalties acquired in childhood, such as identification

---

[42] Almond and Verba, The Civic Culture, ch. 12, especially pp. 363–374.

[43] Heinz Eulau, Micro-Macro Political Analysis, pp. 244–245.

[44] Related literature concerning the stability of political party identifications also is characterized by "maturational" versus "generational" interpretations. See John Crittenden, "Aging and Party Affiliation"; Neal E. Cutler, "Generation, Maturation, and Party Affiliation," along with Crittenden's reply in the same issue; Norval D. Glenn and Ted Hefner, "Further Evidence on Aging and Party Identification." See also Ronald Inglehart's argument that the preference for "postbourgeois" values and left-wing parties he found among western European youth in contrast to their parents is due to generational factors; "The Silent Revolution in Europe: Intergenerational Change in Post-Industrial Societies," especially pp. 1001–1002.

[45] Dawson and Prewitt, p. 56.   [46] Ibid., p. 60.

with the political community, loyalty to the state, and broad ideological positions, are less subject to change in adulthood than orientations toward specific political leaders, policies, and events, and the amount and direction of political participation.[47] This theorizing by Dawson and Prewitt is important, for here we have our first indication that the "maturational" and "generational" approaches need not be mutually exclusive. Furthermore, they predict specific conditions under which earlier patterns will tend to be maintained in adulthood and conditions under which they will be susceptible to change: (a) the earlier the belief is acquired the more resistant it will be to change in adulthood, and (b) general loyalties, identifications, and orientations are more resistant to change than specific beliefs or behavior patterns.

Wide areas of research remain unexplored. No empirical studies have explicitly tested the hypotheses of Dawson and Prewitt. Does earlier childhood socialization establish limits on the amount of change that can occur in adulthood? What is the relationship between childhood and adult political socialization? Does adult political socialization have a varying impact on different dimensions of political orientations and behavior? If so, which dimensions are more amenable to change in adulthood? If experience in adulthood does indeed have important consequences for political belief and behavior patterns, in what way and under what conditions do these changes take place? Should such changes not be found to occur as a result of adult experiences, under what circumstances and how are earlier patterns reinforced and continued?

One of the main reasons these questions have remained unanswered has been the difficulty of studying the problem of persistence and change of political attitudes in adulthood as it should be studied—longitudinally. Political-socialization data, and particularly studies of adult political socialization and the relationship between stages of political socialization, ideally should be longitudinal, i.e., should be collected at different points over an extended period of time. Socialization, political or otherwise, is essentially an on-going process, and the methodology used to study it should reflect its nature. The attempt to use cross-sectional data collected at only one point in time in political-socialization studies has serious limitations. The political-socialization process is dynamic and longitudinal; the data used to evaluate it have been static and limited to one point in time. As a result, the research has generally introduced the time variable through other means. One method has been to project results of data gathered on childhood forward in time. For example, this may be done by comparing the results of a study of a sample of children to

---

47 *Ibid.,* pp. 55–56 and pp. 203–205.

the known, or even to the assumed, characteristics of the adult population. Such a comparison is then normally used to (a) prove the essential stability of the political-socialization process or (b) show the origins in early learning of an important political characteristic of either the system or the adult population. Thus when researchers discovered benign and benevolent images of political authority in the attitudes of American children, they assumed these images provided a basis for the American adult's view of political authority (assuming some modifications with age) and thus helped to explain the essential stability of the political system in the United States.[48]

The drawback to this method, of course, is that it projects known data about children in one generation forward in time, on the basis of data on adults in other generations whose own earlier socialization experiences are unknown. In the example above, the children in generation B are expected, as adults, to have views on political authority based on their current benevolent images because adult generation A—whose actual childhood images of political authority we do not know—seems to hold these views now. The only way such an inference makes sense is to assume that the political-socialization process is essentially stable and unchanging from generation to generation, i.e., that generation A was socialized in childhood in the same manner as the present generation and that generation B will be socialized in the same manner as generation A as they grow up. Both of these assumptions not only result in a somewhat tautological argument, but are untested, unproven, and quite tenuous. How tenuous may be indicated by the current view of the same American children and adolescents who were studied in the early 1960s and found to hold benevolent images of political authority and to adopt the party identifications of their parents. Now as young adults they are said to be alienated from political authority and registering as independents in greater numbers than ever before.[49]

A second major way in which political scientists have sought to use cross-sectional data to analyze the longitudinal political-socialization process has been to begin at the adult end of the process and work back. Almond and Verba begin with the political orientations of adults and then, by the use of retrospective questions, attempt to de-

---

[48] David Easton and Robert D. Hess, "The Child's Political World," and Fred I. Greenstein, "The Benevolent Leader: Children's Images of Political Authority," especially pp. 47–48 and p. 57. To their credit, these authors explicitly recognize that their conclusions depend on an untested inference and call for research on the problem. The point, of course, is not that the inferences made in these two excellent pioneering studies of childhood political socialization were necessarily erroneous at the time, but that cross-sectional studies force such inferences to be made at all.

[49] A discussion of the contradiction between the conclusions of the earlier literature and later events is found in Greenberg (ed.), pp. 1–14.

termine the earlier political-socialization experiences that formed those orientations.[50] Answers to retrospective questions, however, may be subject to the distortions of memory and selective perception.

Both these methods—projecting forward and relying on recall—have their methodological advantages and their limitations. The former approach allows the collection of more reliable data about the political-socialization process in childhood and adolescence, but our knowledge of the end product of the process, the all-important adult political orientations and behavior, remains speculative. The recall method can supply reliable data on adult beliefs and behavior but somewhat less reliable data on the earlier formative process. Following the sample through time and collecting data at various points is far preferable to either of these methods. But as Stephen Douglas has pointed out, "Actually, although most abstract discussions of socialization do take the longitudinal perspective, the practical obstacles to empirical longitudinal research on socialization have been prohibitive in political science." [51]

The main type of longitudinal study, the panel, best illustrates these practical obstacles. The panel study tests a sample at one point in time and then follows that sample and retests it later.[52] The panel has distinct advantages over the cross-sectional study in that it can (1) record changes over time, (2) record the reasons for the observed changes, (3) collect more information, and (4) produce more accurate and reliable results.[53] All of these advantages are especially important in socialization research. Yet because the panel study often involves prohibitive commitments of time and resources it has not been used in the study of political socialization. Few political scientists have the time, resources, or desire to plan a panel study covering even five years of a sample's life, much less ten, twenty, or thirty years. Thus most studies have approached socialization through the cross-sectional method, sometimes with pseudo-longitudinal variations,[54] and the panel study's use has been confined primarily to short-term reinterviews in pre- and post-election voting studies.

A longitudinal methodological alternative to the panel has been

50 Almond and Verba, ch. 12, especially p. 329.

51 Stephen A. Douglas, *Political Socialization and Student Activism in Indonesia*, p. 109.

52 Hans Zeisel, "The Panel"; Charles R. Glock, "Some Applications of the Panel Method to the Study of Change."

53 Zeisel, pp. 340–341.

54 The most common variation is to study three or four grade levels in schools at one point in time. A variation closer to a truly longitudinal study is to reinterview the same type of sample, but not the same respondents, at a later point in time. See Douglas, pp. 19–24. These types of studies are improvements on simple cross-sectional research but still suffer from the same limitations as the latter.

used successfully in other disciplines but has never been used by political scientists: the "follow-up" study. The follow-up resembles the
panel but attempts to trace and locate a past sample and gather new
data on it, rather than following a present sample into the future.[55]
The prime advantage of the follow-up is that the researcher can use
the surveys and data previously gathered by himself or other social
scientists, or both. Thus, rather than collecting data on a sample of
children now and waiting years for them to mature, as in a panel
study, the follow-up study involves tracing a sample of children previously interviewed by oneself or others and reinterviewing them now.
The classic example of this method is Theodore Newcomb's follow-up
of his own Bennington College sample cited above.

The follow-up particularly suits the study of *shūshoku tenkō*, concerned as it is with possible change in belief and behavior through
time. As Herbert McClosky has argued about panel studies in a point
equally applicable to the follow-up, "Although no panel survey has
so far addressed the issue of conversion directly, it would be an excellent device for observing political changes over time and for un-
covering the influences that induce those changes." [56]

THE STUDY

This work provides a longitudinal case study of Japanese student activists and their postgraduate experiences in order partly to answer
some of the questions arising from the literature of political socialization, youth, and student movements. It will treat the political socialization process as a life-long one and investigate the relationship between adult and earlier learning on a number of dimensions of political belief and behavior. A follow-up methodology was used to determine the extent of postgraduate change in a sample of students involved in varying degrees in the 1960 anti-Ampo demonstrations, and
retrospective data were elicited primarily to determine the political-
socialization experiences leading to the students' becoming activists.
The methodological significance of this study therefore lies in its attempt to incorporate a follow-up technique, and thus a true longitudinal approach, into its research design. Further details concerning
methodology and the sample are presented below and in the "Note"
at the end of this book.

The original set of respondents upon which my follow-up study is
based were interviewed in 1962 by Professor Tsurumi Kazuko. The re-

[55] Bruce K. Eckland, "Retrieving Mobile Cases in Longitudinal Surveys," p. 52.
[56] Herbert McClosky, *Political Inquiry: The Nature and Uses of Survey Research*, pp. 41–42.

sults of her research have been reported in a number of articles [57] and in her book, *Social Change and the Individual: Japan Before and After Defeat in World War II*.[58] Professor Tsurumi most graciously offered me access to the data from her original survey, permission to use these data for my study, and aid in relocating members of the sample.

In 1962, Prof. Tsurumi administered an interview-questionnaire to one hundred students at four university campuses in Tokyo— Tokyo University's Hongo and Komaba campuses, Keiō University, and Chūō University—and also to a few other former leaders of Zenga-kuren from various universities. Most of the respondents were still undergraduates; a few, primarily the former leaders, had already grad-uated. The main goals of the survey were to identify the ideological and affective "postures" of the student activists who took part in the 1960 anti-security-treaty campaign and compare these to the ideological and affective postures of the average students of the same generation and to the Communist intellectuals of the 1930s. Accordingly, Prof. Tsurumi selected a sample that would include a number of different types of students. With the help of student self-government associa-tions (*jichikai*) and the administration at each of the four campuses, she attempted to identify and select respondents in equal numbers for three categories of students: those active in, those interested in, and those "apathetic" to the student movement. The assignment of se-lected students to each category was later revised on the basis of ques-tions in the survey asking the student's own evaluation of their ac-tivity and interest. The results of this selection and categorization process produced a final sample of 47 active, 30 interested, and 23 "apathetic" students.[59] An interview schedule of over one hundred items that included questions concerning the students' background, personality, goals, activity, beliefs, and ideology was then administered to the sample.

My own research was an attempt to locate eight years later as many as possible of these students of the "Ampo generation" inter-viewed by Dr. Tsurumi and reinterview them in order to ascertain changes in beliefs, behavior, and ideology. For this purpose, in late 1969 and early 1970, I developed a questionnaire in Japanese which was pretested on a small sample of respondents of similar background

---

[57] Kazuko Tsurumi, "The Japanese Student Movement: (1) Its Milieu," and "The Japanese Student Movement: (2) Group Portraits"; in Japanese, "*Jiko Kyōiku no ba toshite no Gakusei Undō* (The Student Movement as a Place of Self-Educa-tion), (1) and (2).

[58] Chs. 9–11.

[59] Kazuko Tsurumi, *Social Change*, pp. 307–314. Further details on the study and the sample may be found here and in the Tsurumi articles cited above.

to those in the original survey. On the basis of this pretest the questionnaire was then revised to its final form. This instrument consisted of 117 items (with many subparts). Although many of the questions required the respondent to choose among a set of given answers, I also used open-ended follow-up questions wherever possible to provide more extensive and detailed information than the fixed-choice questions alone could supply. For the same reason, I decided to conduct open-ended depth interviews (in addition to the structured survey-interview) with a selected group of respondents. These additional interviews, which were held following the administration of the formal survey questionnaire, allowed me to probe more deeply into some of the answers given to the survey questions, and also to ask additional questions to elicit more detailed information on the respondents' lives, beliefs, and activities.

While these survey and interview instruments were being developed, pretested, and revised, and indeed almost until the last questionnaire had been administered, I undertook to relocate the original sample and elicit their cooperation for the reinterviews. As I began to accumulate information about the whereabouts of the 1962 sample, it soon became obvious that part of it would have to be eliminated from the follow-up. For reasons both practical and theoretical, I decided to confine my follow-up to only the seventy-seven male former students known or thought at the time to be living in the major cities of Honshū—Tokyo, Yokohama, Nagoya, Osaka, and Kyoto. Of these I was able to reinterview fifty-four. Because one respondent proved to be very uncooperative during the interview and his responses unreliable, he was eliminated from the final analysis. Therefore, I successfully reinterviewed fifty-three of the seventy-seven respondents being sought for my study, a response rate of close to 70 percent (68.8 percent), which is a fair return on a follow-up after eight years.[60] The response rate varied with the university. It ranged between 73 and 79 percent in the cases of the two Tokyo University (Hongo and Komaba) campuses and Keiō University. But I succeeded in reinterviewing only 40 percent of the former Chūō University students and 60 percent of the students from other universities. Because of poor alumni records, I was least successful in locating the graduates of Chūō University; hence Chūō is somewhat underrepresented in the follow-up.

It is important to realize the limitations as well as the advantages

---

[60] The successful response rate is probably higher than the 68.8 percent indicated. It must be remembered that among the seventy-seven respondents being sought were many for whom I could find no recent address at all. Consequently, if any of these people were living in the nonurban areas excluded from the survey, they would not have been included in the attempted follow-up and the response rate would have been higher.

of conducting a follow-up study utilizing a sample with the characteristics described above. First, the original sample was not selected randomly. As described previously, Dr. Tsurumi selected her respondents in order to provide roughly equal samples of different types of students, not to represent numerically an actual cross-section of students. Extreme care therefore must be used in generalizing the results to the larger student population. The small size of the follow-up sample adds another reason for caution in interpreting results. Third, the sample is a homogeneous one. Confined to urban males of the same generation, the usual demographic variables used in political-science and socialization research—urban-rural distinctions, sex, and age— cannot be used in the analysis. Finally, the original sample was elite, drawn primarily from the university campuses in Tokyo mentioned above. The final follow-up sample is even more elite, with its over-representation of Tokyo University's two campuses and Keiō University and the small return from Chūō. The sample consequently does not represent students from all types of campuses throughout the country.

On the other hand, using this sample for the purposes of this follow-up study presents a number of advantages. The non-randomness and small size of the sample are by no means inimical to the goal of studying former student activists longitudinally. Because the original sample was selected to include different types of students, we can make comparisons over time between students of varying degrees of activism. Although the proportion of each type of student in the sample may not be representative of the student population as a whole, there is no reason to assume that those in each category are not representative of that type of student. In this study we are not interested in describing the proportion of all students who were more or less active, but rather in explaining the change over time of each type of student. In addition, there is a question as to whether *any* survey treating present or former student radicals can be conducted with a random sample, because of the difficulties involved in identifying the activists and securing their cooperation.[61] Furthermore, the small size of the sample proved to be an advantage in at least one respect: it allowed me to administer a more detailed interview schedule and thus to obtain a more detailed study of the respondents and the political-socialization process than could have been accomplished with a large sample. Whatever the limitations of the selection method and size of the original

---

[61] Takahashi Akira describes the difficulties he encountered in attempting to obtain a sample of different types of activists for his study of a later generation of students. See "Nihon no Gakusei Undō no Shisō to Kōdō" (Thought and Behavior of the Japanese Student Movement), part 2, *Chūō Kōron* (The Central Review), June, 1968, p. 173.

sample, I know of no other study of the 1960 generation of students that provides such comprehensive and reliable information about so many students on which to base a follow-up study as does the Tsurumi survey.

The homogeneity of the sample is also an advantage. Although using this homogeneous sample prevents analyzing interesting relationships based on the standard demographic variables, it allows concentrating on how the dynamic variables of the political-socialization process, and not its parameters, operate on the most important and typical former student activist—the urban male.

Finally, the elite nature of the sample typifies the student activist population of the 1960 generation and provides a more important basis for considering the system consequences of the political socialization process than would a more general sample. Data and reports on the major demonstrations in 1960 show that students from the four campuses in this study supplied a high proportion of the radical "mainstream" Zengakuren [62] activists involved. The two Tokyo University campuses from which the majority of the sample is drawn were probably the two most active in the 1960 demonstrations.[63] Indeed, Packard says Tokyo University "was at the heart of the movement," [64] and many of the student leaders of 1960 came from Todai (Tokyo University). Although students from these universities may not epitomize the average Japanese student, they typify the main activists of 1960. Moreover, the postgraduation fate of students from these universities is most crucial to the operation of Japanese society and the political system, for the elite of Japan is drawn from the graduates of these universities. Todai graduates hold a disproportionately high percentage of the top positions in politics, business, bureaucracy, and academia in Japan. Keiō graduates are well represented in the top

---

[62] The "mainstream" of the Zengakuren in 1960 were those factions that had rebelled against the leadership of the Japan Communist Party and were more radical and active in 1960 than the Communist-affiliated "antimainstream" (or "Yoyogi") faction. Of the twenty-eight students in the sample who belonged to a faction of the student movement in 1960 or at the time of the 1962 interview, or both, twenty-two had been affiliated with "mainstream" factions at some time. The remainder were either members of the "antimainstream," pro-JCP faction, or the "structural reform" faction. See Packard, *Protest in Tokyo*, pp. 98–101, and Tsurumi, *Social Change*, p. 330; also footnote 67 below.

[63] For example, in the June 18, 1960, demonstrations, the Hongo campus of Todai mobilized 3,000 mainstream students, Komaba 1,800, Chūō 2,000. Only Hōsei University and Waseda University among the many other universities represented supplied about as many participants. Keiō University was less active, supplying few mainstreamers but a goodly number of antimainstreamers. Todai Zengaku Kyōtō Kaigi (ed.), *Toride no Ue ni, Warera no Sekai o* (Our World on Top of the Fortress), pp. 592–595. The source for these figures, presented in a table in this activist-edited book, is not given.

[64] Packard, p. 264; see also p. 266.

business firms in Japan.[65] If my sample is elite, it accurately reflects the active elite of the student movement and the future elite of Japanese society.

In analyzing and presenting the data which follow in subsequent chapters, I have categorized the sample according to activity in the student movement. Dr. Tsurumi based her categorization on subjective self-evaluations. As I felt that more "objective" indices of activity —the holding of high positions in student federations and membership in factions of the student movement—provided more reliable expressions of college political activity, I categorized the sample into the following types of students, on the basis of behavioral indicators: LEADERS, ten former students who held high office in Zengakuren or its regional or offshoot campus federations; [66] ACTIVISTS, eighteen former students who had belonged to major factions in the student movement; [67] INTERMITTENT ACTIVISTS, eighteen students who never belonged to a major faction in the student movement but who briefly participated in the anti-Ampo demonstrations in one form or another; and NONACTIVISTS, seven students who neither belonged to a major faction of the movement nor participated in anti-Ampo demonstrations. The leaders and the activists (LA) on the one hand, and the intermittently active and nonactive (INA) students on the other, will be treated as the two main types in most of the analysis that follows, although when significant differences between the subtypes appear, they will be noted in the text. Slightly over one-half of the sample (twenty-eight persons) consists of former committed activists and leaders, all of whom had participated in the Ampo demonstrations, and slightly under one-half (twenty-five persons) of "nonactivists," most of whom had been mobilized to participation during the security-treaty crisis of 1960 although they were never members of factions in the student movement. My categorization, which distinguishes between "hard-core" leaders and activists and students who were accessible to occasional mobilization by Zengakuren during the crisis, conforms to the usual description of types of student participants in demonstrations in Japan, if not to their actual proportion in the student body. Packard estimates that in 1960 about 5 percent of the students at

65 *Journal of Social and Political Ideas in Japan*, V, 2–3, December 1967, pp. 298–301; Herbert Passin, *Society and Education in Japan*, pp. 131–136.

66 The regional federation was Togakuren, the offshoot federation, Zenjiren. All the leaders were either chairmen, vice-chairmen, chief secretaries, or on the Central Executive Committee of Zengakuren or one of these two other related organizations.

67 These factions include the "Bund" (Communist League), Revolutionary Communist League, Socialist Student League, Socialist Youth League, and their later offshoots, in the mainstream; the antimainstream, pro-JCP faction (later the Democratic Youth League); and the structural-reform faction. See footnote 62 above.

Tokyo University were full-time activists and 20 percent were aggressively involved though not necessarily as Zengakuren officers. About 40 percent were usually politically apathetic but were easily aroused to participation and manipulation by the activists at the height of the crisis, and about 35 percent of the students were completely uninvolved.[68]

The survey-interviews and the depth interviews were administered to the sample between April and June of 1970. I was assisted in this by five native Japanese assistants. Twenty-three of the fifty-three respondents were also selected for the depth interviews following the standard questionnaire. In all but one of these cases I was personally present (along with my chief assistant), but to insure accuracy these depth interviews were also recorded on tape. The remaining thirty respondents received only the standard questionnaire, administered by my assistants.

JAPANESE STUDENT ACTIVISTS AS A CASE STUDY

As has been indicated, I did not arbitrarily choose Japan as the setting for a study of adult political socialization and Japanese student radicals as the subject of that study. Academic and journalistic sources, as well as popular belief, indicate that an extreme postgraduation conversion of political beliefs and behavior characterizes a significant segment of Japanese student activists. This indication contradicts the hypotheses advanced by many political scientists concerning the decisive influence of earlier, preadult experiences in the political-socialization process. A change of the magnitude described in the *shūshoku tenkō* literature is obviously inconsistent with these assertions. A systematic study of the fate of former student activists in Japan consequently provides a major test of the hypothesis that significant changes in earlier acquired political identifications and patterns do not occur in adulthood. Whether or not the complete "about-face" of the Japanese student activist proves as widespread as is commonly believed, such a study potentially can help to answer even greater theoretical questions and add immeasurably to our knowledge of the political-socialization process. Comparing former students who did undergo great change after graduation, even if they are a small minority, with those who did not, and with variations in between, offers an opportunity to identify the configurations of socialization experiences associated with changes in adult political patterns and those associated with the maintenance of earlier patterns.

Moreover, it also offers the opportunity to test directly the

[68] Packard, p. 265; also p. 96.

"maturational" versus "generational" models, and the attempt of Dawson and Prewitt to reconcile them. As I shall point out, the Ampo student activists grew to adulthood in a period of rapid social change. How did this change affect the formation of their beliefs and behavior? How formative were the experiences of their youth? How persistent was the youthful rebellion: was it a passing functional transition to adaptation in adulthood, or a long-lasting reaction against, and attempt to change, the relationships in adult society?

This research can also contribute to our understanding of the political process in contemporary Japan. To begin with, it can provide us with further knowledge about the transmission of Japan's polarized political culture and its future prospects. No microlevel empirical studies of the sources of this bifurcated polity have hitherto been conducted. A study of how individuals become part of the subculture of the left as protesting students and of what happens to them upon entering adult society may provide some clues as to how individuals are recruited and socialized to roles within the political subcultures of Japan.

Moreover, this study can provide insights into the political consciousness and activity of an important group in Japanese society. The story of the 1960 students is also that of an influential part of a neglected generation. The "Ampo generation" is a part of the "midwar" generation in Japan. The defeat and occupation of Japan at the end of World War II created a generation gap of which Japanese themselves are extremely conscious, to the extent that they constantly refer to the *"sengo"* (postwar or *après guerre*) generation and to the *"senzen"* (prewar) generation. But it is the little discussed "midwar" generation that is perhaps most interesting. Born and in part brought up during the war and the Occupation, but coming to maturity in an independent and much-changed Japan, they are neither the fish of their fathers' generation who reached adulthood under the Emperor system nor the fowl of their younger brothers' generation who know the Occupation only through their history books and who take prosperity for granted. Because their generation experienced the defeat, the Occupation, and the present system in their formative years, their biographies are themselves invaluable to an understanding of political socialization and the effect of major changes in society on the political belief and behavior of individuals. Their present pattern of belief and behavior is also of great significance for the future of the Japanese political system. Whether they have remained revolutionaries or have made their peace with society, students of this generation, and particularly the graduates of major universities, are now coming to occupy the key "middle level" of leadership in organizations and social groups throughout Japanese society.

The results of this research are presented in the chapters that follow. These chapters are arranged chronologically: first, I will take up the process of political socialization in childhood and adolescence that produced the various types of students; second, I will present the setting for the students' crucial transition to adult society; third, I will examine the maintenance and change of the sample's orientations and behavior since the first survey, or if you will, the adult resocialization between interviews. One major theme runs throughout these chapters —the micro and macro processes of Japanese society that contributed to the development of the sample's beliefs and behavior. On the one hand, the individual changes over time as he passes through different social agencies: the family, school, peer group, workplace. Much of political-socialization research has been concerned with this level. But on the other hand, these social agencies themselves, and the inter-actions that take place within them, are structured by the broader society and culture and reflect and transmit the more general processes of social and historical change. In addition—and here we come to a problem relatively neglected in the study of political socialization— events and changes in the political and social systems themselves often impinge directly on the individual and may be as important as inter-vening social agencies in influencing the development of his beliefs and behavior. A study of a longitudinal process such as political sociali-zation must focus on the intersection of these two levels of social change. The nexus between the two levels, the macrolevel of changing Japanese society, culture, and politics, and the microlevel of passage through particular socialization agencies, tells the story of the political socialization of the Ampo generation.

2

THE FAMILY AND POLITICAL SOCIALIZATION

THIS RESEARCH on political socialization and Japanese student activists focuses on the much neglected aspect of adult political socialization. Nevertheless, before considering what happened to our sample of former students after graduation, we must consider their earlier political socialization experiences, the process which made committed student activists of some but not others of our sample. Earlier political socialization, i.e., before graduation from college, deserves attention in this study for three reasons. The following justifications will also serve to outline the major themes of this and the following chapter.

We cannot consider adult political socialization as operating in a vacuum. By their very nature, the questions involved in the study of adult political socialization—questions of change, maintenance, and replacement of beliefs and behavior—are inseparable from the results of previous stages of political socialization. We must see how closely the backgrounds of former activists and nonactivists parallel each other before we can deal with any changes in these two groups after graduation. Before considering whether student activists remained in the left subculture after graduation, we must see how they were recruited and socialized to that subculture in the first place.

A second reason for examining pregraduation socialization here is the contribution that this can make to the study of the origins of student political activism. The burgeoning literature on student activism includes a number of important works describing the formation process of student activists in the United States and other countries. The studies of Kenneth Keniston and Richard Flacks on the backgrounds of American student activists in the last half of the 1960s are among the most important of their kind because they are based on empirical evidence collected through surveys and interviews with the activists themselves.[1] One goal of these chapters, then, will be similarly to investigate the formative influences on our sample's student beliefs and activities.

The data collected from my sample can do more than help us understand the formative process of student activists: it can be used for the related but more significant purpose of testing hypotheses about and providing data concerning the more general political-socialization process in Japan. It can of course be argued that a sample of student activists, who form such a small and atypical stratum of the population, is not the best one to use to investigate the overall political-socialization process in a given country. There is certainly truth to this argument, and no claim is made here that this study is an exhaustive inquiry into the political-socialization process in Japan. Nevertheless, I believe that the political-socialization literature has too long concentrated only on statistically "average" samples. We should also study the statistically "deviant" to gain insights into the process of political socialization. Furthermore, the study of political socialization in Japan hitherto has been confined to only a few articles [2] using limited samples and concerning one or two specific orientations. One aim of this study, therefore, is to bring together the findings of this small body of research, relate it to my own findings, and formulate hypotheses for future testing.

A FRAMEWORK FOR STUDYING
POLITICAL SOCIALIZATION

A convenient framework for specifying the main variables and relationships involved in political socialization and for organizing my data may be summed up thus: political socialization is a process concerned with who learns from whom (agents), how (methods), and with what results (products).[3] The "who" of this study is obviously our sample of students, but I shall provide additional description by in-

[1] Kenneth Keniston, *Young Radicals: Notes on Committed Youth;* Richard Flacks, "The Revolt of the Advantaged: An Exploration of the Roots of Student Protest."

[2] Yasumasa Kuroda, "Agencies of Political Socialization and Political Change: Political Orientation of Japanese Law Students"; Tadao Okamura, "The Child's Changing Image of the Prime Minister"; Akira Kubota and Robert E. Ward, "Family Influence and Political Socialization in Japan: Some Preliminary Findings in Comparative Perspective"; and Robert Hess, "The Socialization of Attitudes toward Political Authority: Some Cross-National Comparisons" explicitly examine the political-socialization process, using empirical data. A general study of the political-socialization process, using secondary sources, will be found in Frank Langdon's *Politics in Japan.*

[3] This framework is a modification of that proposed in Dawson, "Political Socialization," p. 19.

vestigating the social characteristics and backgrounds of the sample. One major aim of this investigation will be to ascertain whether the activists in the sample differed from the less active on these points.

The agents of political socialization include the social groups and institutions touching the individual and influencing the development of his political beliefs and behavior. Among these agents are family, school, teachers, and peer groups. The relationship between agent and the individual's political orientations has been the most-studied aspect of the process. The family and the schools have been the most-studied agents, but very few studies have explicitly analyzed the role of the peer group in the political-socialization process. Kenneth Langton, however, has found in his seminal examination of the impact of that group on political attitudes that it can have an important influence in resocializing working-class students toward higher-class political norms and in increasing the political efficacy of students from a medium to a high sense of efficacy.[4] The peer group as a political-socialization agency has been relatively unexplored but nonetheless may play an important role in developing political orientations and behavior. In analyzing the process by which our sample of students developed their attitudes and behavior, therefore, I made sure to examine the influence of the peer group as well as that of the family and schools.

Another agent of political socialization that has been neglected but which I have included in my study is that of political events and experiences themselves. Almost all attention to agents in the political-socialization literature has focused on the primary groups mentioned above—family, school, and to a lesser extent, peer groups. The attitudes and behavior acquired in these primary groups, however, may often be modified, reinforced, or changed by the individual's direct contact with the political system. At some point in his life the individual's attitudes must be tested by direct experience with the political process, and this interaction may affect his beliefs. Whereas young children rarely participate directly in politics, adolescents and college students often come into close contact with the political process. But even the beliefs and values of young children may, through the primary groups in which they are located, be influenced by the larger events of the political system. As Verba has pointed out, "One is forced to consider the historical experiences of a nation from the point of view of their impact on political beliefs."[5] Wars, revolutions, depressions, and other crises all may affect the formation of political beliefs and the basic values underlying those beliefs. Inglehart's discovery in western Europe of intergenerational differences in basic values

---

[4] Langton, *Political Socialization*, chs. 5 and 6.
[5] Sidney Verba, "Comparative Political Culture," p. 554.

underlying political orientations, which were related to different levels of economic scarcity during the generations' formative years, underlines this point.[6] Certainly, in looking at the process by which our sample of 1960 students acquired their political orientations, we cannot neglect the impact of the wider social and political environment. That generation of Japanese students, after all, experienced in their formative years some of the most dramatic social and political changes and events of any generation in any nation in the world: the defeat in war and total destruction of the prewar value and political system, the postwar economic breakdown, an occupation by a foreign army, a wholesale and conscious attempt to remake society's values, and the numerous political protests and incidents culminating in the Ampo crisis. A study of the political socialization of this generation would be deficient if it neglected the impact of these events. We shall be concerned here with the relative roles of all the above-mentioned agents at various stages of the political-socialization process.

The third aspect of the political-socialization process, the methods of political socialization, or the "how" of political socialization, is the least-studied part of the entire process. As Dawson and Prewitt have put it, "A major gap in political socialization theory . . . concerns the actual learning mechanism." [7] Unfortunately, inasmuch as this study, like most previous research, relies upon an attitude survey and interviews and not on participant-observation, we can add little to political-socialization theory in that area. However, my data do allow for a brief consideration of two of the main forms of political learning: direct and indirect. Direct political learning occurs when the content of the political orientations acquired is explicitly political, as in the transmission of political-party identification; indirect political learning occurs when the predispositions acquired are not explicitly political but subsequently influence political orientations and behavior, as, for example, when nonpolitical experiences in the family are later generalized to politics.[8] In the data presented below we shall deal with both types of political learning and the relative influence of each in the formation of our sample's view of the political world.

The results or products of the political-socialization process are the various dimensions of political belief and behavior that the individual has acquired at a given point in time. The most obvious con-

---

6 Ronald Inglehart, "The Silent Revolution in Europe: Intergenerational Change in Post-Industrial Societies."

7 Dawson and Prewitt, *Political Socialization*, p. 80. There are exceptions, however. See, for example, the application of learning theory to explain the development of attitudes of political legitimacy in Richard M. Merelman, "Learning and Legitimacy."

8 Dawson and Prewitt, pp. 63–80.

cern of this research is with the socialization experiences associated
with the development of student activism. More specifically, since
Japanese student activists are highly politicized, politically active,
"progressive" in orientation and identification with political parties,
and Marxists or Marxist sympathizers, we need to examine the development of these characteristics in our sample. I am intentionally attempting to deal with a wide range of dimensions of political belief
and behavior. Most studies of political socialization have concentrated
on only one or two dimensions. We thus have many studies exploring
in detail the relationship between various agencies and a specific
political orientation but few attempting to ascertain whether the impact of the several agencies varied with different orientations and
behavioral characteristics. The family may be influential in the formation of party identifications, but does it have the same influence on
the development of political behavior? The school classroom may be
an important source of attitudes toward authority, but is it equally
important in the development of political ideology? In this chapter
and the next I shall investigate which agencies have the most impact
on which dimensions and by what methods at different stages of the
process of political socialization.

THE ROLE OF THE FAMILY

No agency of political socialization has been as much studied for its
effect on political orientations and on student activism as the family.
But neither has the role of any other agency received such diverse
interpretations.

The literature and popular belief about the socialization of
student activists abound with explanations involving the role of the
family. As Kenneth Keniston has noted, two of the most popular are
the "radical-rebel" hypothesis and the "red-diaper baby" hypothesis.
The former states that the student activist's rejection and defiance of
political authority is really a displacement of his rebellion against
parental authority. The "red-diaper baby" hypothesis, on the contrary,
sees student activists as coming from politically radical families who pass
on their left-wing values and their example of political activity to their
offspring.[9] In effect, the first hypothesis sees not just a lack of transmission of familial role models but the positive rejection of them, whereas
the latter views student activism as resulting from the almost complete
adoption and imitation of parental values and behavioral models.

Recent research has suggested that both hypotheses are oversimpli-
fied. As Lane and others have pointed out, for rebellion against parents

---

[9] Keniston, pp. 46–48.

to be displaced into political rebellion, politics must be salient in the family. In any case, little evidence has been found of adolescent political rebellion in the permissive American family.[10] More significantly, Keniston's own research and that of Flacks indicate that student activists tend to come from politically liberal families of upper-middle-class status and to have parents of higher levels of education than those of nonactivists. Activists usually have been raised permissively and have close and warm relationships with their mothers, who nonetheless put pressure on them for high academic performance.[11] Rather than rebelling against their parents' beliefs, they have, according to Keniston, adopted their "core values," "basic assumptions concerning desirable human relationships, feelings and motives." [12] However, the "red-diaper baby" hypothesis is also inadequate, because many of the activists' parents were not "radical" but just more "liberal" than the average without being politically active.[13]

These findings on the impact of the family on the formation of student activists agree in part with the more general literature on family and political socialization. Few would deny that the family has an important indirect impact on the formation of political orientations by influencing the development of the individual's basic personality traits and cultural values and by placing him within a network of social and economic relationships that in turn affect the development of his political self.[14] There is less agreement, however, over the role of the family in the direct transmission of political orientations. Findings from studies in the United States and other countries suggesting that the family influences the formation of party identification and feelings of political efficacy have been cited by some researchers as evidence of the frequent transmission of political values from parent to child.[15] Yet Jennings and Niemi's study of a wide range of political values found that, except for party identification, there was little agreement between the political values of the students and their parents in the families they studied.[16]

---

[10] Robert E. Lane, *Political Ideology*, pp. 270–272; Dawson and Prewitt, pp. 118–120.

[11] Keniston, pp. 14–15, 48–54, 306–310; Flacks, pp. 186–188.

[12] Keniston, p. 112.

[13] They also argue that activists differ from their parents in attempting to implement or "act out" the values and beliefs that their parents held but did not necessarily put into practice. See Keniston, pp. 111–117; Flacks, pp. 188–191.

[14] Dawson and Prewitt, pp. 109–110.

[15] See summary by Dawson and Prewitt of the literature and the references cited, pp. 110–118.

[16] M. Kent Jennings and Richard G. Niemi, "The Transmission of Political Values from Parent to Child," especially p. 183. See also the reevaluation of the literature on the influence of the American family by R. W. Connell, "Political Socialization in the American Family: The Evidence Re-examined."

My data and sample, like most of the other studies of political socialization and the family, cannot supply any definitive conclusions as to the role of the family in political socialization in Japan. Nevertheless, they do allow us to investigate the family backgrounds of the committed activists and the less active students of the 1960 Ampo generation, to test the "radical-rebel" and "red-diaper baby" hypotheses on a Japanese sample, and to evaluate the role of the Japanese family as an agent of politicization, model of activity, and transmitter of party identification.

FAMILY BACKGROUND AND AUTHORITY

The data I shall present first concern the family backgrounds of our sample of students and will be used to investigate whether the leaders and activists differed from the other students in terms of the socio-economic status of their families. Although neither the 1962 nor the 1970 survey attempted to discover the income level of the families of the students, Prof. Tsurumi did query her respondents as to the occupations and educational background of their parents. I categorized the responses concerning their fathers' occupations into three levels of socioeconomic status: High (managers and executives, those in professional, technical, and artistic professions), Medium (white-collar workers and public servants), and Low (shopkeepers, small-scale proprietors, and farmers). The results showed that three-quarters of our total sample came from high- and medium-status families, and that 56 percent came from the highest category (managers, professionals, etc.). This is not surprising when we consider that much of Japan's tremendous postwar growth in higher education, which theoretically should open the door to college for students from lower-status families, has taken place only within the last ten years,[17] that scholarship aid to college students is minimal in Japan, and that Tokyo and Keiō Universities—from which most of the sample is drawn—are elite, prestigious institutions. Indeed, a survey of university students in the early 1960s in Japan, as in our sample, showed that almost three-quarters were of "higher-class origin" and only one-quarter of "lower-class origin." [18]

More significant are the differences I found between categories of students. Although an almost equal percentage of all categories of students came from managerial and professional families (the range

---

17 Herbert Passin, *Society and Education in Japan*, p. 110, presents figures for 1960 based on the *Japan Statistical Yearbook*. These show total enrollment in universities and graduate schools as about 711,000; the 1970 *Yearbook* (Tokyo: Bureau of Statistics, Office of the Prime Minister, 1970), p. 121, gives the figure 1,260,000 for 1968.

18 Passin, p. 121.

was 52 to 60 percent), the intermittent activists were far less likely to come from the middle-status category than any of the other groups (6 percent of the intermittent activists; from 23 to 30 percent of the other groups), and far more likely to come from the lower-status families (39 percent; between 10 and 23 percent for the other groups). Thus, although students of all degrees of activism came primarily from middle- and upper-status families, more fathers of intermittent activists were shopkeepers and farmers than were those of the leaders, activists, or even complete nonactivists. A corresponding result was found in terms of father's education, as the adjoining table shows:

	Leaders (percent)	Activists (percent)	Intermittent activists (percent)	Nonactivists (percent)
Father with at least some college education	75	78	44	100
Father with only high-school education or less	25	22	56	0
Total	100% (n = 10)	100% (n = 18)	100% (n = 18)	100% (n = 7)

Again, the intermittent activists (but not the nonactivists) differed significantly from the committed activists in our sample in terms of the social status of their families as measured by father's educational background.

The data presented in the table indicate that our student activists are somewhat more likely to come from a higher socioeconomic, more educated strata of society than are our intermittent activists. But do the types of students also differ in their intrafamily authority relationships? Is the activist's family more permissive in its child-rearing than the less active student's, or is there some truth to the "radical-rebel" hypothesis that student rebellion expresses defiance toward strict parental authority? Prof. Tsurumi asked our respondents what each of their parents' attitude was toward them when they were children, giving them a choice of "strict," "average," "laissez-faire," or "indulgent." By considering "laissez-faire" and "indulgent" attitudes to be permissive and grouping these responses into one category, we obtain the results shown in table 1. In this and all following tables, unless otherwise specified, leaders and activists will be designated by LA and referred to in the text as "activists" or "committed activists"; intermittent activists and nonactivists together will be designated in the tables as INA and often referred to as the "less active."

The relationship between father's attitude and activity in the student movement is not significant, and that between mother's attitude and activity only weakly so. However, there are differences in the

TABLE 1.   RELATIONSHIP BETWEEN PARENTS' ATTITUDES TOWARD RESPONDENT
AS CHILD AND LATER ACTIVITY IN THE STUDENT MOVEMENT (IN PERCENT)

| | Activity in the student movement | | |
	LA	INA	Total
Father's attitude:			
Strict	26	48	37
Average	43	22	33
Permissive	30	30	30
	99% [a]	100%	100%
	(n = 23)	(n = 23)	(N = 46) [b]
$X^2 = 3.1$; p > .10			
Mother's attitude:			
Strict	23	20	22
Average	35	64	49
Permissive	42	16	29
	100%	100%	100%
	(n = 26)	(n = 25)	(N = 51) [c]
$X^2 = 4.9$; p < .10			

[a] Due to rounding.

[b] N does not equal 53 because 4 activists and 1 intermittent activist were raised in families where a father was not present and 1 leader and 1 intermittent activist answered "Don't remember."

[c] N does not equal 53 because 2 activists responded "Don't remember."

activists' and the less active's backgrounds. Although an equal proportion had fathers who were permissive, more activists were raised in an average manner rather than strictly, while more of the less active came from homes where paternal discipline was greater. In the case of the mother's attitude, it should be noted that for the sample as a whole maternal discipline tended to be less strict than paternal discipline: only 22 percent of those responding said their mother's attitude was "strict," compared with 37 percent in the case of the father. This, of course, is in accord with the sociological and anthropological descriptions we have of the Japanese family which emphasize the close emotional-dependency relationship between mother and child, particularly in the case of male children, the lack of physical punishment to assure obedience, and the father as enforcer of community standards for the children.[19] According to Befu: "Japanese parents, especially the mother, tend to be much less authoritarian vis-à-vis children than American parents." [20] More important, the types of students differed markedly when it came to "permissive" mothers: whereas a large proportion of the intermittent activists and nonactivists saw their mother's attitude as "average," almost three times as many activists (42 as

[19] Ezra F. Vogel, *Japan's New Middle Class*, ch. 12.

[20] Harumi Befu, *Japan: An Anthropological Introduction*, pp. 155–156.

against 16 percent) said that their mothers had been "permissive." We should also note the number of activists who were not included in the percentages on father's attitude because they were raised in families where a father was not present (see note b, table 1).[21]

Other evidence also indicates that although the sample as a whole came from nonauthoritarian families, the families of activists tended to be somewhat less authoritarian than the others. We repeated two questions from the Almond and Verba cross-national study[22] in which the respondents were asked first whether they felt it all right to complain when their parents decided something to which they were strongly opposed, then, if they did complain, whether their parents' decision would have changed. Only one of the activists and two of the less active felt that it would have been difficult to complain, but 30 percent of the less active responding felt that the decision would not have then changed, whereas only 11 percent of the activists responding felt this way.

The data presented here indicate strongly that the "radical-rebel" hypothesis of student activism is as inappropriate to our sample as it has been to other samples of student activists. Student activists tend to come from relatively permissive family backgrounds in which the nonauthoritarian environment of the family would give little motivation for defiance of parental authority. It is also clear, however, that the family backgrounds of the activists and the less active are not different enough to account by themselves for the later differences in political activity.

THE TRANSMISSION OF POLITICAL INTEREST, ORIENTATION, AND BEHAVIOR

If activists do indeed tend to come from permissive, upper-status families, do they also tend to become interested in politics in the family, adopt their parents' political orientation, and imitate their parents' political activity? Is the "red-diaper baby" hypothesis valid?

We asked the respondents in the 1970 survey whether, from the time they were children until they were about 16 years old, their parents were interested in politics. Those who responded positively, who said that one or both parents had been interested in politics, were

---

21 Langton, however, finds that children in mother-only families tend to be less interested in politics, lower in political efficacy, and more authoritarian than children from normal families. See Langton, pp. 30–39, and Dawson and Prewitt, p. 121. It should be noted that Langton found mother-only family structure to have an effect only on working-class offspring's political efficacy, and my sample is obviously not in that category.

22 Almond and Verba, *The Civic Culture*, pp. 533; 330–332.

then asked the political orientation of the interested parent(s) (conservative or progressive) and whether the parent(s) were active politically at the time. The results of the questions concerning interest and orientation appear in table 2. Slightly over half of the respondents had no parent interested in politics during the respondent's childhood and early adolescence. Of the half of the sample who had parents one or both of whom were interested in politics, three-quarters had progressive parents. Comparing the leaders and activists with the intermittent and nonactivists, we see that no relationship exists between being a committed student activist and having had parents interested in politics. Indeed, there was a slight tendency toward a negative relationship. Furthermore, there was little difference between the committed activists and the less active in the political orientation of those who had at least one parent interested in politics: if at least one parent was interested in politics, the likelihood was two or three to one that he would be progressive.

TABLE 2.   RELATIONSHIP BETWEEN PARENTS' POLITICAL INTEREST AND
ORIENTATION, AND ACTIVITY IN THE STUDENT MOVEMENT (IN PERCENT)

Parents' interest and orientation	Activity in the student movement		
	LA	INA	Total
One or both parents interested in politics:			
Conservative	11	17	14
Progressive	33	35	34
Parents not interested in politics	55	48	52
	100%	100%	100%
	(n = 27)	(n = 23)	(N = 50) [a]

[a] N does not equal 53 because two INA did not remember whether parents were interested in politics and one LA answered "Other" to the question on political orientation of interested parent.

Inasmuch as most of our sample, whether activist or less active, were progressive in orientation as students,[23] this overwhelming margin of progressive over conservative in politically interested parents may indicate some transmission of political orientation when the family was politicized. However, it must be remembered that 66 percent of the sample had parents either not interested in politics or conservative in orientation; hence the family cannot account for the transmission of progressive orientations in two-thirds of the sample.

---

[23] This is apparent not only from the fact that most of the less active also participated in the Ampo demonstrations, but from the analysis of their political-party support described below.

The relatively low level of politicization of the sample's families is also indicated by data about the frequency of political discussion in their families. As table 3 shows, in only 10 percent of the sample's families was politics discussed often, and in 31 percent sometimes. Of more importance is the fact that no relationship exists between activity in the student movement and political discussion in the family: the more politicized leaders and activists were actually *more* likely to come from families where politics was hardly discussed than were the less politicized intermittent and nonactivists. That the less active were more likely to come from families where politics was discussed will be taken up in more detail in the next chapter. It is clear, however, that in the case of the activists, we shall have to look elsewhere to find the most important politicizing influences in their lives.

There is no need to present in table form the data on parents as role models of political activity. Only three of the respondents with at least one parent interested in politics said that that parent was politically active also.

As an agent of politicization and a role model of political activity, especially for our activists, the family seems weak indeed. Half of all the students, including leaders and activists, did not come from families where even one parent was interested in politics, and practically no one had parents who were politically active; the most politicized and active students were more likely not to have discussed politics in their families than were the less politicized and active. On only one count, the transmission of a general left-right (progressive-conservative) orientation, is there slight evidence that the family plays some role. However, this is true only if we exclude over half the sample who had

TABLE 3.   RELATIONSHIP BETWEEN FREQUENCY OF POLITICAL DISCUSSION
IN THE FAMILY AND ACTIVITY IN THE STUDENT MOVEMENT (IN PERCENT)

Frequency of political discussion in family	Activity in the student movement		
	LA	INA	Total
	11	8	10
	21	42	31
	68	50	60
	100%	100%	101% [a]
	(n = 28)	(n = 24)	(N = 52) [b]

a Due to rounding.

b N does not equal 53 because one intermittent activist responded "Don't remember." The question read as follows: "From the time you were a child until you were about 16 years old, did you ever discuss political or social problems in your family? Did you discuss them often, sometimes, not much, or hardly at all?"

parents not interested in politics. Our activists can hardly be called "red-diaper babies." And none of our sample's future political roles could be predicted on the basis of their parents' political orientations.

THE TRANSMISSION OF POLITICAL-PARTY PREFERENCE

The few political-socialization studies conducted so far in Japan have focused on the family and the transmission of political-party identification, but with contradictory results. Kuroda's study of Japanese law students showed no relationship between the party preference or political involvement of the students and that of their parents. Most law students, regardless of their parents' preferences, favored the Socialist Party.[24] Kubota and Ward, however, argue that their data on a small sample of child-parent pairs "establishes a probability that in a particular area, the generational transmission of party identification, the Japanese family does play an important and demonstrable role." [25] The latter study also presents tentative evidence that the transmission of party identification may vary with the party preference of the parents, Communist Party supporters and their offspring showing the strongest consistency across generations, followed by the supporters of the Socialist Party and the conservative LDP, in that order. Also, children of parents belonging to labor unions tend to have the same party identification as their parents.[26] In short, although both authors find "progressive" parents to have children of similar party preference, Kuroda argues that other and later agencies bear more of the burden of political socialization in Japan, whereas Ward and Kubota see the family's role, even if limited, as still quite important in the transmission of all party preferences.

In the Tsurumi study of 1962, she asked her sample whether they had voted in the November 1960 general election for the House of Representatives and if so, how they voted. If the respondent had not voted in that election, she then asked how he would have voted if he had. By combining all those who actually had or would have voted for a party in that election we can get a rough approximation, even if not a totally satisfactory one, of our sample's party preferences in 1960 when most of them were college students. For the sample as a whole, almost three-quarters (74 percent) voted for either the Socialist (61 percent) or Communist (13 percent) parties. The leaders and activists, as we would expect, were slightly more left-wing in their party preferences, 85 percent voting Socialist (63 percent) or Communist (22 percent); the remainder had no party preference. But the less active

---

24 Kuroda, pp. 329–330.   26 Ibid., chart on p. 148; pp. 155–156.
25 Kubota and Ward, p. 167.

were by no means conservative in their party preference; only 8 percent voted for the ruling, conservative Liberal Democrats. The majority's preference, as in the case of the committed activists, was for the Socialist Party (60 percent). If there was a difference between the groups at all, it was that more of the intermittent and nonactivists favored the moderately progressive Democratic Socialists (20 percent) over the Communists (4 percent) and that fewer of these students expressed no preference at all (8 percent). Both the active and less active, therefore, were progressive in their party preferences at the time of the 1960 general election.

My interest in the problem of the transmission of political-party identification in the family led me to include in the 1970 survey a question asking the respondents if they remembered which political party their parents had supported when the respondents were young (from childhood to age 16). Because the LDP was not formed from the merger of two conservative parties until 1955 and the Socialist Party was split from 1952 until the same year into a right-socialist and left-socialist party,[27] all responses indicating that parents supported the LDP or its forerunners, or were generally conservative in their party preference, were classified as "conservative"; parental support for the left or right (i.e., the DSP) Socialists, the Communists, or the "progressive" parties in general was classified as "progressive." Combining the students' 1960 preferences in the same way, we obtain the results shown in table 4. Except in the case of respondents whose parents were progressive, there was little correspondence between parental party preference when the respondent was younger and the respondent's own preference in 1960. Whether the respondent remembered his parents as having supported a conservative party, no party,[28] or ideologically opposing parties, he was likely to be progressive in his own party support by the time he was in college. And as mentioned above, most of the progressive support was for the Socialist Party. The data then strongly support Kuroda's findings that, except for Socialist-supporting parents, there is no strong relationship between parental party preference and student party preference.[29]

---

27 The Right Socialists split off again in 1959 to become the Democratic Socialist Party.

28 In this table, the respondents who answered that they did not know or remember their parents' party preference were included in the "none" category. Ordinarily, such responses would be excluded from the data, but in this case their inclusion is justified on the grounds that we are dealing with the transmission of party preference. The inability to remember their parents' preference is as meaningful an indicator of a lack of salience of party preference in the family and a lack of transmission as an answer of "none."

29 The lack of transmission in the family was also indicated indirectly in other ways. Notice that twelve respondents either could not remember their parents'

TABLE 4.　RELATIONSHIP BETWEEN RESPONDENTS' 1960 PARTY PREFERENCE
AND PARENTS' PARTY PREFERENCE DURING RESPONDENTS' CHILDHOOD (IN PERCENT)

Respondents' party preference (1960)	Parents' party preference				
	Conservative	Mixed [a]	Progressive	None	Total
Conservative (LDP)	13	0	0	0	4
Progressive (DSP, Soc., Comm.)	80	100	90	75	84
None	7	0	10	25	12
	100% (n = 15)	100% (n = 3)	100% (n = 22)	100% (n = 12)	100% (N = 52) [b]

[a] "Mixed" parental party preference designates those families where one parent supported a progressive party and one parent supported a conservative party or no party.

[b] N does not equal 53 because one respondent gave his family party preference as "Other."

Two major problems remain. The first is to explain why my study, as well as Kuroda's and Ward and Kubota's, indicates that progressive-party supporters, particularly Socialist and Communist supporters, seem to transmit their party preferences to their children more often than do LDP supporters. One plausible explanation would emphasize that progressive-party supporters have higher levels of politicization, given the nature of a progressive party's appeal and the social basis of its support in Japan. The left-wing parties are more ideological and are the perpetual "out" parties; hence they are unable to attract supporters on the basis of any concrete benefits of governmental output they might deliver. Supporters of the left parties would therefore tend to be more politicized and more committed to the parties and what they stand for than would supporters of the LDP, many of whom support the ruling party chiefly because of benefits it is capable of dispensing, because it is the ruling party, or because of their place in a traditional network of personal relationships (kankei) causing them to deliver their vote more on the basis of identification with a primary

party support or said they supported none. In addition, of those who did remember some party allegiance, twelve responded with expressions of doubt, indicated that the party preference was not really an identification with the party as much as with particular candidates ("This doesn't mean they supported the party—they had a personal relationship to the candidates."), or, as in one case, said that the children persuaded one of their parents to vote for a party and not the other way around. Thus almost half the sample indicated in some way that party identification was relatively unimportant in their families.

and secondary group than on the basis of party label.[30] Furthermore, this argument would run, inasmuch as the left-wing parties derive much of their support from the urban, white-collar stratum with high educational background, the added political knowledge and interest that comes with education would lend greater importance to party labels and their meanings for many of the supporters of the left parties. In short, an explanation of this nature suggests that supporters of left-wing parties, for the reasons mentioned, are more highly politicized than supporters of the LDP and therefore more likely to transmit political information such as party identification to their children.

In order to test this hypothesis, I divided the respondents into two categories, those who said that their parents supported a progressive party while the respondent was growing up, and those who stated that their parents did not, i.e., whose parents supported a conservative party or no party. I then ran this variable against two variables that would indicate the level of politicization of their families: their parents' interest in politics and whether politics was discussed in the family when the respondent was younger. The results lent support to the idea that parents who supported the progressive parties were more politicized than parents who supported the conservatives or no party. The relationship between parental party preference and parental interest in politics was significant ($X^2 = 4.86$, $p < .05$), 68 percent of the progressive-party parents being interested in politics compared with only 36 percent of the others. There was also a relationship between parental party preference and discussion of politics in the family, which, although weaker than the above relationship ($X^2 = 3.68$, $p < .10$), showed that 57 percent of the respondents with progressive-party parents said that they discussed politics in their families often or sometimes, in contrast to only 30 percent of the respondents whose parents did not support the progressive parties. My data thus indicated that parents who supported the Socialist, Communist, or Democratic Socialist parties were indeed more politicized than other parents.

It still remained to be proved, however, that the high rate of progressive-party transmission was actually the result of this greater

---

[30] Scott C. Flanagan, "The Japanese Party System in Transition"; also Nobutaka Ike, *Japanese Politics: Patron-Client Democracy*, pp. 99–104. Flanagan applies his theory of *kankei* to both progressives and conservatives; I am using it here, however, to test whether there is any justification for asserting that it applies more to the conservatives and that the progressives' party preference is due more to party identification. As we shall see, the results will indicate that *kankei* may account for the party preference of both, and be applicable to the political socialization of party preference as well as voter mobilization.

politicization of progressive-party parents; i.e., that these same politicized left-party supporters were transmitting their party identification
to their children more effectively than the left-party supporters who
were not politicized. To test this, I grouped together all the respondents and parents whose party preference was similar (conservative-
conservative, progressive-progressive, none-none) and all the respondents and parents whose party preference was dissimilar (conservative-
progressive, no party-party support, and the reverse of each of these)
as an indicator of transmission of party preference. This variable was
then cross-tabulated with the party preference of parents and the
indicators of politicization. The results in terms of political discussion
with parents are included in table 5. Those results show immediately
that the hypothesis that parents who support progressive parties
directly transmit party preference to their offspring because they are
more politicized is not verified. Progressive parents who did not discuss
politics with their children were as likely to have children who shared
their party preference as those who did discuss politics. Parents who
did not support a left party were likely to have offspring whose party
preference was different from theirs whether they discussed politics in
the family or not. A similar result was obtained using political interest
as an indicator of politicization: whether or not their parents were
interested in politics, children of progressive parents strongly tended
to share their parents' party preference and the children of non-

TABLE 5.   RELATIONSHIP BETWEEN COINCIDENCE OF PARENTAL AND
RESPONDENTS' PARTY PREFERENCE, PARENTS' PARTY PREFERENCE,
AND POLITICAL DISCUSSION IN THE FAMILY (IN PERCENT)

Parent-respondent party preference	Parents' party preference				
	Progressive		Other		Total
	Family discussed politics [a]	Family did not discuss [b]	Family discussed politics [a]	Family did not discuss [b]	
Similar	92	89	22	15	48
Different	8	11	78	85	52
	100%	100%	100%	100%	100%
	(n = 12)	(n = 9)	(n = 9)	(n = 20)	(N = 50) [c]

[a] Those respondents who said politics was discussed in their families "often"
or "sometimes." See table 3.

[b] Those respondents who said politics was discussed "not much" or "hardly at
all." See table 3.

[c] N does not equal 53 because the three respondents who had parents of mixed
party preference (i.e., one parent was a progressive-party supporter and the other
was not) were excluded from the tabulation. See note 1 in table 4.

heir own parents.[33] Of particular importance may be the socializing
effect of a college education. We know that the college environment
has a liberalizing influence.[34] Those who attain higher levels of education would thus be exposed to experiences, environments, and groups
likely to encourage the adoption of a progressive-party identification.
In Japan, for example, surveys have shown that a majority of Japanese
students support the Socialist Party whereas only 23 percent support
the LDP, a proportion almost the reverse of that of the population as
a whole.[35] The impact of higher education and the college environment would also thus explain why, whatever their parents' political
identification, most of my sample and that of Kuroda supported the
left-wing parties, particularly the Socialist: offspring of conservatives
and progressives alike were subject to the same influences after leaving
the family.

Parents who supported the progressive parties and who were interested in politics and discussed it with their children may well, of
course, have transmitted a progressive-party preference to their offspring, or at least an inclination toward one. But if the argument of
the impact of later environments and agencies is correct, then these
later agencies served to reinforce and maintain that preference originally acquired in the family. Where a salient party identification in
the family was lacking, weak, or not transmitted, these later agencies
introduced or substituted a progressive preference. The lack of any
strong party identification in the family was common in my sample.
Almost one-quarter of the sample's parents lacked a party preference
or had preferences to weak that the respondent could not remember
them; [36] almost another quarter of the sample who gave a parental
party preference indicated that the identification of their parents with
a party was weak. Consequently, almost half the sample would be particularly amenable to the influence of later agencies because they received no cues or very weak ones from their family concerning party
preference.

If the explanation just advanced is valid, it also helps account for
the contradictions between the findings of Ward and Kubota and
those of Kuroda and myself. My sample and Kuroda's both consisted
of only the highly educated. Consequently, given the diverse party
identifications of the parents and the push of later experience and the
college environment toward left-wing parties, one would expect a high
rate of inconsistency between parental party preference and respon-

33 Martin L. Levin, "Social Climates and Political Socialization."
34 Roberta S. Sigel (ed.), *Learning About Politics*, pp. 375–377.
35 Cited in Philip Altbach, "Japanese Students and Japanese Politics," p. 183.
36 See table 4.

progressive parents did not. Indeed, among those whose paren
ported the progressive parties, those with parents not intere
politics were *more* likely to come to a progressive-party pre
(100 percent) than those with parents interested in politics (87 p
Students whose parents did not support progressive parties eve
adopted a preference that differed from that of their parents, p
interest of the parents having absolutely no effect (88 percent a
a party preference different from that of their parents wheth
parents were interested in politics or not).

Although all of the studies of the transmission of party id
tion in the Japanese family indicate the coincidence of party
ence across generations to be greatest when parents support
the progressive parties, the evidence here leads to the conclusi
this coincidence of party preference is unrelated to parents'
political interest or amount of discussion of politics in the
hence by inference it is also unrelated to the direct transmi
party identification by parents. We must seek other explana
why children of families who support left parties tend to ad
same party preference as their parents when they grow older
process, we must also deal with a second major problem: att
to reconcile the contradictory evaluations of the role of the fa
the transmission of party preference.

The evidence presented above indicates strongly that ma
lies did not transmit salient party identifications to the resp
Rather, I suggest that the children from these families adopt
party preference as a result of other influences in their envir
This argument sees the adoption of party preference in Jap
two-stage process rather than as simple and direct acquisiti
party identification in the family. Later experiences lead to the
tion of a left-wing orientation or identification with a pri
secondary group other than the family which is leftist-leani
latter case is essentially the *kankei* theory applied to progre
well as conservatives.[31] This leftist orientation or identificat
leftist-leaning groups is then generalized to a progressive-part
ence. In his study of law students, Kuroda similarly hypothes
"socialization agencies in the wider environments, in additio
family, are responsible for the political party preference of
students." [32] Other studies and data reinforce the plausibilit
explanation. Levin presents evidence, for example, that the hig
climate of opinion and even the national political scene can i
party preferences of students regardless of the party prefei

---

[31] See preceding note.   [32] Kuroda, p. 330.

dents' party preference, the only consistency being shown by children of progressive-party supporters. Kubota and Ward's sample, on the other hand, was drawn from a stratified national probability sample from which they chose 177 child-parent pairs, the offspring being aged 15-19. This sample would exclude the impact of higher education on political orientations and thus on party preference: it would contain many offspring who would not enter, or had not yet entered, college. Many of the respondents would also still be living at home and hence would be more likely to be subject to parental cues as to party preference where they existed, so that the correspondence between the party preference of parent and child would be increased. In other words, Kuroda's study and mine probably exaggerate the inconsistencies between parents' and respondents' party preference because we deal with only college-educated youth subject to the left-wing influences of the college environment; Kubota and Ward probably exaggerate the consistencies because their sample excluded such influences, which today touch one out of every five youths in Japan.[37]

An additional point about the studies of parental transmission of party identification in Japan must be made. None of these studies, including my own, really prove or disprove "transmission." We have all dealt with coincidence of party preference between parent and child. Although my study has come closer to the problem of transmission by presenting data about parental interest in politics and political discussion in the family as an intervening variable, it still does not get to the heart of the problem: whether parents are transmitting cues as to party preference to their offspring, and if so, with what effect.

The final determination of the actual influences on the adoption of party preference in Japan awaits a study with a large sample taking into account the roles of both the family *and* later agencies. Such a study must demonstrate that actual transmission does or does not take place in the family and not rely on demonstrating only coincidence. The admittedly limited evidence presented here, however, suggests that our sample did not acquire their party preferences from their parents.

SUMMARY: THE ROLE OF THE FAMILY

Despite the problems involved in making any conclusive statement about the role of the family in the political-socialization process in Japan, some generalizations about its role, particularly in the political

---

[37] Of the total college-age population, 19.4 percent (24.2 percent of the males) attend some type of college. See Kazuko Tsurumi, "Student Movements in 1960 and 1969: Continuity and Change," p. 1.

socialization of student activists, can be made. My data indicate that the family's role may be more important as an indirect than as a direct agency of political socialization. For the activists we are studying here, this means that the family played a large role in the formation of their political beliefs and behavior by placing them in a network of social and economic relationships that increased the likelihood that they would be motivated to enter college, and by providing them with the material and psychological means to do so. That the activists came from upper-status families and had highly educated parents is undoubtedly related to their becoming college students at all. That they came from relatively higher upper-status households as compared with the intermittent activists, and that they had somewhat more permissive parents, especially mothers, coincides with the findings concerning American student activists in the 1960s.[38] The reasons for these relationships need further research. On the other hand, their later political activity cannot be fully predicted on the basis of the relatively small differences between the activists' and the less actives' family background.

It was beyond the scope of this study to explore whether basic values having later political implications were being learned in the family. In my depth interviews, some of the respondents indicated that few values their parents had taught them had relevance for their adult lives, but others indicated that pacifistic attitudes or an emphasis on the value of social trust were clearly transmitted in the family. A fuller study of this interesting problem might reveal that some of the later orientations of the students were founded on nonpolitical core values transmitted by parents, as Keniston found in his study of American students.

Nor could I study the full effect upon later political relationships of the close and interdependent nature of Japanese family relationships. But all observers have noted with Langdon that "emphasis on personal loyalty, small-group or face-to-face preference, and distress at the difficulty of influencing outsiders are common behavior traits first learned within the family."[39] These characteristics learned in the family have been seen as setting the pattern for all of Japan's social organization with its emphasis on small groups, personal communication, and close relationships within a group but distrust of those out-

---

[38] Studies of American students conducted since the spring of 1969 indicate, however, that activists no longer necessarily come from liberal middle-class families. See Lucy N. Friedman, Alice R. Gold, and Richard Christie, "Dissecting the Generation Gap: Intergenerational and Intrafamilial Similarities and Differences," pp. 335–337.

[39] Langdon, p. 204.

side.[40] Few could deny the indirect influence of the family in this regard.

Despite these gaps in our knowledge of the family's role in indirect socialization, my data clearly point to the weak explanatory power of family variables in the *direct* transmission of political orientations. The family's role as a direct transmitter of party identification, as an agent of politicization, and as a model of political behavior seems quite limited. The most-politicized, active students who supported left-wing parties often came from families of nonpoliticized, nonactive parents who did not transmit a party preference. Only in the transmission of a general "progressive" orientation was there even slight evidence of family influence. Even this, however, was true only in the minority of cases where the family was interested in politics.

The relatively weak role of the family in direct political socialization is more understandable when put into historical context. Although I cannot completely agree with Sumiya Mikio's assertion that the postwar Japanese family "has abandoned its responsibility to socialize the child or stabilize social values" and has abandoned its role completely to education,[41] his assertion may have truth to it in terms of political values. In more complex and differentiated societies, the socialization of the young, including their political socialization, often devolves on later agencies, closer in time to the adult world and more capable of preparing youth to enter it. In the case of Japan this tendency in political socialization was undoubtedly reinforced by the defeat in the Pacific war and the changes brought by the Occupation. In prewar Japan the family was integrally tied to the nationalist ideology and was used as an important agency of direct political socialization.[42] With the defeat and the discrediting of prewar political values and everything associated with them,[43] politics might naturally have become one of the most uncomfortable topics of conversation in the respondents' families, and their parents might have been considered dis-

[40] Chie Nakane, *Japanese Society*, chs. 1–3; Koya Azumi, *Higher Education and Business Recruitment in Japan*, ch. 2; Nobutaka Ike, *Japanese Politics: An Introductory Survey*, pp. 25–36.

[41] Sumiya Mikio, "The Function and Social Structure of Education: Schools and Japanese Society," p. 129.

[42] Kazuko Tsurumi, *Social Change*, pp. 103–107.

[43] Feuer, *The Conflict of Generations*, p. 199, refers to this as the "De-authoritization of the Elders." Feuer implies that the result is rebellion against parents. As we have seen, there is little evidence to indicate that the activists in the sample were rebelling against their parents, at least in the sense of rebellion against parental authority. The possibility exists that their parents' lack of politicization contributes to their activism in other ways once they themselves become politicized. This gap between the depoliticized family and the students' own politicization experiences will be discussed later in this study.

qualified as respected transmitters of political culture.[44] Even where politics was discussed and this disqualification did not take place, later agencies—the school, teachers, and peer group—would be better prepared to teach the young about the new political world than were their parents, socialized as they were into the old world. It is to these later agencies that we must turn to find a more complete account of the origins of our activists' beliefs and behavior.

[44] On the depoliticization of the family in the postwar period, see Ishida Takeshi, "Katei to Seiji" (The Family and Politics), p. 5.

3

BECOMING A STUDENT ACTIVIST

WE MOVE now from an examination of the role of the family in political socialization in Japan to a consideration of the part played by other agencies. While growing up, a child everywhere is subject to other influences which, besides those of the family, shape his view of the political world. He attends school and comes into contact with elders other than his parents, elders in positions of authority and who, because of their function as official cultural transmitters, may surpass his family in implanting knowledge, beliefs, and models of authority of the outside world. He is also grouped in the classroom with others of his age. Some of his classmates become his friends outside of school, and with them he grows older and discovers and interprets the world—a world which he also experiences directly and from which he may draw his own inferences as he grows older. It is with these agencies of political socialization—school and teachers, peer groups, and contact with the wider society itself—that this chapter is concerned. The results about family political socialization that were presented in the previous chapter impel us to look to these agencies to determine how some of our students became radicals and active in the student movement. I shall explore three dimensions of political belief and behavior in this chapter: politicization, participation and the belief in democracy, and the development of ideology. My data will be presented in the same order in which most of my respondents experienced it, beginning with their first awareness of politics and ending with their adoption of Marxism.

DISCOVERING THE WIDER WORLD

As I pointed out at the beginning of the previous chapter, little attention has been given to direct contact with the political system itself as a political-socialization experience, or to the impact of political and social change on the development of the political learning of individuals. Such neglect seems inconsequential when studying stable systems in which major crises, rapid social change, and incongruities between earlier agencies and the political system are rare. But in the modern world, the number of such systems untouched by the upheavals of war, political protest, and rapid modernization is diminishing. In any case, postwar Japanese history during the fifteen years from sudden defeat in World War II to the 1960 Ampo crisis hardly justifies including Japan in the ranks of those few.

Many Japanese who had suffered through the deprivations accompanying the closing years of the war reacted to Japan's defeat in the Pacific war with varying mixtures of relief and resignation.[1] To others, however, particularly the young just old enough to know about the war but not old enough to see through the consistent government propaganda promising Japan's inevitable victory or at least heroic defense of the home islands, the sudden surrender came as a shock and at one stroke negated an entire value system and social organization.[2] Into the vacuum stepped an occupying army, the first in Japan's long history, bringing in its wake new goals and values, new standards for regulating and judging social relations, and a new political system. The Occupation left few aspects of society and politics untouched. Land reform, equal status for women, a new legal and educational system, economic reorganization, the legitimation of labor unions and political protest, a new "no-war" constitution, and the value of democracy were all introduced, made into law, and disseminated through the schools and the media during the first few years after the war.[3] The defeat also created another vacuum less easily filled—the tremendous economic void following the wartime bombings, loss of markets, and shortages. The poverty and misery of the later war years continued into peacetime and were worsened by black-marketing, inflation, and the influx into the cities of returning soldiers and evacuees. The Occupation policy, until 1948, of emphasizing economic democraticization and decentralization rather than economic recovery did little to improve these conditions. The Communists emerged from World War II with increased prestige because some of them had resisted the wartime ideology. Blessed by the early Occupation's political tolerance, they gained a following through programs and a

---

1 Kazuo Kawai, *Japan's American Interlude*, pp. 4–10, analyzes the reaction of Japanese to defeat and the reasons for their acceptance of the Occupation.

2 The most moving, personal account of the meaning of the defeat for youth in Japan at the time is found in Makoto Oda, "The Meaning of Meaningless Death." Oda is a writer and leader of the new left in Japan.

3 Kawai, pp. 24–5; chs. 6–11.

philosophy that appealed to many Japanese in the midst of the miserable postwar economic conditions and spiritual vacuum.[4]

These important events in the first few years of the Occupation were to be followed by others. One was the "reverse course" of the Occupation, consolidating rather than expanding the immediate postwar reforms, emphasizing economic recovery, and cracking down on left-wing influence, as in the famous "Red Purge" of 1949 in which thousands of Communist unionists in all fields were dismissed from their jobs.[5] The Korean War soon followed, with its dual consequences of reviving the Japanese armed forces (first as a "police reserve" and later as "self-defense forces") and beginning the postwar economic boom. Labor disputes and increasing left-wing disillusionment with the Occupation resulted from the "reverse course" (which now also included the feared rearmament of Japan) and culminated in "Bloody May Day" of 1952. The "Bloody May Day" incident, which followed by a few days the end of the Occupation and during which hundreds of left-wing demonstrators battled police in front of the Imperial Palace, was only the beginning of a succession of protests and clashes between the Left and Right subcultures in the course of the 1950s which led up to the Ampo crisis itself. The 1950s saw a Ban-the-Bomb and peace movement, debate over article IX (the "no-war" clause of the Japanese constitution), and protests over attempted revisions of the powers of the police, over the autonomy of teachers, over the teaching of "ethics" in the schools, and over the building of a new runway at an American airbase.[6] That decade embraced also economic recovery and growth, the split of the Socialists into two parties and their later reunification, the merging of the conservative parties to form the Liberal Democratic Party, and the rise of an autonomous student movement, breaking away from the control of the Communist Party in rebellion against its authoritarian organization, but retaining its Marxist orientation.

It would indeed be unusual if our students, whose childhood and adolescence were spent in the midst of this social and political turmoil and change, could remain completely untouched by it. In fact, my survey and interviews disclosed that these major changes and events in

---

4 Concerning the relationship between Occupation economic policy and the influence of the Communists in the first few years of the Occupation, see Chalmers A. Johnson, *Conspiracy at Matsukawa*, pp. 13–22.

5 See Johnson, pp. 23, 60; Rōyama Masamichi, *Yomigaeru Nihon* (Japan Revived), p. 113; Robert E. Ward, "Reflections on the Allied Occupation and Planned Political Change in Japan," pp. 502–506. Ward's interpretation differs from most in that he views the changes in Occupation policy as mainly the result of a natural consolidation process and merely a shift in emphasis, rather than a great change in policy and a result of the onset of the Cold War.

6 See Introduction, footnote 12.

postwar Japanese history also played two important and direct roles in the political socialization of my respondents. Many of the respondents, particularly the leaders and activists, first became aware of the wider political and social world through the effect of one or more of the events described above. Moreover, these events, directly and indirectly, also contributed to the adoption of Marxism. In this section I shall describe the effect of these changes and events in stimulating my respondents' first interest in politics. A later section will deal with their effect on the development of ideology.

In my 1970 survey I asked my respondents when and how they first became interested in politics. These data and related questions asked during the depth interviews indicate that the years between middle school and the last year of high school or entrance into college saw the first awakening of the activists' interest in politics and broader social issues. Few of the leaders and activists expressed an interest in politics before middle school, but almost all became interested in politics soon after entering college. The intermittent and nonactivists, on the other hand, tended first to become interested in politics either in primary school [7] or not until their college years, if they were interested in politics at all.

The responses to the question of how the activists first became interested in politics, as well as discussions during the depth interviews, all pointed to the major role of broader social change and major political events in stimulating an initial interest in politics. The particular conditions or events that awakened the activists to the wider world were almost as numerous as the individuals themselves, but common themes emerge. The leaders and activists who had been in middle and high school at the end of the war or during the Occupation were most influenced by the aftermath of the war and the social and economic dislocation that even the most financially secure families experienced. The respondents themselves often had personal contact with this dislocation. A leader of Zengakuren, whom I shall call A, described as follows the discovery of poverty, hypocrisy, and other social evils that led him to think for the first time in social and political terms:

> Around 1947, various evil facts were revealed, like poverty and inequality among people. Also it was known that those people in higher positions who had proclaimed that they had been fighting a holy war had actually been embezzling and turning goods into illegal channels. It was not just these

---

[7] The earlier interest in politics for some of the less active is undoubtedly due to their having parents more interested in politics and who discussed politics more with them. See ch. 2, tables 2 and 3, and the remarks below concerning the relative roles of different agencies.

people who were at fault but the evils resulting from the social structure of the time. Death from hunger, poverty, and blackmarketing have to do with the way society itself is. It was around that time that I began to think that those problems are caused by the structure of the society, and therefore, in order to solve them, the structure itself has to be changed.[8]

E, another leader, explained how his discovery of poverty had the same result. He spoke of the poverty of his family after the war, and went on to say:

I couldn't study or go out and I began to wonder why I had to work. When I was in high school various experiences came together and caused me to realize that the reason that this kind of thing happened was that the society was evil.[9]

E also described how the "Red Purge" directly affected him in his first year in high school:

At that time, teachers whom I had some contact with were returned soldiers who went to war for Japan without thinking about it deeply. But they realized it had been wrong and were troubled by it, and we were exposed to that. So what they said was odd and contradictory, and though they were adults over thirty we were confronted with their troubles. That remains with me strongly. It was these people who were fired during the "Red Purge." At another time a teacher told us that he went to war and fought, but when the times changed he thought about it deeply and realized that rearmament, or in the popular language of the time, "reverse course," shouldn't be permitted. When he was fired in the "Red Purge" he said to us that we might not understand what he meant now, but when we came of age to understand, never to forget what he said. It impressed me very much.[10]

Other leaders and activists also described how the influence of the war and the existence of poverty stimulated their first interest in social and political problems: "In middle school I thought about the difference between rich and poor." "When the war ended I asked myself, 'Why was the state destroyed so simply? What would be from now on? What was war, anyhow?'" The Korean War, the impact of which some respondents felt strongly because of its geographic proximity and relevance to their recent postwar educations stressing antiwar themes, was cited by a few.

Even a few of the intermittent activists, such as K, discovered politics in a way similar to the activists:

. . . at the next school I went to I had a friend whose family was poor, and his elder brother became a member of the Self-Defense Forces. At that

---

8 Interview with A, April 18, 1970.   10 *Ibid.*
9 Interview with E, May 2, 1970.

time it was considered an awful thing, and he was abused by everyone. I talked with my friend about it many times, and it was the first time I experienced an interest in social or political problems, like why we have to have Self-Defense Forces, or why my friend's family who were rich before the war had their house burned down in the war and became poor. He showed me what was left of the family estate, and it was the first time I questioned why the war occurred.[11]

But K was not a typical intermittent activist: the influence of the war and poverty in the first step to political thinking was much more typical of the leaders and activists, especially the older ones.

Other committed activists, including many too young to have been influenced by the immediate postwar conditions, said that their interest in politics was first aroused by major left-wing struggles in the 1950s: the Ban-the-Bomb movement, the problem of the Police Duties Bill, and the Sunakawa struggle.[12] B, a leader in the student movement, described his first concern about politics in terms that connect the influences of war and political unrest:

The Korean War itself influenced me quite a bit though. . . . Up till then we were educated that "war is bad" and "peace, peace" was emphasized. Then the Korean War occurred, and though I didn't know much about Occupation policy or how it changed, within the country public feeling was in a turmoil, what with labor strikes and their suppression, and I had an uneasy feeling that there was unrest in the world.[13]

Many of the leaders and activists, then, demonstrated a great sensitivity to war, political turmoil, and economic inequalities, and from this sensitivity came their first interest in broader political and social issues. Of course, this initial interest cannot be equated with complete "politicization." Like B, these middle- and high-school students might have felt "uneasy" over the political turmoil that existed, or like K or E begun to question why wars occurred or why poverty existed, but these first insights and questions would have to grow and be reinforced by other agents. The events that stimulated an initial interest in political and social questions seem to have established what Keniston calls "enduring sensitivities for later development," [14] rather than sudden, full-fledged politicization. We should note, however, that in the later development of this initial interest in, and sensitivity to, the wider political and social world, such major political events as war and protest movements were again to play a role. Later in this chapter we shall be considering the extent to which the respondents discussed

---

11 Interview with K, April 18, 1970.
12 See Introduction, note 12.
13 Interview with B, April 25, 1970.
14 Kenneth Keniston, *Young Radicals*, p. 76.

politics with their teachers and peers. It is interesting to note now, however, that the problem of war and the major left-wing struggles and incidents of the 1940s and 1950s were among the topics most frequently discussed with these agents. Major crises, important events, and direct contact with social and political conditions thus serve a dual function in the politicization process: they stimulate an initial interest in political and social questions, and then, along with other agents, help develop this interest into a deeper and more enduring concern for politics.

The significance of these findings is twofold. To begin with, they reaffirm the evidence that student activists are extremely sensitive during their early youth to broader social conditions and events, particularly those involving violence and socioeconomic differences. If we make allowances for differences in historical and cultural context, the themes described above are remarkably similar to those that Keniston found when he asked his sample of American student activists about their earliest memories:

> In these recollections, two crucial themes stand out. First, these earliest memories are to an unusual degree connected to the broader social scene: the end of the war, a well-publicized riot, the interviewee's favored social position. This sensitivity to the social scene recurs throughout these young radicals' lives. Second, the issue of violence, external and internal, runs through these early memories. . . .[15]

Keniston here is discussing an earlier period of childhood for his American students, whereas I have indicated that these same themes seem to have become prominent only in middle and high school for my activists. Nonetheless, the similarity in themes is striking and points to a conclusion that student activists become aware of violent events, wars, and social differences fairly early and that this awareness and sensitivity is the first step to full-scale politicization and activism later on. In their first awareness of political and social problems we may very well be seeing the origins of the strong feelings against war and injustice as well as the orientations toward protest as a means of alleviating war and injustice that they were to demonstrate as student activists. Takahashi, who found that his sample of Japanese student activists of the 1960s also exhibited this social sensitivity and awareness of contradictions in their precollege youth, describes these budding characteristics as an undeveloped "feeling of humanism." [16]

---

15 *Ibid.*, p. 50. Keniston also refers to examples of personal and internalized violence that were not investigated or indicated during my interviews.

16 Takahashi Akira, "Nihon Gakusei Undō no Shisō to Kōdō" (Thought and Behavior of the Japanese Student Movement), parts 2 and 3, *Chūō Kōron*, June 1968, p. 183, and August 1968, p. 269.

As we shall see later in this chapter, the more developed "humanism" that evolves from this sensitivity to social tension and societal differences is an important stage in the development of Marxist ideology among the activists.

These findings illustrate, moreover, the important contribution that larger social events can play as an agent of political socialization in Japan. Shinohara Hajime has suggested that because discussion of politics is apt to be infrequent in the Japanese family and social-science education in the schools is mere "intellectual cramming," the development of political concern through crises and incidents may be quite common even among contemporary Japanese youth. Also, examples from compositions of Japanese school children on the subject of "Japan in the World," which he excerpts as illustrations of youth's distrust of adult politics in Japan, dwell on the problem of the Vietnam War.[17] All this raises the interesting possibility that the development of an interest in politics in the same manner as my leaders and activists—through crises, incidents, and wars—may be a fundamental characteristic of childhood and adolescent political socialization in postwar Japan. Indeed, the effect of continual changes in postwar Japanese political history has led another political scientist to refer to political socialization in Japan as the "political socialization of upheavals."[18]

AGENCIES OF POLITICAL SOCIALIZATION

The question of whether the early awareness of the political world that we found characteristic of our activists in the previous section became further developed during their middle- and high-school periods, and if so, in what agencies, is the subject I turn to now. The problems I shall deal with are whether the activists became further politicized during this period in comparison with the less active students, and which agencies made the greatest contribution to developing that political interest and forming the political beliefs of each group. As an indicator of both the respondent's politicization and the relative impact of agencies, I use frequency of discussion of politics, a particularly good indicator for this purpose because discussion depends on the interaction of a subject with others. The frequency with which

---

17 Shinohara Hajime, *Nihon no Seiji Fūdo* (The Political Climate of Japan), pp. 19–24. Shinohara emphasizes the communication of these incidents and events through the mass media, whereas I am dealing here with both that type of stimulus and more direct contacts. The point about the effect of larger social and political crises, however, remains the same.

18 Tadao Okamura, "The Child's Changing Image of the Prime Minister," p. 567.

our respondents discussed politics can serve to indicate how politicized they were, and a comparison of the agents with whom they discussed politics most can show which of those agents had the largest role in the development and reinforcement of political interest and beliefs.

In 1962, Tsurumi asked the students whether they discussed politics with their primary-, middle-, and high-school teachers. In 1970, we asked the sample whether they had discussed politics outside the classroom with their friends. The results of these questions appear in table 6. I have omitted discussion with primary-school teachers because only four students in the entire sample said they had discussed politics with these teachers. The table shows that by their high-school years the activists were already more politicized than the less active students. A relationship exists between future level of activity in the student movement and discussion of politics, whether with teachers or peers. Two-thirds to three-quarters of the activists were discussing politics and social problems with their teachers and peers in high school, but only

TABLE 6. RELATIONSHIP BETWEEN DISCUSSION OF POLITICS WITH VARIOUS AGENTS IN MIDDLE SCHOOL AND HIGH SCHOOL AND LATER ACTIVITY IN THE STUDENT MOVEMENT (IN PERCENT)

Discussed politics with:	Activity in the student movement		
	LA	INA	Total
Middle-school teachers			
Yes	46	16	30
No	54	84	70
	100%	100%	100%
	$X^2 = 7.44$; p < .01		
High-school teachers			
Yes	64	36	51
No	36	64	49
	100%	100%	100%
	$X^2 = 4.1$; p < .05		
Peer group [a]			
Yes	75	32	55
No	25	68	45
	100%	100%	100%
	$X^2 = 9.9$; p < .01		
	(n = 28)	(n = 25)	(N = 53)

[a] The questions about the peer group in the 1970 survey read as follows: "About how much time did you spend talking together with your friends about politics and social problems outside of your middle- and high-school classes? Did you talk often, sometimes, not much, or hardly at all?" In order to make the categories of response similar to those asked in the 1962 Tsurumi question on teachers, these responses were dichotomized, "Often" and "Sometimes" being treated as a "yes" response, and "Not much" and "Hardly at all" being treated as a "no" response.

about one-third of the future intermittent and nonactivists were doing so. It seems that the activists' initial interest in the social and political problems dealt with in the previous section did indeed grow into an enduring political concern in these agencies.

Comparing agencies in terms of discussion of politics by the committed activists and the less active, we find a significant relationship between activity and discussion of politics with middle- and high-school teachers and a strong and significant relationship between activity and discussion in the peer group. The activists were more likely to discuss politics with their teachers and much more likely to discuss it with their peers than were the less active students. And whereas a higher percentage of activists discussed politics with their peers than with their high-school teachers, the less active students tended to talk about politics more with their teachers than their peers.

In the light of the percentages presented in chapter 2 concerning political discussion in the family and those in table 6, agencies of political socialization can be ranked in terms of their influence on each of our subgroups:

Rank	LA [a]	INA [a]
1.	peers (75%)	family (50%)
2.	high-school teachers (64%)	high-school teachers (36%)
3.	middle-school teachers (46%)	peers (32%)
4.	family (32%)	middle-school teachers (16%)

[a] Percentage in parentheses refers to those discussing politics with the agent.

The peer group was the most important agent for the activists, the family the least important; [19] the family was the most important agent for the less active, the peer group third. The data presented here reaffirm the preceding chapter's conclusions: other agencies, in this case the peer group and high-school teachers, were more instrumental than the family in the direct political socialization of student activists before they entered college and could substitute for the family's influence when it was lacking. The family's principal role was in influencing about one-half of the less active students during the precollege period.

Other data from the Tsurumi study enables us to investigate the relative role of these agencies, and to determine whether the peer group's influence continued, decreased, or increased, after the students entered college. In 1962, Prof. Tsurumi questioned the sample as to

---

[19] If we remember that the activists tended to come from families of high socioeconomic status, these results indirectly confirm Langton's findings in his study of political efficacy among Caribbean secondary-school students. He found that the peer group had a greater impact than the family in moving upper-class children from the medium to the high range of political efficacy. See Langton, *Political Socialization*, pp. 154–160.

whom they talked with most about a number of subjects, including politics. As examples, the question gave parents, siblings, teachers, and friends. The results in terms of the percent citing the agent as one with whom they discussed politics most were as follows:

	LA [a]	INA [a]
Family	7%	16%
Teachers	14%	0
Peers	100%	76%

[a] Multiple or no responses possible.

The committed activists are still more politicized than the less active, and the peer group is still the most important agency of political socialization for the activists. This fact is also borne out by separate data from the Tsurumi study showing that whereas 43 percent of my activists belonged to college circles and clubs whose purpose was the discussion of political and social problems, only 8 percent of the less active belonged to such groups. The less active were much more likely to belong to sports or religious groups or clubs. The peer group, as we have seen, already provided the persons with whom more activists (75 percent) discussed politics in middle and high school. This tendency continued in college, but now *all* the activists said that friends were those with whom they discussed politics most.

It is also readily apparent, however, that at the time of the 1962 survey, the peer group was the most important political socialization agency for the less active as well. Although only one-third of the less active said they discussed politics at all with their peers in middle and high school, approximately three-quarters now gave peers as the persons with whom they most often discussed politics.

Few of either group said they discussed politics most with family or teachers. This is not to say that they never discussed politics with family and university teachers. In a separate question, Tsurumi asked them whether they discussed politics and other subjects with various family members and university teachers. Of the activists, 77 percent, and of the less active, 62 percent, said they discussed politics with their parents, and 64 percent of the activists and 40 percent of the less active said that they did so with their university teachers. In the case of the family this represents a dramatic increase over precollege days in the activists' political discussion with their families (from 32 to 77 percent), and a slight increase for the less active (from 50 to 62 percent). But their responses to the question of which agent they discussed politics with *most* suggest that the increases in discussion with the family may be the result of politicization by peers and the college environment rather than of an independent influence. Baber's survey of college students in Japan in the late 1950s lends credence to this interpretation. He found that although politics was high on a list of topics most frequently discussed with parents, it was low on the list of topics on which they agreed with their parents.[20] In any case, even if the family was influencing the political beliefs of the sample when they were in college, the data above indicate that it was still second to the peer group.

The figures for both groups in discussion of politics with university teachers are almost exactly the same as the figures for discussion with their high-school teachers. The relative infrequency with which the university teacher was cited as the person with whom politics was most discussed, and the fact that political discussion with teachers had not increased since high school, may well be the result of the nature of Japanese postwar education. The tremendous increase in the number of college students in the postwar period and the great burdens placed on the underpaid and understaffed college faculties [21] resulted in even larger lecture classes and even less opportunity for personal contact with professors than in the prewar period. Although the universities in our study have not been so deficient in this regard as some of the more *"masu-pro"* ("mass-production") colleges, smaller classes and the opportunity to talk with teachers informally have still been relatively infrequent. In a 1965 survey published in the newspaper at Keiō University, one of the institutions from which my sample is drawn, only 14 percent of the students said they talked on familiar terms with their professors.[22] A Ministry of Education survey in 1966 showed that whereas contact with teachers increased among upperclassmen to about 60 percent in national and private colleges, in the first few years of college only about one-third of the students had contact with professors. Three-quarters of all students who did not have contact with their professors said they wanted to but couldn't for lack of the opportunity.[23]

My data and supporting evidence thus argue strongly that the peer group, as we would expect, continues to be the greatest influence on the political interest and attitudes of those committed to the student movement. And in college, the peer group replaces the family as the prime agent of political socialization among the less active. Other evidence also indicates that the peer group may play the key mediat-

---

20 Roy E. Baber, *Youth Looks at Marriage and the Family*, part II.

21 Between 1950 and 1960, the number of college students increased from 225,000 to 626,000, including an increase from 80,000 to 194,000 in national universities and 136,000 to 404,000 in private universities. See Azumi, p. 24. Because of the low pay, many professors take part-time lectureships at other colleges to make ends meet, and this contributed to the lack of time and availability for contact with students outside the classroom. See *Journal of Social and Political Ideas in Japan*, V, 2-3, pp. 302-303.

22 Cited in Suzuki Hirō, *Gakusei Undō* (The Student Movement), p. 72.

23 *Ibid.*, p. 73.

ing role in the recruitment of students to activist roles in college. Suzuki found in his sample of activists that the influence of friends and upperclassmen was one of the main factors leading to participation in the movement.[24] Although this problem was not investigated thoroughly in either Tsurumi's study or mine, some respondents mentioned how friends helped mobilize them to participation. After his friends encouraged him to participate, one respondent joined a demonstration with a group of ten other students. In another case, a social-science study circle mobilized their classmates. Still another respondent went to his first demonstration because its purpose was to protest the arrest of a friend in a previous demonstration.

A number of reasons may be advanced to explain the peer group's increasing influence in college in political socialization and recruitment. In the case of the activists, the pattern of political interaction with age-mates and friends was already established before entering college, and those active in the student movement would naturally discuss politics more with their coactivists. Then, too, college thrusts all the students, active or not, into a new environment with others of their age with whom they work or live closely. As Sigel has pointed out, this provides the already concerned student with an arena to act out his concern and the less involved with "a ready-made group and an ethos whose norms he may internalize or reject depending on the intensity of his need to belong, the nature of the group ethos, the salience of his career goals, and the permissiveness of the political atmosphere." [25] The environment of Japanese universities is both politicized and permissive, as is evidenced by the existence and degree of student political activity. The extent to which penalties are attached to student activism, and the relation of such penalties to career goals, will be examined in a later chapter. I might, however, note here that such formal penalties as do exist are imposed for being arrested in a demonstration and not for participation *per se,* and that generally both college authorities and the general public are exceedingly tolerant of student political activity. The college environment in Japan, therefore, is quite conducive to the peer group's increased influence as an agent of political socialization.

In addition, Kiefer has argued that the Japanese college-entrance-examination system may encourage the transfer of affect to the peer group: "What the 'examination hell' ritual accomplishes in Japan is the extension of emotional habits learned in the family to the child's *group of age-mates.*" [26] Although family roles are not necessarily un-

---

24 *Ibid.,* pp. 259–260.
25 Roberta S. Sigel (ed.), *Learning About Politics,* p. 379; see also pp. 375–376.
26 Christie W. Kiefer, "Psychological Interdependence of Family, School, and Bureaucracy in Japan," p. 72; emphasis in the original.

dermined in the process, the college-entrance exams serve as a modern
equivalent of a puberty rite, in which the "emotional significance of
his classmates" increases.[27] Consequently, the importance of the peer
group in the political socialization of the students, once they are in
college, rests in part on both the university environment and the prior
socialization process.

By late adolescence, namely the high-school and college years, the
peer group has become the most potent personal agent of political
socialization for these students.

THE SCHOOL AND PARTICIPATION

Robert Lifton has said that the search for *shutaisei* characterized
youth in Japan in the early 1960s. He describes *shutaisei* as composed
of two parts: selfhood, "holding and living by personal convictions,"
and social commitment, "having the capacity to act in a way that is
effective in furthering historical goals" by "joining forces with like-
minded people in order to do so." [28] The 1960 Ampo activists demonstrated both aspects of *shutaisei* in their attitudes toward participation
and authority. They greatly valued participation and the expression of
personal convictions in the face of authority *for their own sake* and not
only as means to a social and political end. Though attempting to implement ideological and political goals, they insisted that "selfhood,"
living by and expressing their convictions, was as important as attaining these external goals. This dual orientation toward participation
as a means to an end *and* as a valued life style distinguishes the activists from intermittent activists of their generation who participated
in the 1960 demonstrations primarily to bring about some specific end.
The emphasis on participation as self-expression also distinguishes the
Ampo anti-Communist Party activists from the prewar and postwar
Communists who were willing to accept the ironclad discipline and
authority of their own party to further ideological goals. The split between the activists who went on to lead the Ampo demonstrations and
the Communist Party was caused not only by differences on questions
of ideology and tactics but also by the refusal of the Party to allow dissent, criticism, and a share in party decision-making to those students
who insisted that opposition to the government did not justify Stalinist authoritarianism within the Party.[29]

---

27 *Ibid.*, pp. 72–73.

28 Robert J. Lifton, "Youth and History: Individual Change in Postwar Japan,"
p. 274.

29 Concerning the issues involved in the split with the Communist Party, see
Kenichi Koyama, "The Zengakuren"; Kazuko Tsurumi, *Social Change*, pp. 309–312,
320–333.

This orientation toward self-expression was still common among former activists even by 1970. I asked them whether they thought they could do anything if the Diet were considering a bill which they strongly opposed. If they said they *could* do something, I asked them whether they thought that they would be successful, and if not, why they would act anyway. Few thought that their acts would be successful, but most said they would oppose the bill somehow. The phrase *"ishi hyōji"* recurred often in these answers. Literally this means "a declaration of intention" and implies the expression of will or opinion. Other former activists said that doing something to oppose the bill was more to express themselves than to accomplish anything or that the action itself had significance. Still others mentioned "personal conviction" or said merely, "just because I oppose it." Only a few connected acts of opposition to any concrete end, such as preventing the passage of the bill or strengthening the revolutionary movement. This trait, characteristic of the 1960 activists, is largely absent from traditional Japanese culture, which tolerated self-expression primarily in such culturally sanctioned areas as art or aesthetics and valued submission to authority and the repression of individual opinions in social relations.[30] In this sense the 1960 student activists were a transitional generation in left-wing movements in Japan. For since 1960, independent expression of political views and emphasis on grass-roots participatory democracy have been increasingly stressed in the student movement and in the multiplying citizens' action groups of the new Left.[31] In this secton I shall attempt to find the roots of these participatory orientations held by the 1960 activists by exploring the school as an agent of political socialization. I shall consider both the direct impact

---

30 The political implications of this cultural trait are studied in Robert E. Ward, "Japan: The Continuity of Modernization," pp. 33–39; Kurt Steiner, "Popular Political Participation and Political Development in Japan: The Rural Level"; Kazuko Tsurumi, *Social Change*, chs. II and III. Historically, however, there has been an elite tradition of resistance and even rebellion against authority, the rebel claiming that he was acting sincerely in the higher interests of the collective. During the Tokugawa period a loyal retainer would express opposition to his lord's policies and claim that he was acting in the higher interest of his lord, the *shishi* of the Meiji Restoration rebelled against the Shogun in the name of restoring the Emperor, and in the 1930s young army officers mutinied or took independent action contrary to orders in the belief that they were merely carrying out what the Emperor would wish if he was only aware of the situation and not misled by evil advisers. This lesser tradition, however, usually did not apply to the vast majority of the population. The more prevalent attitude toward authority survives in postwar Japan among those born and raised before the war. A poll cited by Jean Stoetzel in *Without the Chrysanthemum and the Sword*, pp. 150–151, showed that agreement with the dictum, "never contradict a superior," was the majority opinion among those over thirty and that agreement diminished with decreasing age.

31 Kazuko Tsurumi, "Student Movements in 1960 and 1969: Continuity and Change," pp. 10–12, 24–28; Taketsugu Tsurutani, "A New Era of Japanese Politics: Tokyo's Gubernatorial Election."

of formal classroom teaching and the indirect impact of classroom and school environments in developing participatory orientations and the inclination to express opinions to authority.

Miyata Mitsuo has attributed the democratic citizen's spirit of challenging authority, as demonstrated in the Ampo crisis, directly to the content of postwar education. He argues that the rise of spontaneity in social relations, independent thought, and critical attitudes in Japan, which could be seen in the first decade and a half after the war, were largely the result of education in the schools, especially of the then widely used textbook called *Minshushugi (Democracy)*. This text, issued in 1949, emphasized that a democracy could succeed only if economic and social relations were also democratic and everyone had the "spirit of democracy" within himself.[32] Certainly the Occupation's aim in issuing such texts was to produce citizens who would not be submissive to authority and who would be willing to express their opinions and participate in politics. The evidence from my interviews about the influence of this type of teaching and textbook on actual attitudes is somewhat ambiguous, however. On the one hand, some of the activists admitted that what they had been taught in postwar civics classes had indeed affected their thinking. One respondent even singled out *Minshushugi* as the source of that influence. In addition, the phrase *"ishi hyōji"* discussed above might also reflect that influence, for it is a rather formal phrase of the kind that might be used in the teaching of civics.[33] Some of the activists, however, made it abundantly clear that they had learned merely the structural and organizational forms of democracy in the classroom; they had acquired its spirit and meaning elsewhere. When, during a depth interview, I asked K, an intermittent activist, what he thought the meaning of democracy was, the following exchange took place:

K: What I was taught in school about democracy was destroyed, so I can't answer.

Interviewer: What were you taught about democracy in school?

K: "The separation of powers," "majority rule," etc.[34]

K went on to say that he now thought of democracy as "guaranteeing the people's spontaneity, autonomy, and independence," ideas that, judging from the above response, he did not learn in the classroom. E was even more explicit:

---

32 Miyata Mitsuo, *Gendai Nihon no Minshushugi* (Contemporary Japanese Democracy), pp. 117–121.

33 I am indebted to Mr. Mizutani Osamu of the Inter-University Center for Japanese Language Studies in Tokyo for this information.

34 Interview with K, April 18, 1970.

I think of democracy two ways: one way is what we were taught in school and in the textbooks: democracy is the separation of powers, an Assembly, and the election of representatives. That's what I had in my head as knowledge, and I memorized that they were important. But these are organizational problems. The other way, which I didn't study at school, is democracy viewed as how people in society are affected; I mean how to act when we find that something is wrong—that kind of democracy we didn't study in school. My way of thinking developed through friends or teachers, or when I went to a May Day demonstration without understanding it and became enraged after I was beaten by a policeman and then discussed with my friends how to change such a world.[35]

E's experience is a good example of how direct contact with the political system can often be a more potent socialization experience than intended transmission, as I said previously. But it also makes me doubt that postwar classroom education can be fully credited with developing the strong participatory orientations of the students in my sample. Because my data are only fragmentary, no firm conclusions can be reached. However, the role of direct teaching and the formal educational process in creating participatory orientations appears by no means uniformly great. Classroom teaching that emphasized the underlying democratic spirit supporting democracy as a political form seems to have impressed some of the students. When teachers taught democracy as a form of political organization and required rote memorization, their efforts appear to have left no appreciable mark except a feeling of distaste, and students found their own personal meanings for democracy elsewhere. This interpretation of the impact of classroom teaching on participatory orientations is buttressed by the results of a survey conducted in Japan in the early 1950s. Sofue Takeo found that a majority of Japanese youth, who by the time of the survey had experienced the new democratic postwar education, chose "for the people" rather than "by the people" as the meaning of democracy.[36]

This is not to say that classroom education, combined with the Occupation's entire attempt at resocialization, was ineffective. What is remarkable about my sample's attitude and that of postwar Japan in general is the wide acceptance of the value of democracy, whatever its meaning. No respondent whom I questioned in the depth inter-

35 Interview with E, May 2, 1970.
36 Cited in Stoetzel, pp. 146–147; Ronald Dore, *City Life in Japan*, pp. 239–241, found that in the classrooms he visited, social-studies teachers were often confused and worried about what to teach and therefore took refuge in mere description of the established order; Verba found in his study of Germany that because civics training was strongly oriented toward description of formal and legal structure, it had no impact on participatory or democratic orientations or behavior. See Sidney Verba, "Germany: The Remaking of Political Culture," p. 165.

views about the meaning of democracy or the influence of postwar democratic education on their thinking ever displayed hostility or a negative reaction to democracy as a desirable political end. E and K reacted negatively to their democratic education because it did not go *far enough,* not because they did not value democracy. Whether democracy for postwar Japanese youth means such organizational forms as parliaments or such procedural forms as voting, or means grass-roots participation, democracy itself has been accepted, and much of the credit for this awesome accomplishment of resocialization from the Emperor-system ideology must be given to the Occupation and its reforms. Ironically, this value contributed to the security-treaty crisis in 1960. Kishi's attempt to ram the treaty through the Diet mobilized youth and intellectuals attributing different meanings to democracy because it could be seen as violating both the procedural and the grass-roots meanings of democracy. The treaty issue became a "crisis of democracy" as well as an issue of foreign policy.[37] Tsurumi's data, for example, showed that a significant number of the students in the original survey saw the goals of the Ampo demonstration as concerned with democratic principles and procedures, and not just opposition to the treaty or ideology.[38] I am suggesting, therefore, that formal classroom teaching contributed to the acceptance of democracy as a general value. But I am also arguing that the civics education in the schools cannot alone account for the fact that participation and the expression of opinions were to become central to the meaning they attached to democracy and to their own lives. To explore these questions further I investigated the more indirect socialization experiences of the sample —the opportunity for participation and expression of opinion in the classroom and school.

Almond and Verba in their cross-national study of political culture demonstrated a relationship between participation and authority patterns in nonpolitical situations and later political participation. They found that those who reported being able to participate in family and school were more likely as adults to feel politically competent, i.e., to perceive themselves as able to participate in politics. This subjective political competence in turn was related to higher levels of political activity.[39] In order to test whether such a relationship between participation in school and later political activity existed in my sample of students, I asked questions similar to those of Almond and Verba on authority relations and participation in schools. I asked my respon-

---

[37] George R. Packard III, *Protest in Tokyo,* pp. 270–275, especially comments upon Maruyama's speech, p. 272; Packard also, pp. 242–251, emphasizes Kishi's personality as a factor.

[38] Kazuko Tsurumi, *Social Change,* pp. 337–338.

[39] Almond and Verba, *The Civic Culture,* ch. 12, also pp. 236–239.

dents whether students in their high schools participated in decisions concerning school and school-club matters or whether the teachers decided things. Of those who said that their high schools gave students some voice in decisions I then asked whether they themselves participated a great deal, to a certain extent, or hardly at all. The results appear in table 7.

TABLE 7. RELATIONSHIP BETWEEN OPPORTUNITY TO PARTICIPATE IN SCHOOL
AND CLUB DECISIONS, ACTUAL PARTICIPATION, AND LATER ACTIVITY
IN THE STUDENT MOVEMENT [a] (IN PERCENT)

Opportunity and actual participation	Activity in the student movement		
	LA	INA	Total
Could, and did a great deal	68	20	44
Could, and did to some extent	8	40	24
Could, but did not	0	16	8
Could not	24	24	24
	100%	100%	100%
	(n = 25)	(n = 25)	(N = 50) [b]

[a] The questions read as follows: "In some high schools, the students participate in decisions concerning the school or school-club matters. In some high schools, the teachers decide all matters. How was your high school? Did the students participate in decisions a great deal? To a certain extent? Or, did they hardly participate at all?" Responses of "A great deal" and "To a certain extent" were considered as indicating environments in which the students could participate; "Hardly at all" responses were taken to indicate environments in which the students could not participate. To those who responded "A great deal" or "To some extent," the following question was then put: "And what about you? Did you yourself participate a great deal, to a certain extent, or hardly at all?"

[b] N does not equal 53 because two leaders and one activist responded "Don't remember" or "Other" to one of the questions.

As the table shows, activists and the less active students had the same opportunity to participate. Three-quarters of both groups came from high schools where students were allowed some say in decisions. But activists and the less active differed in the extent to which they took advantage of that opportunity. The future activists were far more likely to participate "a great deal," while the future intermittent and nonactivists were more likely to participate only "to some extent" or not at all. The impression of great participation by the activists in high school was reinforced by references to their activities during the depth interviews. Membership in circles,[40] writing for student magazines and newspapers, and participation in high-school student government were among the various activities mentioned.

---

[40] "Small, voluntary informal groups organized for educational and recreational activities." Kazuko Tsurumi, *Social Change*, p. 213.

Similar results were obtained on questions concerning the opportunity to express opinions to their teachers in middle and high school if their teachers decided something to which the students were opposed. Although most students, the activists and the less active, recalled that they felt they could express their opinions to some teachers,[41] they differed significantly when I asked those who felt they could whether they actually had expressed such opinions: 67 percent of the activists said they did so often, as opposed to only 25 percent of the less active. The remainder responded "sometimes," "not much," or "hardly at all" ($X^2 = 6.62$, $p < .05$). Thus, in terms both of participation in decisions in school or club matters and of expression of opposing opinions to teachers, the future proclivities of the students are clear even as early as middle and high school: although both the future activists and the less active tended to come from schools where they could participate and express opinions, the activists actually did so to a greater extent than the future intermittent and nonactivists. In terms of the classroom and school environment, these results confirm Duke's description of postwar Japanese schools:

The American Occupation fostered the concepts of student inquiry, academic freedom, and student organizations. Today the Japanese student has greater freedom than students in most other countries. Classroom discipline in many schools has become a problem. Students are full of energy and make no attempt to conceal it. In particular, the Japanese junior high school is often a rather noisy place. There is life there, and it is abundant. The students have little inhibition in asking questions, and usually only in some of the classrooms of older "prewar" teachers does one find an atmosphere of strict obedience.[42]

It is important, however, to distinguish between, on the one hand, an environment in which participation and the free expression of opposing opinions are considered legitimate and, on the other, the responsiveness of authority to that participation and dissent. There was

[41] Activists more than the less active. Although only 4 percent of the activists said it would be difficult to do so, 30 percent of the less active felt that way.

[42] Ben C. Duke, "American Education Reforms in Japan Twelve Years Later," p. 534; Dore, pp. 229–233, also provides a description of the primary school he visited which emphasizes the lack of rigid discipline, the opportunity to talk, expression and even criticism in the classroom, and opportunity for participation in the student self-government association. Arthur P. Coladarci's studies of Japanese primary-school teachers reinforce these descriptions. He found that Japanese public primary-school teachers were no more authoritarian than their American counterparts (although they were different in the way they arrived at their overall F-scale rating), and at least verbalize attitudes consistent with the postwar educational reforms. See Coladarci, "Measurement of Authoritarianism in Japanese Education," and "The Professional Attitudes of Japanese Teachers."

evidence that teachers and school authorities, despite their tolerance of opposing opinions in the classroom and of students' participation in some forms of activity, were not always responsive to student dissent and resisted other forms of student participation. Older leaders who had been educated in the immediate postwar period told of some teachers whom they resented for their authoritarian manner or whom they distrusted for their sudden and seemingly artificial "conversion" to democracy.[43] A few students also recounted incidents in which they clashed with high-school authorities over the right of students to engage in political activities. More importantly, one-half of the responding leaders and activists said that some or all of their teachers took an unresponsive attitude when opposing opinions were expressed to them. Thus, even though the general atmosphere of the classroom and schools was conducive to the expression of dissent and to participation, some of the activists found that when they actually dissented or participated, they could expect unresponsive attitudes or even resistance on the part of some in authority. That these activists nevertheless expressed their opinions despite the lack of responsiveness reflects the strength of their participatory orientations.

Two conclusions about the relationship between the school and later participation in the student movement can be advanced. First, the school environment provided a "training ground" for the development of participatory orientations. The reforms of the Occupation, particularly those in education, may have had their greatest effect in the democratization of authority relationships in the school, rather than in the content of civics education. Instead of indoctrinating students into the Emperor-system ideology, the teachers and texts instilled a belief in democracy. Of even more importance, however, was the fact that the authoritarian and discipline-oriented classroom and school of the prewar period were replaced for most of these students by a school offering the opportunity to participate in decisions and to express opposing opinions to their teachers. For some of the activists, the school served as a preparation for later political life in another sense also. These students may well have first learned in the schools that although participation and dissent are legitimate and should be valued, they may have to be undertaken with little hope of response from those in authority. A second conclusion is that even in middle and high school, the future committed activists and the less active had

---

[43] See also Feuer, *The Conflict of Generations*, pp. 200–202. Some of the leaders whom Feuer interviewed were also part of my sample and they repeated to me, as did other older leaders, their feelings of distrust toward teachers who they felt were not sincere in their switch to democracy, or who preached democracy in an authoritarian manner.

already established different patterns of activity. The activists were frequent participants, and the less active only moderate participants.[44]

THE DEVELOPMENT OF IDEOLOGY

Before World War II, Marxism's influence in Japan was confined to a small group of intellectuals. The ideology at first had to compete with democratic liberalism among intellectuals, and then its believers were carefully watched and later persecuted by the government. With the end of the Pacific war, however, Marxism's appeal spread. Among intellectuals, Marxism became the dominant social, economic, and political philosophy.[45] The student movement too, from the formation of Zengakuren in September of 1948, was Marxist-influenced and soon was dominated by the Japan Communist Party (JCP). The anti-JCP factions that arose in the late 1950s and were in the forefront of the Ampo struggle were also predominantly Marxist in orientation, although they had a more eclectic approach to Marxism than the Japan Communist Party and differed from it in their interpretations of the applicability of classical and Stalinist Marxism to Japanese conditions.[46] Even today the Japanese student continues heavily under Marxist influence, each sect passionately and dogmatically clinging to its own brand of the ideology. In our sample, all but two of the leaders and activists (about 93 percent), and one-third of the intermittent activists (but none of the nonactivists) in the 1962 survey chose Marxism as one of the ideas to which they felt most sympathetic. In addition, 70 percent of the leaders, 55 percent of the activists, but only 4 percent of the intermittent and nonactivists were willing to identify themselves as Marxists. All of the leaders and activists were interested in Marxism, as were half of the less active. All or almost all of the activists in the sample, therefore, were interested in Marxism and sympathetic to it, and most considered themselves Marxists. Even some of the intermittent activists were interested in and felt an attraction to

---

[44] An explanation of why, despite similar opportunity to participate and express opinions, activists took greater advantage of the opportunities and participated more than the less active is offered at the end of this chapter and discussed further in chapter 7. I should note now, however, that I tested and found no relationship between permissiveness in the family and frequency of participation and expression of opinion in the schools. Rather, as I shall argue below, the explanation for these differences may lie partially in a discontinuity in the socialization process experienced at that time by the activists, but not until later by the less active.

[45] Brief but excellent accounts of the history of Marxism among Japanese intellectuals appear in Nobutaka Ike, "The Political Role of Japanese Intellectuals"; *Journal of Social and Political Ideas in Japan* II, 1, April 1964; and Lawrence Olson, "A Japanese Marxist," in his *Dimensions of Japan*.

[46] See the references cited in the Introduction, note 14, and note 29 above.

Marxism. In the 1962 survey, Professor Tsurumi also asked the respondents to what ideas they felt most sympathetic at various stages in their lives. By noting the respondents' answers to this question, we have an indication of when the Marxist-oriented first began to turn toward the ideology. The data show that of those who eventually became Marxist-oriented, 59 percent developed their first sympathy for and interest in Marxism after graduating from high school,[47] the remaining 41 percent in middle school and high school. In this section I shall describe how these ideological orientations developed.

Compared with other dimensions of political behavior and belief, ideological orientations have received little attention in the literature of political socialization. However, Richard Merelman in a recent article has provided a framework for studying this problem.[48] Merelman suggests two prerequisites for a person's becoming an ideologue: the development of "cognitive skills which allow him to see linkages between ideas and events" and "a developed morality which allows him to evaluate consistently the ethical meanings of political events." [49] The cognitive skills required include the ability to reason from cause to effect and the belief that the causes in the political world are partly or potentially under human control. Moral development requires both an understanding that rules are man-made for specific purposes, rather than part of an objective order which brings automatic punishment, and an internalization of the individual's own moral norms. The two processes of cognition and moral development are seen by Merelman as closely related: cognitive growth resulting in a realization that human and social forces are controllable and have effects enables the child to recognize the moral relativism that leads to the development of internalized individual morality; internalizing morality motivates inquiry into the causal structure of events.[50]

Few people become ideologues in America, according to Merelman, because few children there experience all the intervening factors that encourage the development of these cognitive and moral prerequisites to ideology. Among a number of factors he considers important are those related to child-rearing practices. On the basis of the child-development literature, he hypothesizes that the requisites for ideological development are more likely to arise in families where

---

[47] All but two after entering college. Two came to their Marxist sympathy during their *rōnin* period of studying to retake the college-entrance exams after graduating from high school and failing the exams once. This conforms to Takahashi's findings that most of the activists in his sample also came to Marxism after entering college. See Takahashi (June, 1968), p. 183 and (August, 1968), p. 269.

[48] Richard M. Merelman, "The Development of Political Ideology: A Framework for the Analysis of Political Socialization."

[49] *Ibid.*, p. 753.   [50] *Ibid.*, pp. 753–757.

parents are warm, permissive, and allow the child to shoulder responsibility early.[51] This hypothesis is quite interesting, given the literature
on child-raising techniques in Japan I have mentioned earlier. If Merelman's hypothesis is correct, it may help to explain the relatively enduring influence of Marxism in postwar Japan and particularly in the
postwar student movement. Japanese child-rearing practices, combined
with the high level and high pressure of Japanese secondary education
geared toward college-entrance examinations which stimulate early
cognitive development, may have provided the combination that has
encouraged the prerequisites to ideological thinking to develop among
a relatively greater number of Japanese than American youth in the
postwar period.[52]

At this point the validation of Merelman's hypothesis about the
sources of development of cognitive and moral prerequisites to ideology and their applicability to Japan must await further research. His
discussion of the prerequisites themselves, however, is more relevant
for the purposes of this study because the future Marxist-oriented
activists in our sample showed signs of having developed these cognitive and moral prerequisites during the same period as, or prior to,
their first sympathy for Marxism.

In a preceding section, we saw that our activists developed a
sensitivity to societal tensions and contradictions during middle and
high school, a sensitivity that has been called a "feeling of humanism."
This "humanism" during these years takes on added significance in
light of Merelman's framework. The activists' early questioning of the
origins of war and poverty and the social events that stimulated their
first interest in politics can now also be seen as the development of the
preconditions for ideological thinking. A's discovery of postwar poverty
and blackmarketing, E's own experience with poverty, and K's wonder-
ing about why war occurs reflect the beginnings both of causal thinking about political and social life and of a moral sense: note the
concern for causes, their perception of the problems as social (human),
their use of the moral term "evil," and consequently the strong feeling
that the problems could be, indeed had to be, changed. In the case of

---

51 *Ibid.*, pp. 758–762.

52 The recent rise of interest in Marxism among some American students and
student radicals might well be the result of changes in child-rearing and education
making their evolution more similar to the Japanese pattern. Permissive child-
rearing practices among upper-middle-class American families combined with an
emphasis in those same families on academic achievement may be producing the
prerequisites for ideological thinking among more American students today. The fact
that Marxism's appeal to American students is still weak and confined to only a
few activists is probably the result of other factors such as the general climate of
anticommunism in the United States or the decreasing relevance of Marxism in
"postindustrial" societies.

the two-fifths of the students who felt sympathetic to Marxism during their middle- and high-school years, this general "humanism" rapidly led to an affinity for Marxism. But do the other three-fifths of the future Marxists who did not immediately embrace Marxism during their precollege years also seem to acquire the preconditions for ideological thinking during middle school and high school? The answers of almost all of these respondents to the question of what ideas they were most sympathetic to during this period show that their adolescent years were also characterized by concerns that involved moral questions, usually combined with a desire to alleviate social problems. B, who was first led to an interest in politics by the Korean War but who did not adopt Marxism until after entering college, said that the Korean War led to his baptism as a Christian. Others also mentioned an interest in Christianity during this period, and still others mentioned humanism, non-Marxian socialism, or existentialism. A "sense of justice" was cited by a few, as were a concern for injured veterans and homeless children, the relationship between war and capitalism, pacifism, the differences between rich and poor, and the outcast problem. Whether they adopted Marxism at this time or not, the adolescent years of the activists were a time when social and moral concerns were paramount.[53]

These concerns of the "late-blooming" Marxists during their middle- and high-school period also suggest a further prerequisite to the development of Marxist ideology not mentioned by Merelman. The diverse responses share a common characteristic. Interest in problems of war, equality, existentialism, humanism, justice, or religion reflects more than just an ability to think in cause-and-effect or moral terms; it reflects a universalistic orientation. It is perfectly possible to attain the ability to think causally about society and politics, see them as malleable to human will, and evaluate political and social events ethically, but to do so in particularistic terms, as do nationalist or traditionalist ideologues. What distinguishes our future Marxist-oriented students is that their early cognitive and moral development is intimately wrapped up with universalistic concerns. Whether this trait is associated with post-war education, changes in the wider environment, or individual characteristics, I cannot say. But it is significant that in our Japanese students such a universalistic orientation should be a forerunner of sympathy for Marxism. Japanese culture has generally been described as particularist, with the criteria governing social rela-

---

[53] Also, of those who chose Marxism as a thought system to which they were sympathetic in the 1962 Tsurumi study and who combined it with some other idea or ideas, humanism was the most popular combination. See Kazuko Tsurumi, *Social Change*, p. 349.

tions based on "situational ethics" and on an orientation to the collective goals of the particular group. The Japanese family is usually held to be the formative model of this characteristic. The acquisition of a universalistic orientation, therefore, can be a necessary "way-station" on the road from the particularism of both the Japanese family and traditional Japanese culture to the universalistic principles of an ideology like Marxism.[54]

I have argued that whether they became sympathetic to Marxism before or after entering college, the future ideologically oriented students in our sample exhibited the prerequisites for ideological thinking, as well as a tendency to think in universalistic terms, during their middle- and high-school years, and that the sensitivity to social events and differences which first arose and developed during this period was an important stage in their inclination toward Marxism. Having these prerequisites, however, merely indicates who has the capability for ideological thinking but not how an ideological orientation is actually acquired. How was the transition from "humanism" to Marxism made? What agencies are most influential in the actual adoption of Marxism by student activists? And why did some show an attraction toward Marxism earlier than others? Tsurumi has dealt with this question in depth in her report on the 1962 survey. We need note here only her findings and the confirmation of those findings both in my subsample and in Takahashi's sample.

Tsurumi asked her sample in 1962 what events, circumstances, or experiences had contributed to the adoption of their views, whether reading influenced them, and what persons and emotional motives led to their views. She also asked them which of these four factors was most decisive in their choice of ideological stands. She found that events, circumstances, and experiences were cited as the most decisive factors, followed by reading and then persons. Furthermore, among those who chose Marxism as an attractive ideological stand, participation in demonstrations and the impact of earlier social events were the most common experiences and events leading them to Marxism. Thirty-six of the fifty-six who were attracted to Marxism cited participation in either the Ampo demonstration or the demonstrations of

---

[54] Going through a period of "humanism" and becoming universalistic in thinking prior to developing an attraction to Marxism seems to be characteristic of Marxist sympathizers of all periods in Japan. The youth of such prewar Marxists as Katayama Sen, Sakisaka Itsurō, Kawakami Hajime, and others contained a period preceding their discovery or adoption of Marxism when they morally and cognitively awoke to problems such as poverty, and sometimes first sought solutions through a universalistic religion such as Christianity. See my "Ideology in Transition: A study of Marxism in Postwar Japan" (unpublished paper, 1972), pp. 12–15. I also examine the great differences in other respects between prewar Marxists' approach to the ideology and that of my students, as does Kazuko Tsurumi, *Social Change*, pp. 345–346, 354–355, and 368.

the late 1950s leading up to Ampo as having turned them to it. Twelve said events of the early 1950s such as the Korean War, the Red Purge, or the May Day (1952) incident had influenced their sympathy for Marxism.[55] My subsample corresponded to these results. Personal experiences—such as participating in demonstrations and the student movement—and wider social and political events were cited by the greatest number of my respondents as being most responsible for leading them to Marxism. Although Japanese students are avid readers of periodical literature, which is often Marxist in orientation, and reading was mentioned as one influence by most respondents, it was mentioned by the fewest number of respondents when they were asked which factor contributed most to their sympathy for Marxism. Demonstrations and social events were mentioned as an influence by an equal proportion of those who came to Marxism before and after entering college. But whereas the reading of Marxist literature influenced almost all who were attracted to Marxism in middle and high school, and the peer group influenced few, the peer group was equally as likely to have contributed to those who developed Marxist sympathies while they were *rōnin* (high school graduates who have failed the college entrance exams and are waiting to retake them) or college students.

These data indicate no simple or uniform route to the development of ideological beliefs. Marxist sympathies develop both before and after entering college, and through a combination of influences. But a few generalizations can be made. Once again we see how wider social events and direct contact with the political system, in this case participation in demonstrations, can be potent socialization experiences. They have the strongest impact on the development of ideological beliefs, whenever Marxist sympathies are acquired. The reading of Marxist literature—in other words, a more intellectual approach to ideology—seems to play a greater role in developing ideological tendencies for those who become Marxist in middle school and high school. The "late-blooming" Marxist sympathizers go through two distinct stages: they develop the prerequisites for ideological and universalistic thinking in middle and high school but first express it in less systematic and nonideological ways. Not until entering the environment of the university and coming into contact with the student movement, demonstrations, and Marxist peers are they led by their social and political concern to an attraction to Marxism.

At whatever stage Marxism is acquired, it serves the same two functions. As Takahashi has pointed out, Marxism to the activists can be thought of as a "new humanism" applying methods of "scientific" understanding to their humanistic and universalistic concerns.[56] In

---

[55] Kazuko Tsurumi, *Social Change*, pp. 350–359.
[56] Takahashi (August, 1968), p. 273.

other words, Marxism provided them with a more integrated and systematic causal explanation of social problems, tensions, and discrepancies, and a universalistic ethical system with which to make moral judgments about them. For these activists with their strong participatory orientations, Marxism also legitimized their participation in political activity and held out the promise that their actions could indeed change the political world.

THE MAKING OF JAPANESE STUDENT ACTIVISTS:
A DEVELOPMENTAL PROFILE OF THE
INDIVIDUAL AND THE PROCESS

The results presented in this and the previous chapter allow us to formulate a developmental profile of the political socialization of student activists in Japan and point out which socialization experiences they share with the less active students and those on which they tend to differ. They also allow us to generalize about the most important stages in the process by which the beliefs and behavior of each type of student were formed, and the relative role of different methods and agencies of political socialization in developing specific orientations and behavior.

The typical student-movement leader and activist in the sample came from a permissive family in which his father had a college education and was employed as a high company official, a professional, or a white-collar worker. His parents tended to be uninterested in politics, although when they were, they were progressively oriented, and whether interested in politics or not, it was likely that they had voted for the Socialist or the Communist Party. There is little evidence, however, that his parents directly transmitted their party preference to him. His family also played the least important role in politicizing him, and, being politically inactive themselves, did not provide him with a model of political activity. Wider social events and his own direct experiences first encouraged in him an interest in, and moral concern about, politics and social problems. Of all the persons with whom he came into contact, his own peer group contributed most to further politicizing him and influencing his beliefs. The environment of his middle-school and high-school classes gave him the opportunity to express opinions to authority and participate in school and club decisions, and he took advantage of these opportunities frequently, just as he committed himself to an activist role in the student movement once in college. As a result of his participation in demonstrations and events, this interest in political and social problems and his participatory orientations would develop into a sympathy for Marxism.

The typical less active student came from a somewhat stricter family than did the activist. His father was more likely to have had only a high-school education and be a shopkeeper than was the activist's father. As in the case of the activist, his parents usually voted for the progressive parties, but with them this meant the Socialists or DSP rather than the Socialists or Communists. He was less likely than was the activist to be politicized before entering college, but if he was, his family had the greatest influence on him. He tended not to be a Marxist, but like the activist placed great value on democracy as a result of Occupation-inspired civics education and changes in the wider environment after the war. He had the same opportunities for expression and participation in school as the activist but took advantage of them only infrequently; when in college, he similarly failed to commit himself to an active role in the student movement but rather was mobilized to demonstrate only in response to a salient crisis such as Ampo.

When we view this developmental profile in terms of stages of political socialization, we can generalize as follows: the middle- and high-school period was the most formative in developing orientations and behavior with political consequences for the activists. During this period they first became interested in politics, developed that interest, acquired both a concern for social problems and the cognitive, moral, and universalistic thinking that was to lead to their Marxist orientations, and learned the role of dissenter and participant. There is no equally important period for the less active. Their interest in politics developed during all stages, from primary school through college. Although democratic education and the opportunity to participate in the high-school environment may have influenced their political orientations, they did not become behaviorally participant until after entering college. For the activists, on the other hand, the political-socialization process was characterized by the concentrated impact of wider societal and political events, the peer group, and school environment during their precollege adolescence. The data thus indicate that for the highly politicized and politically active, adolescence and not early childhood was the most crucial stage in the political-socialization process.

In the framework outlined at the beginning of chapter two, I introduced three key sets of variables for investigating the political-socialization process: agencies, methods, and products. It is now possible to use our data to link these. The family played a great role in indirect political socialization. It placed the respondents in a matrix of social and economic relationships that provided the motivation and the means to enter the university. Moreover, we found a relationship between permissiveness in the family and a tendency to later activity in the student movement. And, although I did not investigate this point, the family may transmit important "core values" of later political significance to offspring, and undoubtedly provides the model for the small, self-contained, face-to-face group pattern that characterizes all of Japanese social and political organization. The family's influence is far weaker when it comes to direct political transmission. This study found little evidence that parents transmit party preference or ideology, or provide a model for political activity. The family plays some role in the political socialization and politicization of the less active, and, in the minority of cases where the parents are politicized, may transmit a vague left or right orientation to the political world.

The school's impact on our students was both direct and indirect. Explicit and direct transmission through teaching and texts seems to have been one source of a general belief in the value of democracy. Teachers played a moderate role in the politicization and political socialization of both the more and the less active. Indirectly, the greatest impact of the school was in providing the activists with an environment encouraging behavioral participation and the expression of dissent even to unresponsive authority.

The middle- and high-school peer group was the most potent personal agent of political socialization for the leaders and activists. The college peer group played a role in the development of Marxist ideology, and also helped to further politicize the less active once they entered the university.

Social and political events and direct contact with the political system made perhaps the most crucial contributions to the process. Directly, these events and experiences began the political-socialization process for the activists, were the most frequently cited content of political discussion, gave the final impetus to acquiring ideological beliefs for the Marxists, and also eventually mobilized the less active to participation in demonstrations. Indirectly, they contributed, by stimulating cognitive, moral, and universalistic concerns, to forming the intermediate stage in the development of ideology.

The findings of this and the preceding chapter, viewed from the perspective of Eisenstadt's theory of the rise of youth groups in modern society, can now be seen as part of two different patterns of development for the activists and the less active. Coincidence alone does not explain why we find the activists discussing politics infrequently with their families but frequently with their peers, participating in school clubs and activities and even in political activities with peers, and being highly sensitive to wider society and hence adopting "universalistic humanism" during their middle- and high-school period. According to Eisenstadt, age groups arise in modern society because the universalistic values of the wider society conflict with the particularistic nature of the family. Schools as organizations based on age-homogeneous groups, for example, arise because "family and kinship age-heterogeneous relations cannot ensure the smooth and continuous transmission of knowledge and role disposition." [57] However, because the formal organization of the school cannot satisfy the emotional and physiological needs of the child and adolescent for, among other things, spontaneity and expression, more independent and spontaneous youth groups become necessary. These additional groups allow for the affirmation of the student's values and dispositions and for his participation in spontaneous activity. As Eisenstadt points out, these groups "in some cases will also have a more direct relation to the symbols of identification of a total society, either the existing one or a new one to which he would like to develop." [58] The importance of the peer group for the activists, and their frequent participation in extracurricular activities, undoubtedly arises from a discontinuity in their lives between the particularist world of their families and their sensitivity to, and adoption of, the ideal universalistic values and symbols of the political sphere they first encountered during middle and high school.

We find a very different pattern prevailing among the less active students. Although they too were exposed to, and seem to have adopted, the values of democracy, they either were not very politicized before college or, if they were, developed their concern in the particularist environment of the family. They did not exhibit the orientation to universalistic values that the activists did, nor did they participate in peer-group activities or interact politically with their peers. They discussed politics most with their families. In other words, the less active students do not seem to have experienced a discontinuity between family and universalistic values during their middle- and high-school years. The peer group became important political-socialization agents for them only in college. In college their politicization increased, and most of them participated in the Ampo demonstrations. On the basis of these facts, we can judge that the discontinuity first experienced by the activists in middle or high school was first experienced by the less active in college. There they reacted to and internalized the universalistic values prevalent in the college environment and the student movement. The increased importance of the peer group in their lives resulted from the attendant conflict that they experienced with the particularist family norms to which they had been especially close during their precollege years.

---

[57] Eisenstadt, *From Generation to Generation*, p. 163.   [58] *Ibid.*, p. 166.

4

ENTERING ADULT SOCIETY

WHEN I first met the respondents in our sample in 1970, their world was very different from what it had been ten years before during the 1960 Ampo crisis, or eight years before at the time of the Tsurumi survey. No longer students, they had entered adult society and found a role for themselves in it. This chapter is concerned with the process of transition to adult occupational roles. It will begin with a description of this process and the alternatives available in the 1960s to Japanese students such as ours, and then proceed to a description of the occupational choices actually made by our respondents.

FROM UNIVERSITY TO OCCUPATION

The college years constitute a hiatus in the life of a postwar Japanese youth. Coming after the severe competition of the entrance exams but before the assumption of occupational roles, college has become something of a waiting room for adult society. This is, of course, true to some extent in all societies, but it is more marked in Japan. Passing the entrance examinations to an elite university virtually guarantees the student a position in the top ranks of Japanese society. Furthermore, because few students ever fail out of, or transfer from, a college they enter, and because many schools are considered direct pipelines to specific occupations or company jobs, the achievement standards of Japanese society and their consequent strains on the individual are concentrated on passing the entrance exams. No wonder, therefore, scholars have paid so much attention to the exam period, focusing on its functions in social mobility and as a puberty rite, on its consequences for Japanese family relationships, and on its influence on student discontent and emotional disturbance.[1] But the college period

---

[1] Ezra Vogel, *Japan's New Middle Class*, ch. III, and "Entrance Examinations and Emotional Disturbances in Japan's 'New Middle Class' "; Kiefer "Psychological Interdependence of Family, School, and Bureaucracy in Japan," and "Social Change

itself, when the student must actually begin to think of leaving the university and finding a job, has been relatively neglected.

The university as a "semiadult"' stage and the importance of not just entering a university but leaving it and finding a job are reflected in the status of college students and in everyday language. College students are not considered full-fledged adults or members of society. Rather, "student life is considered a protected, nurtured existence, isolated from the rest of the world, so that the graduates are young, inexperienced, and innocent of the realities of *"jitsu-shakai,"* [2] "the real world." This conception of student life and the status of college students undoubtedly forms one basis for the belief that once the student radical enters "real society" and becomes an adult he will quickly give up his youthful rebellion. The college student in Japan is expected to be romantic, idealistic, full of youthful energy, inexperienced in life, and therefore, as Lifton has pointed out, to engage in student demonstrations, just as he is expected to give up this childish behavior and settle down after leaving college.[3] Language, too, reflects the notion that the transition from the university to the working world is seen as an entrance to adulthood. One "goes out from school" (*gakkō kara deru*) and "enters society" (*shakai ni hairu*). Being a *shakaijin*, a member of society, or becoming *hitorimae* (or *ichinimmae*), a full man or adult, denotes earning one's own living.[4]

During the 1950s and 1960s, largely because of rapid economic growth, graduating from college became increasingly identified with a

---

and Personality in a White Collar Danchi"; Altbach, "Japanese Students and Japanese Politics."

2 Koya Azumi, *Higher Education and Business Recruitment in Japan*, p. 104.

3 Robert J. Lifton, "Youth and History: Individual Change in Postwar Japan," pp. 284–285. Lifton deals with the contrast between the two periods in terms of "totalism" during the university period and "moral backsliding" after college.

4 The origins of this cultural attitude may lie in traditional age-grading practices, such as the *wakamonogumi* (youth groups) found in rural villages throughout Japan until the Meiji period. Youths at about age seventeen would enter the *wakamonogumi*, a group of age-mates who were self-governing and independent of adults but closely tied in to village functions, and remain in the group until a fixed age or until marriage. Not until they left the youth group would they be considered full-fledged adults. See *Nihon Shakai Minzoku Jitten* (Dictionary of Japanese Social Customs), pp. 1616–1630; *Sekai Daihyakka Jitten* (World Encylopedia), pp. 40–41. Although the traditional age-grading practices seem to resemble the modern age-grading implicit in the role of university students, there is at least one major difference between the two. The *wakamonogumi* served to socialize youth into the kinship-centered, particularist adult village society of traditional Japan in which the gap between the norms of the family and those of adult society was small. The university socializes youth into the universal values of modern technological society, and the gap between these values and family norms may be much larger. On the role of age-grading in traditional and modern societies see Eisenstadt, *From Generation to Generation*. Below I shall argue that there is actually a discontinuity between the university and adult roles in contemporary Japanese society.

particular type of transition to adulthood. In 1950, 48 percent of the work force in Japan was employed in primary industries, 22 percent in secondary manufacturing industries, and 30 percent in tertiary industries. In 1965, the figures were 25 percent, 32 percent, and 43 percent, respectively.[5] Japan was becoming a white-collar society. And the white-collar worker in large business enterprises or governmental bureaucracies, known as a "salary man," became the ideal occupational role model of postwar parents and youth. As Vogel has pointed out, the salary man has represented for most postwar Japanese "the bright new life." [6] The salary man working for a prestigious company or government ministry not only equalled or even surpassed the independent businessman or professional worker in status, but he obtained, as well, security and the benefits of a good and predictable wage. The security assured in a large private enterprise may indeed supply the key to understanding the attractiveness of this role to postwar families that had experienced the upheavals and poverty of wartime and earlier postwar Japan.[7]

The tremendous increase in the number of college students in postwar Japan must be seen in the context of modernization and the rise of the salary man. Technologically advanced industry required more and more educated white-collar workers. In 1959, junior-high-school graduates constituted 62 percent of those entering the work force and college graduates only 7 percent. By 1970, 21.4 percent of the newly employed were college graduates, and 20 percent were junior-high-school graduates. Moreover, economic expansion has lately been more than keeping up with educational expansion. Most college graduates today have little trouble finding employment,[8] although this was not always true in the 1950s. And a higher proportion of university graduates seem to go into the private sector (rather than into government or education) in Japan than in Britain or the United States.[9] The requirements of an advancing and expanding technological economy dovetailed with the strong desires of postwar parents for their childrens' upward social mobility.[10] The strength of these

---

[5] "Results of the 1971 Survey on Labor Forces Announced," *Japan Report*, XVIII, 10, May 16, 1972.

[6] Vogel, p. 9.

[7] *Ibid.*, p. 42. The importance of security in job choice seems to have declined rapidly in recent years with the appearance of youth raised in affluent, stable circumstances. According to one survey conducted in 1956 and again in 1971, high security as a reason for job selection has dropped from 52.5 percent to only 17.2 percent. "Japan and the World Economy Through the 1970's: A Projection," *Japan Report*, Special Supplement, XVIII, 14, July 16, 1972.

[8] *Asahi*, April 7, 1970, p. 12; *Japan Times*, April 26, 1970, p. 14. In April, 1970, soon after graduation, 94 percent of university graduates had found jobs.

[9] Azumi, pp. 89–90.

[10] Ōno Tsutomu, *Demo ni Uzu-maku Seishun* (Youth in a Whirlpool of Demonstrations), pp. 166–167.

achievment drives by parent and child is reflected in the sacrifices that families make to enable their children to take the exams and pay for college, and in the pressure the student is willing to endure to enter universities that will place him in top firms.[11] In short, college students during the 1960s came increasingly to resemble what one author calls "a reserve army of salary men," [12] rather than the traditional *"interi no tamago,"* "budding intellectuals."

As a result, the ties between universities and businesses and the recruitment process to white-collar occupational roles have become more institutionalized as the economy has grown and higher education has expanded. The university placement office and its formal evaluative and recommendation procedures have become at least as important a recruitment channel as direct personal connections, especially for recruitment to large firms. Direct personal connections have remained important primarily for those who do not enter the leading schools or who are not recommended by their university's placement office.[13] Certain types of universities are closely associated with certain types of employment. Government-university graduates tend to enter the more prestigious large enterprises. Of more importance is the fact that business enterprises have developed the practice of drawing their new employees from designated universities, and generally from among only those students recommended by the university. Those who do not come from the designated schools or who fail to pass the university placement office's evaluative procedures and be recommended by it are often not eligible for consideration and evaluation by the leading companies.[14] This practice has been described as "collective nepotism" which favors certain individuals on the basis of membership in a particular collectivity.[15]

The nature of Japanese large business organizations [16] has contributed to a discontinuity between university and adult roles, a discontinuity that politically aware and active students would have to consider in making their career choices. The student will probably be in the company he enters for life. Occupational mobility in Japan seems less than in the United States. In addition, Japanese white-collar workers are much less mobile than blue-collar workers, employees in large companies are less mobile than those in small companies, and

---

11 The average competition rate to enter the 28 national universities has been five applications for every position and as high as eleven to one in the faculties of some schools. *Asahi Evening News,* February 11, 1969, p. 1.

12 Ōno, p. 165.

13 Azumi, pp. 60–66, 68–73, 92.

14 *Ibid.,* pp. 92–94; also p. 62; Ōno, pp. 174–178.

15 Azumi, pp. 100–101.

16 The study of the nature of Japanese business organizations that follows is based on Azumi, chs. 3, 4, and 7; Chie Nakane, *Japanese Society, passim,* especially chs. 2 and 3; and M. Y. Yoshino, *Japan's Managerial System,* chs. 7 and 8.

men are less mobile than women. The longer a white-collar employee has been in a company, the less likely he is to leave.[17] As Azumi has put it:

> For university graduates, . . . especially those from elite universities, lifetime employment is an institutionalized norm. As they enter the job market they are keenly aware that once they contract for employment with a firm, that is the firm in which they will spend the remainder of their working lives—unless they are prepared to take large risks and perhaps losses in their life chances.[18]

The lifelong-commitment norm among the university educated places even greater importance on the occupation choice of the student.

Although the personal paternalism of employers in prewar Japan is no longer feasible in the large bureaucratic enterprises of today, the new recruit knows he will enter an organization characterized by hierarchy, particularism, and ascriptive and pseudoascriptive criteria for advancement in contrast to his egalitarian relationships with age-mates in college, the universalistic orientation of his educational experiences, and the achievement orientation of his precollege days. In Japanese organizations, the relative status of individuals is defined rigidly and clearly, and hierarchy is emphasized. Individuals are related in this heirarchy particularistically, and advancement is based on seniority and prior educational background. It is, of course, easy to exaggerate the particularist, diffuse, and pseudoascriptive nature of Japanese enterprises. For example, the pseudoascriptive elements of the seniority system and of recruitment from selective universities also contain achievement criteria: achievement and skill presumably characterize graduates from quality universities or older employees with years of experience. And, of course, particularist and hierarchical norms may still be found in the predominantly universalistic university environment. Nevertheless, the "mix" of these criteria in the business world and that in the educational world differ substantially, the occupational sphere being more heavily particularistic, ascriptive, and hierarchical, and the educational experience more universalistic, achievement-oriented, and egalitarian.

Perhaps most important of all, the transition to employment as a salary man means a transition to diffuse roles and almost total commitment to the organization and its goals. Specificity of function is quite limited in Japanese organizations, and much of the formal training the new recruit will receive upon entering the company is socialization to company norms, goals, solidarity, and loyalty. Once in the company, the salary man's occupational role will scarcely be differenti-

---

17 Azumi, pp. 34–36.   18 Ibid., p. 38.

ated from other aspects of his life. His performance will reflect upon the people who recommended him and the university he came from; aside from friends from college days, his peer group as an adult will be his friends from work with whom he will spend much of his free time; his social position will be evaluated by others on the basis of the institution to which he belongs rather than on his profession or individual accomplishments. The diffuseness of the occupational role of the salary man is reflected in the recruitment procedures of business firms. Adaptability and loyalty are the qualities most valued by prospective employers. The university placement office and the employer, in their evaluation procedures, pay great attention to the applicant's background, personality, and political views, not merely to his academic preparation. Questions in the exams and interviews include extensive probing into the candidate's family, socioeconomic status, personality traits, emotional stability, judgment, and ways of thinking. Significantly, these evaluations include questions concerning the applicant's political party preference, organizational affiliations, political orientations, and ideological leanings. Emphasizing such criteria makes sense when one considers that employment is for life, that Japanese organizations lack functional differentiation, and that the orientation of the workplace is particularist. But they also reflect a desire on the part of the employer to avoid hiring potential political agitators.[19] The student knows, too, that once in the company his political beliefs and activity may jeopardize his success in the firm. Although white-collar union activity is prevalent and legitimate in large enterprises, union membership must be given up beyond a certain level in the management structure, and too overt an expresssion of political progressivism or unduly active union work can imperil chances for advancement. Such attitudes and activities are often considered antithetical to loyalty to the company, the most important evaluative criterion for career advancement, and therefore a potential conflict arises between occupational role and political beliefs for the politicized white-collar worker.[20]

Economic growth, the nature of Japanese business, the rise of the salary man, the close connections between business and universities, and the resulting process of recruitment to occupational roles in Japan in the last decade have thus helped to create strains in the transition to adulthood and a role conflict for many Japanese students. The occupational world of the salary man and entrance to it, especially in the case of large private enterprise, contrasts with the student's college and precollege experiences and the democratic values legitimized

19 *Ibid.*, pp. 75–87, 100.
20 Wakao Fujita, "The Life and Political Consciousness of the New Middle Class," p. 136.

in postwar Japan. This problem has generational significance as well, as Azumi has pointed out:

> University graduates who spend most of their school years under the "new" system began entering the labor force in the late 1950s and early 1960s. They suffered acutely from the strains arising from the gap between the "new" ideal (equal employment opportunities, independence of spirit, and the like) as taught in school and the "old" reality (collectivistic nepotism, emphasis on connections, importance of ascribed statuses) as practiced by those in power (educated and socialized in a nationalistic collectivistic society).[21]

These characteristics of large business firms in Japan impose a particular strain and role conflict on the more politically aware and active student, like many of those in our sample. While still a student he knows he will eventually be faced with a basic choice of entering the world of large enterprise in which the environment may not be conducive to his political activities or beliefs, or entering another occupation and sacrificing the security, social position, and financial benefits of the salary man. More specifically, the activist is aware of a number of concrete alternatives. He can devote himself completely to political activism and attempt to obtain a full-time position with a labor union or political party. This alternative has a number of disadvantages: the relative scarcity of such positions, the poor financial remuneration, and the social stigma attached to an adult role that barely qualifies as "earning one's living" in a society where the work ethic and the institution to which one is attached are very important. Such a course would, however, permit him to remain true to his political principles and to work actively for them. Alternatively, he can enter a legitimate occupation other than business which would produce less of a conflict with his political beliefs and activity. In one sense, economic and educational expansion during the late 1950s and the 1960s has made this option more feasible. For as positions in business became more plentiful, so did positions in the professions, teaching, law, and journalism, and in these occupations progressive political beliefs and activity might find more support or be combined with one's work. Taking such an alternative, however, means both rejecting the advantages of the life of a salary man and having the motivation and

---

21 Azumi, pp. 101–102. It must be remembered, however, that the nature of Japanese business organization in postwar Japan is not just the result of the carry-over of "traditional" practices. It also represents a response to severe competition and labor shortages in the postwar economy, as well as to labor-union demands. For a general criticism of the tendency of western scholars to attribute Japanese management practices to cultural tradition and to ignore the influences of economic and political factors, see Odaka Kunio, *Nihon no Keiei* (Japanese Management), ch. 1.

skill necessary for the specific professional career. Furthermore, entering these professions also usually means entering a large bureaucracy, perhaps with close connections to the government and perhaps with professional standards that may also conflict with political activity. A third alternative is open to the student activist: he can enter business or government, perhaps hoping that he can "work from within" and combine union activity with the status and rewards of the salary man's life. The problem in this case, aside from the danger that one's political beliefs and behavior may be compromised, is the difficulty of entry. Because of the institutionalization of recruitment channels and the nature of the selection process, the student would have to cover up his background skillfully, take employment in smaller firms where university recommendations are not so important, or resolutely reject his past activity and convince his employer of his future loyalty. Should he be successful in entering a large firm, however, the security and benefits of the salary man would be open to him. For our students from major universities, their future elite positions in society and their careers would be assured.

Let us see how the students in our sample chose, and attempt to discover whether, under the conditions outlined above, our students did indeed enter prestigious large enterprises or government bureaucracies after graduation, as popular belief would have it.

OCCUPATIONS ENTERED

In the 1970 survey, I asked the respondents what occupations they entered. The results, broken down by former activity in the student movement, appear in table 8. They show that the former leaders and activists tended to enter professions, especially professions involving education, research, and writing, whereas the former less active students tended to enter business, especially large enterprise. Almost twice the proportion of former activists—half of them—entered the professions as did the less active, and more than twice the proportion of the less active—two-thirds of them—entered business as did the former activists. It is interesting to note also that whereas the great majority of the less active who went into business overwhelmingly joined large enterprises, almost as many of the former activists who entered business went into small firms as large ones. Among the professions, the most frequently entered by the former activists was higher education, where most were "tutors" (*joshu*),[22] professors, or graduate students in Ph.D.

---

[22] The American equivalent would be a cross between a teaching assistant and a junior faculty member. *Joshu,* although not full faculty members, perform teaching and research duties and after many years in this position may become

courses at major universities, especially Tokyo University. The other activists who entered the professions became reporters for a major wire service and a broadcasting company, or editors of publishing companies. A researcher, a writer, a doctor, and a medical assistant, and one former activist who was in the process of changing jobs from an editor to a researcher, were also represented. The activists who went into business entered diverse types of firms. They took up data processing at a drug company, sales work, or administration, and one was even head of his own small trading company and real-estate agency. The less active students who took jobs in business are now working in banks, construction companies, chemical companies, and as clerks and accountants. Although famous, large conglomerates are fairly well represented among the companies that employed the less active students who chose business, only one of the former activists who went into business is employed in a branch of one of those firms. Contrary to popular belief, former leaders and activists in Zengakuren, at least those in my sample, have not flocked to Mitsui and Mitsubishi.

TABLE 8.　RELATIONSHIP BETWEEN TYPE OF OCCUPATION ENTERED AFTER GRADUATION AND FORMER ACTIVITY IN THE STUDENT MOVEMENT(IN PERCENT)

Occupation entered	Activity in the student movement		
	LA	INA	Total
Full-time political activist	7	0	4
Professions:	54	28	42
Writing, journalism, publishing	(18)	(12)	
Teacher,[a] researcher, university staff	(29)	(12)	
Medical, legal	(7)	(4)	
Government service	11	8	9
Business:	29	64	45
Large enterprise (350+ employees)	(18)	(56)	
Small enterprise (fewer than 35 employees)	(11)	(8)	
	101% [b]	100%	100%
	(n = 28)	(n = 25)	(N = 53)

a Includes two LA who were graduate students in Ph.D. courses at the time of the 1970 interview.

b Due to rounding.

Surprisingly, however, a few (11 percent) of the former activists have entered government service, as have 8 percent of the less active students. And those, former activist or not, who have gone into government service have done well. Their ministries include the two most in-

professors. Although not graduate students, they usually do function as professor's aides. Perhaps the shortest term reflecting their function and status would be "apprentice faculty."

fluential ones in the Japanese government and they all hold positions now as section chiefs, chief clerks, or administrative officials.

Also somewhat surprising, in a different way, is the small percentage of former leaders and activists who have become full-time political activists. Only two have done so: one is a local executive-committee member for a left-wing party, and the other is a top executive in a "new Left" political group that is the parent organization of one of the most active and extreme anti-Communist Party factions in the contemporary student movement. One reason for the low number of student radicals who became professional political activists is undoubtedly the strong connection between a "normal" occupational position in which one can earn a living and the Japanese conception of *hitori-mae*, full adulthood. Moreover, our activists spent their childhood in preaffluent society. E's response to my question during a depth interview of how he personally resolved the problem of making a living and continuing his political activity provides an insight into both these influences:

> It may be an old-fashioned way of thinking, but I thought that when a man comes to a certain age he has to make a living by himself. I thought that a revolutionary or political movement should be carried out at the same time. It's not something that should be done while getting money from others but rather by earning money oneself and then spending it for that purpose. There are some pre-war morals in me. To my way of thinking, a man who can't continue his political activities while earning his own living is pretty hopeless.[23]

The former committed activists as well as the less active had been in their present jobs at the time of the 1970 survey for an average of about five and one-half years. Prior to coming to their present positions, 21 percent of the leaders and activists had held other jobs or been employed with other organizations, as had 16 percent of the less active. This is a very high mobility rate for highly educated white-collar workers, even taking into consideration that mobility is higher in the first few years of employment than later on. Some of this mobility was the result of purely personal considerations—feeling incapable of doing their prior job, feeling that another job would be more suitable to their temperament, or dissatisfaction with low wages. In other instances, however, the job change was directly related to politics. One student, for example, had a job with a company and was fired when his past record as a Zengakuren leader came to light. Another student voluntarily changed jobs when he found that his old job interfered with his participating in demonstrations and political activity.

---

[23] Interview with E, May 2, 1970.

Nevertheless, despite the relatively high mobility rate, most students wound up in the type of occupation which, while still in college, they had anticipated entering. Prof. Tsurumi had asked the sample in 1962 how they would like to earn their living after graduation. A comparison of their answers to that question with their occupations in 1970 shows that the correspondence between type of occupation selected in the 1962 survey and actual occupation in 1970 ranged between 75 and 100 percent. Three-quarters of the committed activists who thought they would like to enter the professions in 1962 actually did so; 86 percent of the less active who wanted to enter business actually did so. The only exceptions were activists who wanted to become full-time political activists (only two out of four actually did so) and the less active students who wanted to go into professions (55 percent did so). Most of those whose type of occupation differed from their responses as students wound up in business.

Although the reasons the students gave for choosing the occupations they did were extremely diverse, and not a few indicated that they came to their present occupations almost by accident or out of necessity, many of the committed activists and even intermittent activists gave answers indicating that their choice of the professions over large enterprise was quite intentional. The motivations of these students tended to be of three kinds. One was the desire to enter an occupation where one could be involved in social and political matters. Another was the desire for a relatively free work atmosphere. And the third, probably related to the second, was a general antipathy to entering the salary man's world of commercial enterprise. Some examples will illustrate. A former leader now a *joshu* at a major university stated: "I was interested in the economics of underdeveloped countries." "Interpreting economic phenomena is important for understanding society," another former leader said in explaining why he had gone into academic life. Another student, now a researcher of Asian economics, said flatly: "I didn't want to become an ordinary salary man." The former activist in the midst of changing jobs to become a researcher said, when interviewed, that he was doing so in order to "be able to do my own research and express myself." One intermittent activist who became a reporter did so because "the job is free and I can be a witness to history." And a former intermittent activist entered the same profession because "I was somehow fascinated by the interest of a job in which I myself would know the movement of society and transmit it exactly to people." Even one small businessman, a former leader, said he formed a trading company that deals with mainland China because he was interested in China. An interest in social problems, a desire for autonomy, and an antipathy to the world of large private enterprise thus seem to have motivated many of our former activists and even some of the intermittent activists to enter such occupations as teaching, research, and journalism.[24]

Political goals after graduation were related to choice of occupation. In a question concerning preferred goals after graduation, Prof. Tsurumi gave the respondents a list of choices involving indifference to, defense of, or working to change the capitalist system; the latter two general goals also included the subchoice of whether they would be willing to sacrifice their own personal happiness in the process. Two-thirds of the students who picked the professions as their occupational choice when they were still students chose the goal of working to change the capitalist system. Moreover, two-thirds of the students who actually did wind up in the professions after graduation held the goal of changing the capitalist system, as did four of the five students who entered government service. By comparison, the figure for those who thought they would like to enter business was 47 percent, and for those who actually did so, 50 percent. Of the seven students who said they would be willing to sacrifice their own personal happiness to change the capitalist system, six entered careers in the professions. In addition, Prof. Tsurumi in 1962 asked her sample what they wished to have realized in their lives by the time they were forty. Eleven activists but only one of the less active mentioned that they wished to combine political activity with an occupational career. Of these, three-quarters, all activists, chose a future occupation in the professions rather than in business.

The occupational choices of our sample do not indicate that former activists become professional revolutionaries after graduation, but neither do they confirm the popular myth that most become part of the "establishment" in business and government. Few of our former student radicals dedicate their lives to their political goals to the extent that they were willing to forego a normal occupational career. If we add the former activists who entered business to those who entered government service, they constitute an impressive 40 percent of that group. However, whose who chose a career in business did not join large, prestigious conglomerates but rather entered less well-known or smaller companies. Moreover, the majority of the former activists entered professions, particularly the "intellectual" professions of teaching, journalism, and publishing, and not private or public bureaucracies. It was the less active students, particularly the

---

24 Interestingly, even some of those who went into government service seem to have been trying to avoid becoming salary men in large enterprises while desiring a role in solving political and social problems. For example, one former activist, now in government said: "I didn't want to go into the commercial field; I wanted to be useful at the country's center."

intermittent activists [25] who were not members of the student movement but who had participated in the Ampo demonstrations, who found jobs in the large, famous enterprises or in government service.

The data indicate that the careers preferred by the students while they were still in college were generally the ones they eventually followed. In terms of motivation to enter occupations, many of the students who entered the professions or government service seem to have been trying to avoid taking up careers in large private enterprise, and hoped to work to change the capitalist system after they graduated. Most of those activists who planned to combine political activity with an occupation chose a profession as their career. All this indicates that the students, particularly the activists, who wished to and did enter the professions were seeking an occupational environment that would allow them to fulfill their personal political values.

It remains to be seen whether their change of role and adult experiences changed the political beliefs and behavior of the sample.

[25] As compared with 42 percent of the nonactive students, 72 percent of the intermittent activists entered large business firms or government work. There was a similar difference between leaders and activists. Whereas only 30 percent of the leaders went into business or government, 44 percent of the activists did. The professions were entered by 60 percent of the leaders, compared with 44 percent of the activists.

5

CHANGE AFTER GRADUATION

THUS FAR we have seen the development of many of the political beliefs and much of the political behavior of our respondents; we have also traced their occupational alternatives and choices. Now we must concern ourselves with questions of whether, and to what extent, the political beliefs and behavior of the student period changed in adulthood.

GENERAL ORIENTATIONS TOWARD POLITICS

The respondents were asked to choose the general left or right political orientation that best fitted them, with a choice of "extremely conservative, conservative, progressive, extremely progressive." Broken down by former activity in the student movement, the results appear in table 9. The former activists are still conspicuously left wing in orientation, all but one of them identifying themselves as progressive and half of them considering themselves "extremely progressive." Although a majority of the former less active students also consider themselves progressive, only 8 percent are very leftist in orientation. Perhaps the most interesting aspect of these data, aside from the general continuity in progressive orientations of activists that they show, is the sizeable percentage of the former less active who now consider themselves "conservative" or are unwilling to place themselves in a left-right continuum at all. No less than 41 percent of the less active students responded in these ways, most of whom identified themselves as conservatives. The possibility that this reflects a shift toward more conservative beliefs among this type of student is increased when we consider that only one of the students who now says he is conservative failed to participate in the 1960 Ampo demonstra-

TABLE 9.   RELATIONSHIP BETWEEN POLITICAL ORIENTATION IN 1970 AND
FORMER ACTIVITY IN THE STUDENT MOVEMENT (IN PERCENT)

Political orientation, 1970	Activity in the student movement		
	LA	INA	Total
Conservative [a]	0	33	16
Neither	4	8	6
Progressive	46	50	48
Extremely progressive	50	8	30
	100%	99% [b]	100%
	(n = 26)	(n = 24)	(N = 50) [c]

[a] No respondent identified himself as "Extremely conservative."

[b] Due to rounding.

[c] N does not equal 53 because two LA and one INA responded, "Don't know."

tions—all the rest were intermittent activists. If there has been a trend toward conservatism in the sample in the last 8 to 10 years, it has been among the intermittent activists and not among the former Zengakuren leaders and activists or the completely nonactive students.[1]

The political beliefs we consider next are central to political life: the individual's perception of his government and of his ability to influence it. Are the former activists still politically alienated or have they come to trust the government and its leaders and to believe it to be responsive to their needs and demands? Do they still believe they can and should do something to influence government, and if so, is that "something" still to protest and to demonstrate? Do they believe that their actions will be effective? Many of these questions have been studied and measured in political-science literature through the concept of political efficacy [2] and the related notion of "subjective political competence," [3] both of which have been shown to be highly correlated with political behavior, or through the idea of cynicism toward political leaders.[4] For example, the classic definition of political efficacy is provided by Campbell, Gurin, and Miller:

Sense of political efficacy may be defined as the feeling that individual political action does have, or can have, an impact upon the political process,

[1] Only 28 percent of the former nonactivists identified themselves in 1970 as conservatives or refused to identify themselves as either progressive or conservative.

[2] Angus Campbell, Gerald Gurin, and Warren E. Miller, "Sense of Political Efficacy and Political Participation." On socialization to a sense of political efficacy, see David Easton and Jack Dennis, "The Child's Acquisition of Regime Norms: Political Efficacy," including the vast bibliography cited in footnote 4, p. 27.

[3] Almond and Verba, The Civic Culture, especially chs. 7 and 12.

[4] See, for example, Robert Agger, Marshall N. Goldstein, and Stanley A. Pearl, "Political Cynicism: Measurement and Meaning," and Edgar Litt, "Political Cynicism and Political Futility."

i.e., that it is worth while to perform one's civic duties. It is the feeling that political and social change is possible, and that the individual citizen can play a part in bringing about this change.[5]

Easton and Dennis, however, have pointed out that the concept of political efficacy and the usual scale of items used to measure it actually contain at least five related but separate ideas: a sense of the direct political potency of the individual, a belief in the responsiveness of the government to the desires of individuals, the idea of the comprehensibility of government, the availability of adequate means of influence, and a general resistance to fatalism about the tractability of government to anyone, ruler or ruled.[6]

Aberbach, in a study of alienation and political behavior, recognized the disparity between measures usually lumped together in the term "political efficacy" and devised two separate measures of political alienation. One he called "political trust," which involved items concerned with cynicism toward officials and politicians and the feelings of governmental responsiveness to the people. The other measure, which he called "political efficacy," contained only items measuring the perceptions of the ability of individual citizens to comprehend and participate in the decisions of government.[7] In other words, Aberbach separated the aspect of "political efficacy" concerned with cynicism and perceptions of the responsiveness of government from the individual's sense of his own potential for political participation. Interestingly enough, applying these two measures to voting in the 1964 election in the United States, he found that while political distrust alone can spur negative voting in national elections under certain conditions, perceived individual political powerlessness was unrelated to political distrust;[8] in other words, a man lacking a sense of personal political efficacy was not necessarily politically cynical and did not necessarily believe in the unresponsiveness of government. Similarly, Edgar Litt found in a study of the attitudes of Boston citizens that "a high level of political cynicism may exist independent of the belief that one may exert some influence upon these politicians who are regarded as hacks unconcerned about satisfying any notion of a community interest."[9] The above studies, then, argue strongly for separating measures of political cynicism and responsiveness from measures of personal political efficacy and treating the two as independent concepts; the relation between them should be considered an empirical question. I have taken this approach in the data presented below.

In my survey, I gave my respondents a series of questions con-

5 Campbell, Gurin, and Miller, p. 170.   8 *Ibid.*, pp. 98–99.
6 Easton and Dennis, pp. 28–29.   9 Litt, "Political Cynicism," p. 319.
7 Joel D. Aberbach, "Alienation and Political Behavior," p. 92.

cerning their perceptions of politicians and officials, the responsiveness of government, and their own political capabilities. The items used were in random order, interspersed with other questions, and were variously phrased positively and negatively, to avoid response set. The respondents were asked to "strongly agree," "agree," "disagree," or "strongly disagree" with each of these statements. The "political trust" items consisted of the following statements:

Cynicism:
(1) "There are few dishonest people in government who take graft." (Agreement = high political trust.)
(2) "Diet members spend most of their time trying to get re-elected." (Disagreement = high political trust.)
Responsiveness:
(3) "In the long run, I think the government and Diet sufficiently take the desires of the average person into account in deciding policy." (Agreement = high political trust.)
(4) "Only some people and special groups influence the policies of the government; it ignores the interests of the majority of people." (Disagreement = high political trust.)

The measures of personal political efficacy consisted of the following statements:

Comprehensibility of government:
(1) "Politics and government are difficult and people like me don't really understand them very well." (Disagreement = high political efficacy.)
Political fatalism:
(2) "The things the government does are like the weather—there's nothing the average person can do about them." (Disagreement = high political efficacy.)
Political potency:
(3) "People like me don't have any say in what the government does." (Disagreement = high political efficacy.)

If our former students have become less politically alienated since their college days, we would expect a large percentage in 1970 to indicate a lack of cynicism toward politicians and government and a belief in the responsiveness of government; if they have become more quiescent about their own participation in politics, we would expect many of them to score low on the items measuring political efficacy. Table 10 shows the first of these hypotheses to be invalid. The sample as a whole exhibits widespread political cynicism and a belief that government is *not* responsive to the thoughts, wishes, and interests of most of

TABLE 10.   RELATIONSHIP BETWEEN HIGH POLITICAL TRUST AS ADULT AND
FORMER ACTIVITY IN THE STUDENT MOVEMENT (IN PERCENT)

High political trust, 1970	Activity in the student movement		
	LA	INA	Total [a]
Lack of cynicism toward:			
1. Officials	4	16	10 (N = 51)
2. Diet members	4	8	6 (N = 50)
Belief in responsiveness of government:			
3. Desires of average person reflected in policy	22	44	33 (N = 52)
4. Special groups: Interests of majority	15	21	18 (N = 51)

[a] N does not equal 53 because in each question some respondents answered, "Don't know."

the people in Japan but rather responds only to special-interest groups. On no item does more than one-third of the sample exhibit a high degree of political trust, and on those items concerned with cynicism toward leaders and the influence of special interest groups, less than one-fifth of the sample believes that officials are honest, that politicians are concerned with more than their own political careers, or that the interests of the majority are served by the government.[10] Furthermore, on all the items a greater percentage of the activists than of the less active show low political trust. Clearly, the sample, and particularly the former members of the student movement, are still politically alienated ten years after the 1960 anti-Ampo movement. They believe that government officials are corrupt, that party politicians are interested only in the preservation of their careers, and that government and Diet are unresponsive to the majority of Japanese citizens because special interests have an undue influence on policy-making.

The sample's feelings about the nature of government in Japan came out clearly in the depth interviews. I frequently asked my respondents what the first thing was that popped into their minds when they thought of "government," what the functions of government are,

10 There was one item asked in the survey-interview of 1970 whose results have not been reported, and in responding to which 44 percent of the LA and 57 percent of the INA did exhibit high political trust. The item read: "Representatives and officials don't care very much what people like me think." Disagreement with the statement indicated high political trust. The higher percentages on this item may well be due to the ambiguity of the statement. Easton and Dennis, p. 31, see this statement as a measure of perception of the responsiveness of government. On the other hand, Aberbach, "Alienation," p. 92, possibly reasoning that if a person believes that the government cares what he thinks it is because he believes in his own political importance, includes it as a measure of personal political efficacy. Because of the ambiguity of the statement it was excluded from the analysis.

and what things they thought government ought never to do. The following examples of responses illustrate the images of government that many of the sample held in 1970. J, an intermittent activist and now a university professor, said:

> My first impression—power. It's not a neutral mechanism, but an authoritarian organ which is operated by a controlling class. . . . The present government is the organization which integrates the whole society for a certain social class. I wonder if the people who operate the present government are helping the country or if they are representing certain limited interests. To my way of thinking, I hope in the future there will be a government which represents the interests of the majority. . . . Despite the fact that they don't represent the interests of the whole, they pretend they do—but they shouldn't. This kind of thing has to be changed.[11]

H, a former leader of Zengakuren, also said that "power" was what he thought of when I pronounced the word "government." He went on to say:

> The basic form it ought to take? It ought to act as the agent of each individual. . . . The government should not exist only to protect the special interests of certain people or to increase such interests.[12]

To U, a former intermittent activist, now a reporter, the two things in which government should never indulge were "war and protecting the interests of special people." [13] To K, a former intermittent activist, now a bank clerk, "Fools—vulgar and authoritarian" [14] was the image of government that first came into his mind. B, a former leader, now a university tutor, answered the question concerning the basic role and function of government in this way:

> In society there is the opposition of various interest relationships, so from the position of a third party the government pretends to regulate these interests fairly but actually controls these special-interest relationships.[15]

These images of government may well reflect the influence upon the thinking of our respondents of Marxism or the Japanese value that the collective interests of the group should take precedence over selfish, private interests, or both of those influences. Interestingly enough, however, these responses also indicate hostility based on a discrepancy between the respondents' ideals and the professed goals of the government on the one hand, and what the respondents believe are the real actions of the government on the other. For example, J's saying, "Despite the fact that they don't represent the interests of

---

11 Interview with J, April 25, 1970.   14 Interview with K, April 18, 1970.
12 Interview with H, May 23, 1970.   15 Interview with B, April 25, 1970.
13 Interview with U, April 16, 1970.

the whole, they pretend they do," or B's statement that "the government pretends to regulate these interests fairly but actually controls these special-interest relationships," seem to reflect a strong belief that the government is violating the ideals of government as a public agency responsive to the will of the people—ideals held by the former students and to which the government also professes loyalty. This belief was also strongly apparent in the depth interviews when I asked the respondents about democracy in Japan. The most frequent response I received was that Japan was a democracy in form, but not necessarily in actual operation.

In any case, in 1970 most of the respondents continued to feel a deep and abiding alienation from a government they deemed unresponsive and hypocritical, and which they viewed as violating the legitimate aims of democratic government through its attempt to control society for its own benefit or that of special-interest groups.

The hypothesis that the former students experience a decrease after graduation in their sense of their own political efficacy is also not confirmed, as table 11 shows. On all items a majority of the sample scores high in political efficacy. Again, the percentage of former activists who score high on these items is larger than that of the less active. Three-fifths of the former leaders and activists believe they can have a say in politics, 86 percent believe there is something the average person can do about government, and 93 percent believe politics and government are readily understandable. As did the studies cited above, we find a paradoxical gap between political trust and political efficacy. Although our former students, particularly the activists, believe in their own political capabilities and that citizens can do and say something about what the government does, they have little faith that their actions will be translated into government policy or that the government will be responsive. Rather, they believe that the government will pursue its own interests or those of special groups.

This perceived disparity between the political potential of the

TABLE 11. RELATIONSHIP BETWEEN HIGH POLITICAL EFFICACY AS ADULT AND
FORMER ACTIVITY IN THE STUDENT MOVEMENT (IN PERCENT)

High political efficacy, 1970	Activity in the student movement		
	LA	INA	Total [a]
1. Comprehensibility of government	93	83	88 (N = 51)
2. Low fatalism	86	64	75 (N = 53)
3. Political potency	61	52	57 (N = 51)

[a] N does not equal 53 on some items because some respondents answered, "Don't know."

individual and his actual political power was apparent in the results
of another question asked in 1970. We asked the respondents, "Let's
suppose that the Diet is considering the passage of a bill which you
strongly oppose. What do you think you could do? If you could do
something, what kind of thing would it be?" We asked those who said
they could do something if they thought their actions would probably
succeed in influencing the passage of that bill. These questions provide
us with a measure of our respondents' belief in their potential to act
against government policy, the extent to which they believe such an
act would be effective, and the specific type of political acts they would
choose.[16] The results showed that (1) the former activists and the
former less active students differed in the extent to which they believed
they could do something if they opposed a Diet bill, and (2) in both
groups, those who thought they could do something did not believe
they would succeed in influencing the passage of the bill they opposed.
The great majority of the former activists (93 percent) said they could
do something to oppose such a bill, compared with 54 percent of the
former less active students. Regardless of these respondents' former
activity in the student movement, almost four-fifths thought that if
they did act their action would fail to influence the outcome of the
Diet decision: 79 percent of the former activists and 77 percent of the
former less active who thought they could act felt that their actions
would fail. These results lead to the same conclusions as those on political efficacy; although our former students, the activists more than
the less active, score highly in subjective political competence, in other
words, feel that they themselves have the opportunity and capability to
act politically, they do not believe that their actions will influence the
decisions of government.

The particular means of action which the subjective political
competents would choose in opposing a Diet bill are presented in
table 12. Because many respondents gave more than one answer, the
percentages exceed 100 percent. Most of the activists who thought that
they could act to oppose a Diet bill chose to do so through collective-

---

[16] These same questions were used by Almond and Verba. They called the
belief in one's ability to influence governmental decisions, as I have indicated
above, "subjective political competence." As with political efficacy, the term may be
construed as including both the belief that one can act and the belief that this
action will probably be effective. Although Almond and Verba use the term almost
synonymously with "political influence," they did ask separate questions concerning the belief that something could be done and its likelihood of success. Unfortunately, although they imply a relationship between the two questions, they
do not present data showing the actual extent to which the belief in the ability
to do something is connected with a belief in the success of such an action if
attempted. See Almond and Verba, ch. 7 and especially pp. 200 and 196. Here we
use the term to denote *only* the belief that one can do something to oppose a government bill and not to mean a belief in the effectiveness of such opposition.

TABLE 12.   RELATIONSHIP BETWEEN CHOSEN MEANS OF ACTION BY RESPONDENTS
SAYING THEY COULD DO SOMETHING TO OPPOSE A DIET BILL AND
FORMER ACTIVITY IN THE STUDENT MOVEMENT (IN PERCENT)

Means of action chosen, 1970	Activity in the student movement	
	LA (n = 24)	INA (n = 13)
Collective protest (demonstration, mass move-		
ment, mobilization of masses, strikes, etc.)	79	46
Communication of opposition to others		
(discussion with friends, informing people		
through writing, speeches, media, etc.)	42	54
Petition or contribution campaign	17	8
Voting (or abstention from voting)	4	15
Nonspecific expression of intent to oppose	21	15

protest actions such as demonstrations, mass movements, strikes, etc.
(79 percent). On the other hand, the greatest proportion of the former
less active students (slightly over half) favored communicating their
opposition to others (for example, through discussion with friends,
writing, making speeches, etc.) rather than taking collective-protest
action.

One further note is in order regarding the relationship between
the belief that one can protest a bill and actually having done so. All
of those former students, activist and less active alike, who said they
could not do anything to express opposition also said they had not
actually tried to influence the passage of a Diet bill during the four
or five years prior to the survey in 1970. Among those who thought
they could do something, however, the former activists were much
more likely to have acted on this belief than were the former less active
students. About three-fourths of the activists in this category (77 percent) have actually attempted to act in opposition to a Diet bill during
the last four or five years, whereas only 43 percent of the less active
who thought they could act have actually done so. The former
activists not only demonstrated greater belief in their capabilities
for political opposition than the less active, but also were more likely
to have put those beliefs into practice.

To summarize, our data show that although almost all of the
members of our sample displayed a high degree of political alienation
in 1970, the former activists, in particular, demonstrated a high degree
of political efficacy and political competence. They believed that
government was understandable, that citizens like themselves could
have a say in policy making, and that they as individuals could take
action, along with others, to oppose governmental policy they dislike.
The former students, however, did not believe that their government

was responsive to the majority of citizens or that their political acts could actually influence government policy. The activists, despite their pessimism, were more likely than the less active to have taken some action to oppose a Diet bill and to favor demonstrations or other collective-protest actions to express their opposition.

POLITICAL PARTICIPATION

So far we have found little evidence of widespread change in the activists' leftist orientations, political alienation, and participatory beliefs. We come now to the crucial question of whether they experienced a similar lack of change in political behavior. We shall consider first their activity in political organizations and groups, and then other forms of political protest and behavior.

MEMBERSHIP AND ACTIVITY IN POLITICAL ORGANIZATIONS

Our former students tend to be joiners. All but 18 percent of the activists and 8 percent of the less active belonged to one or more organizations in 1970, and a majority of each group belonged to two or more. In addition, almost two-thirds of the former activists and slightly over half of the less active belonged to smaller and less formal groups as well. The question, though, is whether these groups were political. We found that this was not usually the case. Only 32 percent of the former activists [17] and 8 percent of the less active were active members in explicitly political organizations. Furthermore, only 21 percent of the leaders and activists and only one of the former less active students were active participants in citizen-action groups as of 1970. Thus, even though the former activists were still more likely to commit themselves to membership in political organizations and groups than the less active, only a minority of them were doing so, most belonging to sports and recreation or other nonpolitical groups and organizations. In addition, 43 percent of the activists and 56 percent of the less active were active union members. The larger proportion of the less active in labor unions is undoubtedly due to their tendency to enter large-enterprise firms rather than the professions as did the activists. In this respect, then, the activists' political behavior has changed since their college days. Many fewer activists have been willing to commit themselves to activity in political organizations after graduation than committed themselves to membership in the factions and organization of Zengakuren.

---

[17] Interestingly enough, of the activists who were active members of political organizations, two-thirds had held an office in that organization.

POLITICAL ACTIVITY

We asked the respondents in the 1970 survey a series of questions designed to discover in what type of political activity, if any, they were engaged as adults. The respondents were asked whether they had engaged in a particular form of political activity within the two years before the survey. Specifically, we inquired as to whether they had contributed money to a political candidate, political organization, or the student movement,[18] signed a petition related to politics, attended a public debate or other political gathering, collected signatures or contributions themselves, distributed leaflets or given a speech concerning politics, elections, or social problems, and participated in demonstrations. The results appear in table 13. Two main points emerged from the data: most of the former activists had engaged in these political activities in the two years prior to the interviews in the spring of 1970, and they were more likely to do so than were the former less active students. Of the former activists, 82 percent had made a financial contribution to a political group or to the student movement,[19] and 71 percent had signed a petition or attended a public debate related to politics. More interesting are the last two items, which involve more than the relatively passive action of donating money, signing a paper, or listening to a speech. They require the individual to take an active political role. By the end of the decade after the 1960 Ampo crisis, 61 percent of the activists were still participant enough to collect signatures, distribute leaflets, and give speeches for a political cause; 71 percent of them were participating in demonstrations despite the years that had passed since their student days.[20] In contrast, only 40 to 52 percent of the former less active

---

18 This includes the student medical-aid movement, contributions to which help provide medical attention for radical students injured in demonstrations.

19 All but two of these respondents had given both types of contributions. Those two had given only to the student or student-aid movement.

20 Those who collected signatures, distributed leaflets, and gave speeches had also taken part in demonstrations. All but one of the activists and one of the less active students who had engaged in one or more of the former activities had also been in a demonstration. About three-fifths of the activists were thus participating in both types of active political behavior, and an additional 18 percent were participating only in demonstrations. Lester W. Milbrath, *Political Participation*, pp. 17–22, has suggested that the more active political roles requiring greater commitment and expenditure of time and energy should be seen as part of a hierarchy of political involvement: persons who engage in such activity may be called the "gladiators" of the political arena, in contrast to the more passive "spectators." Milbrath, however, does not see demonstrations as fitting into the hierarchy of political involvement in the United States. Such activity should definitely be included in any assertion of such a hierarchy in Japan. Whereas our activists are clearly "gladiators" as adults, our intermittent activists are clearly "spectators."

TABLE 13.   RELATIONSHIP BETWEEN TYPES OF POLITICAL ACTIVITY AND
FORMER ACTIVITY IN THE STUDENT MOVEMENT (IN PERCENT)

Political activity, 1970	Activity in the student movement	
	LA (n = 28)	INA (n = 25)
Made a contribution	82	52
Signed a petition	71	52
Attended public debate or political gathering	71	40
Collected signatures or contributions; distributed leaflets; delivered speech	61	20
Participated in demonstration	71	20

students had participated in the relatively passive forms of political activity within two years of the survey, and few (20 percent) had engaged in either of the more active forms of political behavior.

These results strongly challenge the notion that committed student activists give up political activity after graduation. Certainly, between one-fifth and two-fifths of the activists on a given item have not continued to be politically active. But the majority have kept participating, and nearly three-quarters continue to attend demonstrations. On the other hand, students who were not members of the student movement but whom the 1960 Ampo struggle stimulated to brief participation, or the completely nonactive students, have reverted to, or perhaps I should say have maintained, the basically nonparticipatory pattern of their college days. The activists' continued political activity is not related to adult membership in political organizations. Only a relatively small percentage have joined such organizations, and those who have not are still more likely to be behaviorally participant than are the less active. For example, whereas 58 percent of the former activists not belonging to a political organization as adults have participated in demonstrations, only 17 percent of the less active who are not members of such organizations have done so; 69 percent of those former activists who are not members of labor unions continue to attend demonstrations, but only 9 percent of the nonunion less active students have participated in a demonstration.[21] Former student political activists thus tend to continue political activity after graduation, but in a different manner. As adults they no longer act as members of on-going radical political organizations

---

[21] However, activists who are members of political organizations are more likely to go to demonstrations than those activists who are not. All of the former activists now belonging to political organizations have participated in a demonstration in the last two years. Membership in a union, however, does not seem to affect activists' political participation: 75 percent of those who are members, compared with 69 percent who are not, have participated in a demonstration.

and groups. Now they are more likely to participate informally in political-protest activity.

The results presented in the last two sections of this chapter show another facet of the political beliefs and behavior of our activists. Political scientists have frequently sought to describe political involvement and participation in terms of an "expressive-instrumental" continuum.[22] An orientation to political participation in which action is taken to bring about a clearly defined end may be thought of as "instrumental" political action: the individual expects that his participation will help bring about a specific goal. "Expressive" political action is taken more for its own sake than for the particular result it may attain: participation is its own reward. Our former activists' orientation to political action is clearly closer to the "expressive" end of the continuum. They feel that they should participate but do not believe that such participation will be influential in bringing about desired change. They prefer the expressive and symbolic action of demonstrations and collective protest to more instrumental opposition. They frequently engage in such expressive action—not necessarily as members of an on-going political organization pursuing definite ends, but as individuals expecting few results from their participation other than the symbolic affirmation of their own principles. The activists' participatory drives and tendency to self-expression that we found evidenced as early as middle school and high school have continued into adulthood.

POLITICAL-PARTY PREFERENCE

In an earlier chapter I explored the party preferences of the sample when they were in college and the formative process behind those preferences. To determine party preferences during the respondents' college years, they were asked which party they had voted for, or would have voted for, in the 1960 general election. During the 1970 survey, I asked the sample the same question—what party they had voted for, or if they hadn't voted, what party they would have voted for—in the December 1969 general election. Their responses concerning the two elections will be used to measure roughly changes in party preference over the last 9 years, and these data appear in table 14. If we combine those voting for any of the three progressive parties (DSP, JSP, or JCP), 68 percent of the former activists and 86 percent

---

22 See, for example, Milbrath, pp. 12–13 and 87–88. Gabriel A. Almond and G. Bingham Powell, Jr., *Comparative Politics: A Developmental Approach*, p. 87, make a somewhat similar distinction between the "instrumental" and the "affective" styles of interest articulation.

of the former less active students who preferred a progressive party in 1960 still do so today. Of the students who have deserted the progressives, 70 percent (or all but three) have not decamped in favor of the conservative LDP but instead prefer no party, and almost all of these are former activists. Looking more closely at changes in preference among progressive-party supporters, we found that only 56 percent of the activists and 73 percent of the less active who had preferred the Socialists in 1960 still supported them in the 1969 election. In other words, although there had been some change among those who had preferred the Communists and the DSP in 1960, most of the loss of progressive-party support shown in table 14 took place among former activists who had preferred the JSP in 1960: 31 percent of these students expressed no party preference in 1969. We find, therefore, the following changes in party preference: a large decline in preference for the Socialist Party; a greater decrease in support for the Socialists among the former activists than among the former less active students; and a shift to no party at all or to another progressive party rather than to the LDP.

When the party preferences of the sample in 1969 are compared with their actual voting behavior, another interesting pattern emerges. Whether former activist or less active student, all who said they would vote for the LDP or the Communists actually voted for the party they preferred in the 1969 election. Moreover, all of the students (all but one a former activist) who said they had no party preference did not vote. Among those preferring the Socialist Party, however, there is evident a massive abstention rate in ballots cast. Of the former activists and the former less active students who said they preferred the Socialists, 58 percent and 38 percent respectively did not bother

TABLE 14.   RELATIONSHIP BETWEEN PARTY PREFERENCE IN 1960 GENERAL
ELECTION AND 1969 GENERAL ELECTION, BY FORMER ACTIVITY
IN THE STUDENT MOVEMENT (IN PERCENT)

Party preference, 1969	Party preference, 1960					
	LA [a]			INA		
	LDP	Prog.	None	LDP	Prog.	None
LDP	0	5	0	50	9	50
Progressive	0	68	0	50	86	50
None	0	27	100	0	5	0
	100%	100%	100%	100%	100%	100%
	(n = 22)	(n = 5)	(n = 2)	(n = 2)	(n = 21)	(n = 2)

[a] N does not add up to 28 because one LA who preferred the JSP in 1960 preferred the Kōmeitō in 1969.

to turn out and vote for them in the 1969 election. There was, therefore, not only a defection from the Socialist Party in the course of nine years among our sample but also a marked lack of support from Socialist sympathizers at the polls. Again, this tendency is more marked among the former activists than among the former less active students.

ATTITUDES TOWARD THE SECURITY TREATY

Opposition to the United States-Japan mutual-security treaty in 1960 united in a common cause committed student activists of Zengakuren and a large number of students who normally were politically inactive. Whether because of antiwar sentiments, a perceived threat to democratic principles and procedures, or opposition to the personality and tactics of Prime Minister Kishi, students not members of the student movement joined with Zengakuren activists who unalterably opposed the treaty and all it represented. How did our two types of students view the treaty in 1970? Was the treaty issue as salient to them a decade later? Did they participate in or plan to participate in anti-Ampo demonstrations in 1970 as most of them had in 1960?

In order to ascertain the extent of the sample's opposition to the Ampo treaty in 1970, I repeated a question that had appeared in a nationwide public opinion poll conducted by the *Asahi Shimbun* in 1969.[23] It asked the respondents what they thought it best to do about the treaty.[24] The choices given the sample, from which they were asked to choose only one answer, were:

(1) Change the mutual-security treaty so that it cannot be ended again for ten years.
(2) Without revising the treaty, continue it with the condition that it can be ended if we want to do so.
(3) Revise the treaty so that the American army will come only when necessary.
(4) Don't terminate the treaty immediately but aim toward ending it when the opportunity presents itself.
(5) Terminate the treaty.

These alternatives were the same that faced the Japanese government and people as the end of the ten-year extension of the treaty, which had gone into effect in 1960, approached. The first two answers are

---

23 October 1, 1969.
24 The question read: "The Japan-United States mutual security treaty's first term will expire next year, and afterwards, if Japan says it wants it terminated, it will be after one year. What do you think is best to do with this treaty from now on?"

basically protreaty responses, the first expressing a wish to once again adopt the fixed, long-term treaty arrangements that had been in effect during the preceding decade, the second suggesting that the treaty be continued in the form that would automatically go into effect as of 1970 if no action were taken by the Japanese government. The last two answers represent antitreaty postures, one a gradualist approach to ending the treaty and the last an absolute opposition. Response three is an interesting compromise as it would provide for American commitment to defend Japan in an emergency but without the stationing of American forces on the islands. Not a single respondent chose this compromise alternative. Rather, a large majority of the respondents wished to terminate the treaty in one of the two ways suggested, as table 15 shows. Interesting differences appear, however, between the former activists and the less active students. The total-opposition response, with its advocacy of outright termination of the treaty, was chosen by 88 percent of the former activists but only 36 percent of the less active. And whereas only one former activist took a protreaty stand, nearly one-quarter of the former intermittent and nonactivists wished to see the treaty continued in effect, most under the new arrangements beginning in 1970. It is evident, therefore, that whereas both types of students wanted to see the treaty terminated, the former activists were still more strongly antitreaty.

I did find, however, a decline of interest in the treaty issue among a substantial number of both types of former students. In response to another question, 64 percent of the activists and 56 percent of the less active said that their interest in the treaty issue in 1970 was greater than or the same as it had been in 1960; 36 percent of the activists and 44 percent of the less active said that their interest had declined.

TABLE 15.   RELATIONSHIP BETWEEN ATTITUDE TOWARD THE SECURITY TREATY IN 1970 AND FORMER ACTIVITY IN THE STUDENT MOVEMENT (IN PERCENT)

Attitude toward Ampo, 1970	Activity in the student movement		
	LA	INA	Total
Fixed 10-year extension	4	4	4
Continue without revision; termination possible	0	20	10
Revise for U.S. forces in emergency only	0	0	0
Move toward termination	8	40	24
Terminate	88	36	62
	100%	100%	100%
	(n = 25)	(n = 25)	(N = 50) a

a N does not equal 53 because three LA answered "Other" or "Don't know."

Because the 1970 survey was conducted prior to the days near the end of June when demonstrations would reach their peak, we had to allow for future as well as past participation in the 1970 anti-treaty movement in attempting to ascertain our respondents' participation in 1970 demonstrations against the treaty. We thus asked them first whether, during the six months prior to the interview, they had "participated in any demonstration which had as its main object opposition to the security treaty?" To those who said they had not, we then asked: "Do you think you will participate in the future (this year) in any kind of demonstration related to the security treaty? Will you participate? Might you participate? Probably won't? Won't participate?" Grouping together all those who said they had or probably would or might participate in antitreaty demonstrations, we found that 71 percent of the former activists had joined or thought they would join protest demonstrations against the treaty. Of these, four-fifths had already done so. By comparison, only 24 percent of the former less active students had joined or would join the antitreaty struggle, and only half of this group had already participated in a demonstration. Interestingly enough, among the less active students the intermittent activists who had joined in the 1960 demonstrations were *less* likely to do so in 1970 than the former nonactive students who had taken no part in the 1960 antitreaty movement (17 percent and 43 percent, respectively). The trend toward conservatism after graduation which we found among our intermittent activists and toward greater progressivism among the former nonactivists in the case of political orientation are duplicated here in the likelihood of participation in demonstrations against the Ampo treaty. Furthermore, even when we control for decline of interest in the treaty issue, activists were still more likely to participate than the less active, although loss of interest in the treaty issue does tend to decrease participation within each category. Half of the activists whose interest had declined had participated or thought they would do so, compared with only 9 percent of the less active students for whom the treaty was no longer so salient an issue.

Although the treaty issue's intensity has faded somewhat during the decade, among the large crowds protesting the Ampo treaty in 1970 were most of our former leaders and activists of the student movement of ten years before. But one would look in vain for the faces of most of our intermittent activists. For these students, the crisis-filled days of May and June 1960 may have been their one and only involvement in such political-protest activity.

IDEOLOGICAL BELIEFS

The dimension of change to which we now come—that of changes in beliefs about Marxism and related values—is particularly interesting. The rapid development of Japan toward becoming an affluent, consumer-oriented, and white-collar society establishes the conditions which many have predicted lead to the "end of ideology" and a decline in the appeal of Marxism.[25] These changes in the wider society have come about simultaneously with our students' entering into adult occupational roles and leaving the sheltered, Marxist-influenced environment of the university and the student movement for direct and "practical" contact with affluent, capitalist society. All these societal and personal developments would lead us to expect that the sample's Marxist beliefs would be highly susceptible to change after graduation. Fortunately, Prof. Tsurumi's 1962 survey contained many questions concerning Marxism and related beliefs and thus allowed me to explore in detail the extent and nature of change that has taken place on this dimension.

The first series of data that I shall present deal with the changes in the appeal of Marxism as an ideology and the importance of Marxism in our respondents' thought and belief system. Three questions asked by Tsurumi in 1962 can be used to gauge the importance of Marxism to the sample. One question, which asked the respondent whether he considered himself a Marxist, tapped the most intense level of appeal, a willingness to identify oneself in terms of the ideology. The second question presented the respondent with a list of fourteen philosophical or ideological viewpoints ranging from Marxism through liberalism, existentialism, and nationalism and asked him to choose those to which he felt closest. This question measured whether and to what extent the respondent felt an attraction to Marxism.[26] The third question simply asked whether the respondent was interested in Marxism. The responses to these questions serve as a spectrum of the intensity of Marxism's appeal, from strong identification through general attraction to mere interest. As we should expect, the 1962 data show that the less intense the level, the larger the proportion of the sample who responded positively. The activists tended to score higher on each of these levels than the less active: 64 percent of the activists and 4 percent of the less active were willing to identify themselves as Marxists, 93 percent of the activists

---

25 A fuller discussion of the "end of ideology" and its application to Japan will be taken up in the next chapter.

26 See ch. 3, where this measure was used to assess the development of Marxist orientations in our sample.

and 24 percent of the less active felt an attraction to Marxism, and all of the activists but only 56 percent of the less active were interested in Marxism. The same questions were repeated in the 1970 interviews. By combining the answers to these questions in the two surveys, we can obtain variables measuring the extent of maintenance and change of belief in Marxism and the direction of change on each level. In the tables that follow, we can show the extent to which the Marxist-oriented activists and less active students "retained" or "lost" their Marxist beliefs, and the extent to which the non-Marxist-oriented students "remained" that way or "acquired" Marxist beliefs in the eight years between the surveys.

Table 16 presents the data for changes in Marxist beliefs. Almost two-fifths of the activists are still willing to identify themselves as Marxists in 1970. However, one-quarter of the activists have lost their identification with the ideology, and no activists have newly acquired a Marxist identification; hence a full 61 percent of the former activists are now non-Marxist on this level. By comparison, 80 percent of the less active students remain unwilling to see themselves as Marxists, and another 4 percent have lost the Marxist identification that they professed in 1962. However, a net increase in Marxist identification has occurred over the last eight years because a surprising 16 percent of the less active have acquired a Marxist identification they lacked as students. Although Marxism has lost some of its appeal for a proportion of the activists on this measure, the activists are still more willing to identify themselves as Marxists than are the less active, and Marxism's appeal has gained a bit among the less active students.

Table 16 also shows changes in attraction to Marxism. Whereas almost all the activists felt an attraction to Marxism in 1962, one-quarter have lost it. Most of the less active students have remained impervious to the appeal of Marxism, and the majority of those who were attracted to Marxism in 1962 have turned away from it, a loss not offset by a gain among some others.

We find a slightly different pattern in changes in interest in Marxism. The data indicate that 89 percent of the activists have retained an interest in Marxism and only 11 percent have completely lost interest in the ideology. On the other hand, although substantially fewer of the less active students were interested in Marxism in 1962, more of them (almost one-quarter) have now lost interest. Few have displayed increased interest in Marxism.

Marxism's appeal has declined a bit between surveys for those whom it previously attracted, and except for a few of the less active students, those who were not attracted to the ideology as students have remained resistant to it. Moreover, the data above reflect only

TABLE 16.   RELATIONSHIP BETWEEN CHANGES IN MARXIST BELIEFS, 1962–1970,
AND FORMER ACTIVITY IN THE STUDENT MOVEMENT (IN PERCENT)

Change in identification as Marxist	Activity in the student movement		
	LA (n = 28)	INA (n = 25)	Total (N = 53)
Marxist, 1962:			
Retained, 1970	39	0	21
Lost, 1970	25	4	15
Non-Marxist, 1962:			
Remained, 1970	36	80	57
Acquired, 1970	0	16	8
	100%	100%	101% [a]
Change in attraction to Marxism:			
Attraction, 1962:			
Retained, 1970	68	8	40
Lost, 1970	25	16	21
No attraction, 1962:			
Remained, 1970	4	64	32
Acquired, 1970	4	12	8
	101% [a]	100%	101% [a]
Change in interest in Marxism:			
Interested, 1962:			
Remained, 1970	89	32	62
Lost, 1970	11	24	17
Not interested, 1962:			
Remained, 1970	0	36	17
Acquired, 1970	0	8	4
	100%	100%	100%

[a] Due to rounding.

incompletely the extent to which Marxism's appeal has weakened. Even among some of those who have retained their Marxist beliefs, doubts about Marxism have begun to set in. For example, in the case of B, who continues to choose Marxism as an ideology to which he feels close, his doubts concern the conflict he feels between his basic humanism and the rationalistic and scientific aspects of Marxism, a conflict which he seems to be settling in favor of humanism:

Marxism is scientific socialism which says that a human being's rational consciousness rules his action. That's sort of limited. There definitely are things in action which can't be explained by such rationality, by science. . . . I'm thinking quite a bit now about individual human beings who can't be lumped together quantitatively. I'm beginning to think that if the "proletariat" or the "bourgeoisie" becomes just a "mass"—well, I'm sorry, you just can't leave it like that! [27]

[27] Interview with B, April 25, 1970.

Marxism is by no means dead as an ideology among these former students, as witness the continued interest in it, the nearly three-quarters of the former activists who still find it a sympathetic intellectual standpoint, the 40 percent who identify themselves as Marxists, and the 16 percent of the less active students who have actually come to Marxism only since graduation. Nevertheless, its overall appeal is slowly declining.

A closer look at those who have lost faith in Marxism and those who have gained faith in it since their college days discloses some interesting facets of the change in ideological beliefs. Change on one dimension tended to be related to change on another, i.e., the changes at each level often reflected the gain or loss of faith of the same students in Marxism. For example, three of the four students who showed an increased attraction to Marxism also changed positively in their willingness to identify with Marxism. Half of the students who lost an identification with Marxism also ceased to be attracted to it. The decline in attraction to Marxism seems to progress in stages related to the sample's original eclecticism of ideological beliefs. As Tsurumi has pointed out, eclecticism in the choice of ideological standpoints characterized the anti-JCP Marxist students of 1960.[28] This was reflected in our sample. About 59 percent of those who chose Marxism as an ideology to which they were sympathetic also were sympathetic to at least one other ideology, and only 41 percent were "total Marxists." If we divide our sample according to whether they felt an attraction to "Marxism only," "Marxism plus" another ideology, or were "non-Marxist," an interesting pattern emerges from the data. Almost all of those who lost their sympathy for Marxism in the eight years between surveys were those who were "eclectic Marxists" in 1962; few of the "total Marxists" gave up Marxism completely, as the following results show:

		Attraction to Marxism, 1962	
	Marxism only	*Marxism plus*	*Non-Marxist*
Attraction to Marxism, 1970	*(percent)*	*(percent)*	*(percent)*
Marxism only	46	5	5
Marxism plus	46	42	14
Non-Marxist	8	53	81
Total	100%	100%	100%
(N = 53)	(n = 13)	(n = 19)	(n = 21)

A step-like progression in the decline of Marxism is shown: "total Marxists" have tended to become "eclectic Marxists," "eclectic Marx-

---

28 Kazuko Tsurumi, *Social Change*, pp. 347–349.

ists" have tended to abandon Marxism, and non-Marxists usually have remained non-Marxists since graduation. From these data we can set forth two hypotheses for further research: (1) decline of ideological beliefs is related to the extent to which the ideology serves as a total thought system for the individual; (2) the abandonment of belief in an ideology such as Marxism does not occur suddenly but in stages, the first of which is the transition from a totalist approach to the ideology to an eclectic approach. These data indicate still another way in which Marxism's appeal has somewhat declined: almost two-thirds of those who were attracted to Marxism in 1962 were "total Marxists," but today two-thirds are "eclectic Marxists." Again a definite, but gradual, loss in Marxism's appeal is evident.

Has this weakening of the importance of Marxism in the thought and belief of our sample since 1962 been an across-the-board decline in belief in the major tenets of Marxism, or have certain tenets of Marxism retained their appeal? In other words, have certain aspects of Marxian thought been more resistant to change than others and thus continued to influence our respondents' view of society and politics?

All respondents were asked in 1962 and again in 1970 whether they thought the following points of Marxism were correct: the proposition that history until now has been the history of class struggles, the analysis of the contradictions in capitalism, the inevitability of the collapse of capitalism and the advent of socialism, and the dictatorship of the proletariat. The first two comprise some of the main premises of Marxian theory, and the latter two are predictions based upon those premises. To Marx, of course, the premises and the predictions were inseparable, because the overthrow of capitalism and the establishment of a dictatorship of the proletariat were inevitable results of the class laws of history and the nature of capitalism. But what about our students? Have they been rather selective, albeit un-Marxian in their disenchantment with Marxism?

We find that, indeed, some elements of Marxian analysis have retained a powerful hold on the thinking of many of our respondents, but that others have declined. In 1962 and again in 1970, 89 percent of the activists believed the proposition that history until now has been the history of class struggles, and there has been a slight increase in this belief among the less active, from 48 percent to 56 percent. Little change has occurred over the years, only two of the activists having lost faith in the proposition, offset by two who gained faith; of the less active, 8 percent changed negatively and 16 percent changed positively. Even more interesting is the extent of change in agreement with the analysis of the contradictions in capitalism, for we find that belief in this tenet has *increased* among both categories of students. The activists have increased in agreement from 78 percent to 92 percent and the less active from 56 percent to 68 percent. In both instances, small losses have been more than compensated for by converts: 21 percent of the activists changed positively and 7 percent negatively; 24 percent of the less active changed positively and 12 percent negatively.

By comparison, the two predictions of Marxian theory not only drew less support from the students eight years ago than did the premises, but have further declined since then. In 1962, 68 percent of the activists and only 20 percent of the less active believed in the inevitable collapse of capitalism and the advent of socialism, and by 1970 the figures were 61 percent and 16 percent. Almost exactly the same result was found for the dictatorship of the proletariat: 64 percent agreement by activists and 20 percent by the less active declined to 57 percent and 16 percent, respectively. Once again the number switching to positive beliefs in both cases was not large and slightly more always changed negatively than positively. Two conclusions may be drawn. The premises of Marxian thought had, and have retained, an appeal for both former activist and less active alike beyond the general appeal of the ideology itself: almost all of the activists and a majority of the less active still believe in the class-struggle premise and the analysis of the contradictions in capitalism. Second, the predictions of the inevitable destruction of capitalism and the establishment of a dictatorship of the proletariat, much less popular to begin with, especially among the less active students, have declined even further in the course of time. In short, although the methodological premises of the Marxian world-view have by no means lost their attraction in the last decade, confidence in Marx's predictions based on those premises has eroded.

The weakening of belief in Marxism's predictions and the maintenance of belief in Marxism's assumptions, particularly as shown in the decrease in agreement with the destruction-of-capitalism tenet and the increase in agreement with the contradictions-in-capitalism tenet, are indicative of a tendency we also found in the results of other questions: although the activists' faith in revolutionary change in the capitalist system in Japan has weakened, their antipathy to that system has not. We repeated in the follow-up study a question asked in the original survey: "Do you think there will be a great change in the social system of Japan by the time you are forty years old?" It was believed by 61 percent of the activists and 33 percent of the less active in 1962 that such a change would occur. Today only 18 percent of the activists and 8 percent of the less active believe that such a change is possible in the few years remaining before their fortieth birthdays.

Their pessimism about the short-term prospects for changing the system, however, has not decreased the determination of the activists to continue trying to change it. In the survey of eight years ago, the students were asked to choose among six alternative ways of living for a twenty-year period after they graduated. These alternatives were to defend the capitalist system while pursuing or sacrificing personal happiness, to work to change the capitalist system while pursuing or sacrificing personal happiness, or to pursue personal happiness with no interest in, or regardless of what happened to, the system. Prof. Tsurumi used these data to show that the activists of the 1960 movement were not "ascetic revolutionaries" like the prewar Communists, because a majority chose responses that indicated an unwillingness to sacrifice personal happiness while working to change the system.[29] We repeated this question in our follow-up but will use it here chiefly as an indicator of changes in our students' desire for, and intention to work toward, a change in the capitalist system. Combining all four of the alternatives that present the goal of defending the capitalist system or being uninterested in or indifferent to a change in the system, we get a dimension of the variable which I shall call "status-quo oriented"; combining the two alternatives that indicate the goal of working to change the capitalist system yields the other aspect of the variable called "anti-capitalist-system." In 1962, 78 percent of the activists were "anti-capitalist-system," and 75 percent are so today. A 14 percent change to "status-quo oriented" was accompanied by an 11 percent change against the system, hardly affecting the large proportion of the activists who have as their goal working to change the system. Similarly, among the less active, a 16 percent defection from the antisystem ranks was offset by an equivalent number who now desire such change, leaving unaffected the 40 percent of the less active in favor of a change. To sum up, three-quarters of our student activists even today desire systematic change in Japan and are willing to work to effect that change.[30]

---

29 *Ibid.*, pp. 366–368.

30 In fact, evidence suggested that the intensity of this desire had increased. There was a surprising *increase* in the percentage of former activists who said they would be willing to sacrifice their personal happiness to change the system. Whereas only 18 percent of the activists were willing to sacrifice their happiness to their political goal while they were students, an amazing 54 percent were willing to do so in 1970 as adults. If this question is indeed a valid measure of such sentiments, its implications are great. The common assumption that activists are coopted into the system after graduation because they have more to lose as adults would thus not be true. It might also mean that the 1960 Ampo activists today

The evidence points strongly to the conclusion that although Marxism's appeal for our students has diminished somewhat since they graduated, it has by no means ended. Our students are less "ideological" today than they were ten years ago. One-quarter of the activists no longer think of themselves as Marxists or even feel close to it as an ideology; Marxism has won few converts in the last eight years; even some of those who have not given up Marxism completely may be beginning to question its relevance to their own values and to contemporary society; and an ever-growing number of former students find it impossible to explain social reality by Marxism alone. Especially influential in Marxism's decline may be the increasing likelihood that the ideology's predictions of the overthrow of the present system, by violent or peaceful means, will not be fulfilled in the near future, if ever. If it is true that much of ideology's appeal is its ability to make the individual feel he can play an effective role in the creation of a certain and optimistic future, the loss of faith on this point may be a crucial turning point in the history of Marxism in postwar Japan.

Nevertheless, these changes hardly reflect the "end of ideology" among our students. Interest in Marxism is still high, and three-quarters of the activists continue to cling to it as an ideology with which they sympathize. Of even more importance is the fact that our analysis clearly shows an underlying continuity with respect to ideological orientations in other ways. The Marxist *weltanschauung* of history as class struggle and its analysis of contradictions in capitalist structure remain viable influences on the thinking of our students. The continued appeal of these premises of Marxist ideology may well be related to the maintenance of a strong antipathy to the present capitalist system in Japan and a continued desire to work for its reform. Despite some disillusionment with Marxism, our sample still appears to find it useful as a systematic explanation for the injustices and inequalities in society about which they continue to be concerned. When I asked my students their definition of democracy during the depth interviews their replies were almost identical: equality and the end of differences between rich and poor. In this concern, as well as in their hostility toward a system they perceive as subject to the undue influence of special-interest groups to the detriment of the majority's interests and needs, may well lie the secret of the continued appeal of Marxism's premises. If the relevance of

---

resemble the prewar "ascetic revolutionaries" more, now that they have become adults.

Marxism as a total ideology has waned in the last decade for these students, their basic "universalistic humanism," which led them to Marxism in the first place, has not.

SUMMARY

We have found little change among our activists after graduation: most are still left-wing and many exceedingly so. In orientation and behavior, most are alienated, antitreaty, and politically participant, although they are pessimistic as to the effectiveness of their actions in bringing about change. Nevertheless, they continue to wish to change the capitalist system and their basic universalistic humanistic values have remained strong. The only significant changes we have found are in their increasing doubts about Marxism as a total ideology and in their large defection from the Socialist Party to no party preference. Our findings therefore do not support the popular notion of post-graduation "conversion" among former student radicals, but rather are comparable to Fendrich's findings concerning American former student activists: [31] they enter professional occupations and tend to continue their left-wing beliefs and activities.

The less active students seem to be moving toward conservatism and to be maintaining a non-Marxist outlook, although many still consider themselves progressive, are antitreaty (though less intensely so than the activists), and, surprisingly, seem to have remained more loyal to the Socialist Party than the activists. Behaviorally, they have dropped the intermittent activity of their college days. Thus, as in their pregraduation development, we find great differences in the political-socialization patterns of our less active and activist students.

[31] Fendrich, Tarleau, and Simons, "Marching to a Different Drummer: The Occupational and Political Orientations of Former Student Activists."

6

YOUTH, ADULTHOOD, AND OCCUPATION

IN THE first chapter I briefly reviewed the two streams of social-science theory and research concerning the impact of youth on adult values and behavior and the possibility of change due to adult roles. I referred to the research postulating that the transition to new adult statuses brings about changes in childhood and adolescent belief and behavior patterns to conform to the new roles as the "maturational" model. By implication this model would predict that youthful protest is abandoned in the process of the individual's integration into adult roles. The "generational" model, on the other hand, sees the beliefs and behavior acquired in the preadult period as permanently formative for the individual. Basic values and behavior patterns such as those that lead to youthful protest, would, according to the generational model, persist in adulthood, and although change would be possible it would occur only in less basic belief and behavior patterns. Such change would be caused mainly by general trends in the political and social environment rather than by entrance into new adult roles. We saw that these two models were also implicit in the political-socialization literature, noting the attempt of Dawson and Prewitt to reconcile them. Dawson and Prewitt suggest that although basic identifications acquired early in life are likely to continue, some change in adulthood due to role change is possible, and that we should investigate whether some products of the earlier political-socialization process are more resistant to change in adulthood than others. This chapter will examine the applicability of all these hypotheses to our sample's adult political beliefs and behavior.

On the basis of the data already presented about our activists, a strong case can be made for the generational model over the maturational model. The first and most important evidence of the formative

influence of youth is the relatively small shift in the political characteristics of our activists. Most former activists who were highly politicized, markedly left wing, politically alienated, very desirous of changing the capitalist system, deeply imbued with "universalistic humanism," and consistently active politically in demonstrations as students
have not changed since graduation. A second argument in favor of the
generational model is that the activists seem intentionally to have
sought careers more compatible with the fulfillment and expression
of their earlier values and behavioral dispositions.

The third reason for preferring the generational model is that
many of the orientations and behavior patterns acquired earliest seem
to have been the least subject to change and the most intensely held
after graduation. We have seen that the activists acquired their interest
in politics, universalistic humanism, and disposition to participation in
middle school and in high school. These very characteristics of their
formative years seem to have weathered the transition to adulthood
with little change even in intensity. On the other hand, party preference and Marxism's appeal as a total ideology, both of which orientations, as I have shown, were usually acquired in college as a generalization from more basic beliefs—Socialist Party preference from progressive beliefs and Marxism from universalistic humanism—were the two
orientations that seem to have changed most in adulthood. Indeed, the
changes in these orientations in adulthood—from support of the Socialist Party to no party preference and increasing disillusionment
with Marxism—can be better explained by the effect of general shifts
in the political climate interacting with the way in which these beliefs were first acquired than by the effect of adult roles. Let us
examine the evidence more closely, beginning with party preference.

Changes in the political climate during the 1960s produced a
decline in preference for the Socialist Party. Since 1960 the Socialist
Party has become increasingly torn by factional and ideological strife,
and the resultant polarization has produced a left-wing faction led by
Sasaki Kōzō and a right-wing faction led by Eda Saburō. Since 1960,
Eda has been striving for adoption by the Socialist Party of his proposal
for "structural reform," a plan for increasing the appeal of the party
among all segments of the population, not merely the working class,
and for bringing about reform by nonrevolutionary means. "Structural
reform" has been bitterly resisted by the Sasaki faction, who consider
it tantamount to bourgeois revisionism. Each faction has enough support to stalemate the other but not enough to impose its will on the
party, and intraparty squabbling erupted in bitter and chaotic party
conventions in 1968 and 1970. The Socialists thus increasingly presented to the public in the 1960s an image of a divided party with
outmoded programs, a party incapable of reforming itself and leading

a unified left to electoral victory.[1] The Party's problems seem to have resulted in a general decline in support, especially among younger voters. Shigeki Nishihara argued as early as 1964 that survey data suggested that the younger age groups were giving less support to the progressive parties than previously.[2] A national survey by the National Railways Union in April 1969 showed that the support rate for the Socialist Party among its members was only 55 percent (13.4 percent for the Communist Party), compared with 83 percent two years before.[3] In another survey, the number of respondents saying that they had no party choice in 1970 exceeded those preferring the Socialist Party by 17 percent. In 1965, the difference was only 3 percent. And the evidence suggests that many of those with no party choice were "traditional supporters of the Socialists who could not bring themselves to vote for another party but could not see any point in going to the polls to vote for a party doomed to fail anyway." [4] In the 1969 election, nearly 71 percent of the eligible voters cast their ballots, but among those in the seven largest cities between the ages of 20 and 39—traditional supporters of the Socialists—the turnout ranged between 44 percent and almost 60 percent.[5]

The *Asahi* saw an incident in 1969 as symbolic of the Socialist Party's decline. In the 1960 antitreaty movement the JSP and supporting labor demonstrators were sometimes greeted with confetti and applause en route. On October 21, 1969, in an antitreaty protest preparatory to the 1970 struggle, the lines of demonstrators passed quietly through darkened streets. "The times have changed," said the writer, "but even so, the JSP hasn't changed. They're not even trying to change." [6] Those dissatisfied with the present system have come to see the choice as not necessarily one of LDP vs. JSP. Indeed, a general

---

1 For a general discussion of the problems of the Socialist Party in Japan, see Taketsugu Tsurutani, "The Japan Socialist Party in Transition." The factional conflicts in the JSP and their foreign-policy implications are examined in J. A. A. Stockwin, "Foreign Policy Perspectives of the Japanese Left: Confrontation or Consensus?" For basic material necessary in understanding the beginning of the "structural reform" issue in the party, see *Journal of Social and Political Ideas in Japan*, I, 2, August 1963, pp. 39–50.

2 Shigeki Nishihara, "Are Young People Becoming More Conservative?," p. 139.

3 *Asahi*, October 8, 1969, p. 1.

4 Tsurutani, "The Japan Socialist Party," p. 11. Information and quotation are cited from Shinohara Hajime, "70-nendai to Kakushin no Kanōsei" (The Possibilities of Reform in the 1970s), *Sekai* (The World), March 1970, p. 32.

5 *Asahi*, March 23, 1970, p. 2. The average turnout for the population as a whole declined somewhat more than 4 percent from the 1967 election. Among those in their twenties, the turnout was down 7 to 8 percent.

6 *Asahi*, December 29, 1969, p. 2. This article, entitled "Shakaitō Wa Tachinaoreru Ka (part 1)," interprets the decline of the JSP as due to their continually relying on "postwar" sensitivities of antiwar and "defense of the Constitution" feelings rather than realizing that "in the time of the miniskirt" a new vision and appeal is necessary to gain the support of a new generation.

shift away from the Socialists does not seem to have been translated into support for the LDP. In 1969, for the first time, the LDP in winning its overwhelming majority in the Diet did not receive a majority of the popular vote. Moreover, in the Railway Worker's Union survey cited above, many of those who said their standard of living was "upper middle," and who therefore might be expected to shift from the Socialists to the LDP, were those who were dissatisfied with all the parties and not just the JSP.[7]

The tendency we found among our activists to shift from a preference for the JSP to no party preference thus seems to parallel a general shift in political climate. My data provide further evidence that this change was due to climate and not to a change in role after graduation. I found that as many as 42 percent of those who did not vote in the 1969 general election *had* voted for the Socialist Party in the 1967 general election when they had already graduated and entered adult society. Attributing this shift to the effect of climate rather than role change also makes sense in light of the data presented in chapter two concerning the acquisition of party preference. When party preference is not transmitted early in life in the family but rather is acquired as the result of a general and persistent progressive orientation gained later in life, we would expect both such easy change-overs to no party preference (but not to be conservatives) and weak voting support in response to changing events and conditions.

The increasing doubts about Marxism and the decline in its appeal as an ideology we found among our activists can also be attributed to political climatic changes interacting with the way in which their belief in Marxism was originally acquired. During the 1960s, in a number of published articles by Japanese and Western scholars, the new affluence and industrial and technological trends in Japan were linked to forecasts of Marxism's obsolescence and the "end of ideology" [8] in Japan. Shimizu Ikutarō, himself a Marxist-influenced

---

[7] *Asahi*, October 8, 1969, p. 1. The article sees the trends as a process of "depoliticization" rather than a trend toward conservatism. It also cites, as evidence of alienation from the LDP as well as from the left, the fact that since 1965 the number of Tokyo voters who have agreed in polls to the statement that "Government policy does not often reflect the desires of the people" has consistently exceeded 50 percent. Vogel, *Japan's New Middle Class*, p. 279, also found that in the white-collar community he revisited in 1969 after a ten-year absence, cynicism toward political leaders was still prevalent despite the increase in material prosperity.

[8] The predictions of the "end of ideology" began in the West, of course, with Daniel Bell's *The End of Ideology*, and have been hotly debated ever since. See for example, Daniel Bell and Henry Aiken, "Ideology—A Debate," and Joseph LaPalombara, "Decline of Ideology: A Dissent and an Interpretation," along with Lipset's rejoinder, "Some Further Comments on the 'End of Ideology.'" For differing views on the application of the theory to Japan, see Arata Ishimoto, "Radical

intellectual and a leader of the 1960 anti-Ampo forces, noted the failure of Marxist predictions and condemned Marxists and Marxism for the ideology's lack of meaning in an age of mass society.[9] Shimizu thus became both an "end of ideology" theorist and an oft-cited example of the theory's application to Japanese intellectuals. There were other signs, as well, that the ideology was generally on the wane among intellectuals. For the first time since the war, Marxism's monopoly on intellectual discourse weakened as non-Marxian analyses began to appear in the trend-setting intellectual journals. An enterprising Japanese scholar studying in the United States has confirmed this by content-analyzing the intellectual journals *Chūō Kōron* and *Sekai*. He concludes that his results show the validity of the "end of ideology" thesis in Japan.[10] Marxism's weakening hold on the intellectual community was also shown by the entrance of younger, Western-educated, non-Marxian economists into the faculty at major universities and by the emergence of pragmatic theoreticians who could now openly discuss "balance of power" theories and even think about the unthinkable—the realistic options of Japanese foreign policy, including nuclear armament.[11] Our sample's doubts and disillusionment concerning Marxism and their increasing eclecticism in ideological belief consequently appear to be part of a general trend: Marxism's appeal for intellectuals has declined because of changing conditions in Japan and the world during the 1960s.

These changes in society, international conditions, and intellectual climate have weakened our activists' faith in Marxism, especially its predictions, because they strike at the very motivations that led them to the ideology during their youth. We saw in chapter three that in the process of political socialization to ideological beliefs our activists went through a stage of "universalistic humanism" before acquiring Marxist beliefs. Marxism's appeal lay in its providing a systematic causal explanation of social problems and discrepancies and in its

Intellectuals and the End of Ideology," and the "Introduction" and "Notes by the Editor" to parts II and III of the *Journal of Social and Political Ideas in Japan*, II, 1, April 1964; cf. J. A. A. Stockwin, "Is Japan a Post-Marxist Society?" The signs that Marxism is losing some of its appeal among Japanese intellectuals are unmistakable. However, in view of the data already presented I am inclined to agree with those such as LaPalombara and Stockwin who argue that domestic political or social conditions in specific countries can influence the relationship between economic affluence and the decline in ideology, and that what Bell and Lipset interpret as "the end of ideology" can also be seen as its adaptation to changing circumstance. Marxism, as I shall indicate below, may continue to serve functions for the individual even when its predictions have been discredited. For a similar argument, see Robert E. Cole, "Japanese Workers, Unions, and the Marxist Appeal."

9 Ikutarō Shimizu, "Ideology in an Age of No Ideology."
10 Masaaki Takane, "Economic Growth and the 'End of Ideology' in Japan."
11 *Asahi*, October 13, 1969, p. 1.

promise of fulfilling the universalistic and humanistic values in which these youths strongly believed. Both of those original appeals of Marxism have been weakened by the changing conditions of the 1960s: increasing affluence and the diminishing prospects of a revolution by an impoverished proletariat, the continuing ramifications of de-Stalinization, and the increasing fragmentation of the Socialist bloc.

Our former leaders of Zengakuren most clearly show the effect of these conditions and events in weakening Marxism's claim to "scientific" analysis and predictive validity. One of the intriguing aspects of the data on the decline of Marxism is that former leaders were more likely to change negatively on all measures of Marxism's appeal than were former activists: 30 percent of the leaders and 22 percent of the activists decreased in identification and sympathy; 30 percent of the leaders and 17 percent of the activists showed a decline in interest. This is an especially important change because the leaders were more likely than any other type of student to be Marxist in orientation in their student days. In their positions as top officers of Zengakuren they were the students most deeply involved in studying Marxism's theoretical structure and in formulating ideological policy for the movement. After graduation, they tended to enter the intellectual occupations: fully half of the former leaders, a greater proportion than any other type of student in our sample, entered journalism, writing, publishing, research, or teaching. With their deeper theoretical grasp of Marxism, they were among the first to see how the changing conditions of the 1960s have invalidated Marxism's predictions and its claim to scientific predictibility. Witness the rejection of Marxism by A, a former leader and now an editor of a journal on labor relations:

> The greatest change [in my thought about Marxism] has been to arrive at the conclusion that it is indeed childish by the standards of knowledge in the latter half of the 20th century. Thus while at that time [in his student days] Marxism satisfied my intellectual desires, it can no longer satisfy them all. You could say that now, when I see only the faults in Marxism, it's because I know it so well. When you go into it thoroughly, you also see its weaknesses. Even when I was a Marxist, I saw various weaknesses in it, but now I see them more clearly, even in economics.[12]

G, another former leader in the student movement and now a university professor of "futurology" has also rejected Marxism, having "come to recognize clearly the contradictions in its theoretical structure." [13]

The experience of other leaders not included in my study indi-

---

12 Interview with A, April 18, 1970.   13 Interview with G, June 25, 1970.

cates that this type of change has been quite prevalent among the leaders of the 1960 student movement. Reports of at least three other top leaders show that they went on to graduate school, studied Marxism, became interested in quantitative economics, and finally rejected Marxism. Two of the three came to the United States for advanced study. One died in a tragic fire at the University of Pennsylvania, and the other now teaches at Harvard. The remaining student has recently received his Ph.D. from Tokyo University.[14] Thus, motivated by their interest in Marxist theory, many of the leaders have gone on to study it further after graduation, but their familiarity with Marxist theory and their strongly intellectual approach to it have helped lead them to the conclusion that it is decreasingly applicable to the changing world of the twentieth century. Entering adult society has not led to a decline in their faith in Marxism as much as changing conditions have affected their earlier belief in Marxism's scientific, logical, and predictive capacities.

The increasing eclecticism in ideological belief and the doubts about Marxism's predictions that we found even among those who continue to accept Marxism and its premises can also be explained by the way in which changing conditions have interacted with the respondents' earlier socialization. One of the appeals of Marxism to our activists in their youth was its seeming identification with their universalistic and humanistic values. This "universalistic humanism" has remained an important and integral part of their values even after graduation. In a sense the very continuity of their humanism has made them leery of accepting Marxism *in toto*. Because of the events of the 1960s, many have come to realize that orthodox Marxism's vision of the future may in practice result in a society antithetical to the basic values that led them originally to participate in the student movement and to adopt Marxism. B summed up most eloquently the continuity in the basic values of these students and its relationship, on the one hand, to changing international conditions and on the other, to their loss of faith in Marxism's ability to fulfill those values:

Socialism is losing its appeal. In our time we felt "capitalism is bad" and "socialism is good." But now we have to explain what kind of socialism it is. You don't want to say "socialism in general is the socialism of the Soviet Union." What about Czechoslavakia and Hungary? Or the Cultural Revolution in Red China? We have to struggle against things without having a "vision" of the future. I don't think the sort of vision will appear that can be

14 Tachibana Takashi, "Rokujūnen Ampo Eiyū no Eikō to Hisan," (The Glory and the Tragedy of the 1960 Ampo Heroes), p. 250; Mainichi Shimbun Shakaibu Ampo Gakusei Han (ed.), *Ampo: Gekidō no Kono Jūnen* (The Security Treaty: These Ten Years of Upheaval), pp. 12–13.

expressed in words. Classical Marxism-Leninism was a vision that could be expressed in words. . . . We have to create a vision which goes to the point and says what kind of relationships can be built which get down to the living flesh and blood of human beings. . . .

We used to have the idea that socialism directly relates to liberty and equality, so those who thought that inequality and exploitation and capitalism were inseparable were attracted to socialism. But now we know clearly that socialism like that of the Soviet Union doesn't contain freedom and equality either. In 1960 Ampo the idea that Marxism-Leninism was Stalinist was criticized. But if Japan becomes a socialist country, if you think that a planned economy controlled by a modern "rationalism" like Marxism won't be Stalinism, you're wrong.[15]

While questioning Marxism's predictions, therefore, they continue to believe in those premises of Marxism not in conflict with their concern for democracy, equality, and universal human bonds. Their continued belief in the contradictions in capitalism and history as class struggle still provides them with conceptual tools to explain injustice and inequality and to continue their struggle to eliminate these. But the struggle is increasingly an existential one devoid of "visions" of the future.

In the preceding pages, I have concentrated on presenting evidence that the generational model seems best suited to explaining the political socialization patterns of our activists. They have demonstrated a continuity in belief, especially in basic orientations and values, and have selected postgraduation environments compatible with those orientations and beliefs. Such changes in belief as have taken place seem better explained by new social conditions and climates interacting with orientations and values acquired before graduation. All this evidence fits better with the generational than with the maturational model, for according to the latter, new and specific roles in adulthood cause changes in belief. Given this, however, we are confronted with a central problem concerning our less active students. Most of them had temporarily, if intermittently, engaged in political-protest activity while in college. Why do they seem to have given it up so completely in adulthood? The generational hypothesis alone is of little help here, or rather, by explaining everything it explains nothing. Since the intermittent activists were both inactive and active at various times in their youth—fairly nonparticipatory in middle- and high-school activities, occasionally active politically during college—merely saying that they revert to an earlier pattern of activity is not a completely satisfactory explanation. Clearly, the question of the extent of change in adulthood due to entering new roles must be further explored.

---

15 Interview with B, April 25, 1970.

There is another reason, however—a more important one—for investigating more fully the effect of adult roles on political belief and behavior. We have yet to test the hypotheses of Dawson and Prewitt that (1) while earlier socialization is long lasting, new adult roles can still affect political belief and behavior, and (2) the effect of adult roles may vary with the specific dimension of belief or behavior in question. The first hypothesis essentially asserts that although the generational model may be generally valid, entrance into new adult roles can have a *conditional* effect on belief or behavior, or both. Not viewing our two models as mutually exclusive may indeed be a more theoretically valid way to approach the problem of the relative effects of youth and adulthood on political belief and behavior. The question becomes: under what conditions do adult roles have an effect on the products of the political-socialization process? The second hypothesis answers this question in part by predicting that the effect of adult roles will vary with the type of political belief or behavior pattern.

The findings of developmental psychology allow us to be more specific in predicting the conditions under which new roles will bring about change. Ira S. Rohter has criticized the assumption of most political-socialization theorists that by studying the development of enduring dispositions we arrive at an explanation of behavior as well.[16] He points out that psychologists have seriously questioned such an assumption and found that behavior is not necessarily generalized across situations: "The fact that an individual may display one form of behavior in one situation, and perhaps its opposite form in another, can be accounted for by differences in the situational cues and reinforcement contingencies. . . . Thus we should not expect a person to act similarly across situations if the reward or punishment consequences produced by the same behavior are different." [17] This does not mean that the individual's response is totally the product of current stimuli. His reaction to a specific situation will depend upon his previous experience. According to Rohter, "the antecedent conditions to which the individual has been exposed, together with current situational stimuli, affect his performance in new environments." [18]

On the basis of Rohter's discussion we may hypothesize that (1) behavior may be more affected by adult roles than is belief, but (2) the effect of adult roles may vary with the prior socialization experiences of the individual. I shall attempt to test these hypotheses and determine whether the adult roles that our former students entered had any effect on their political beliefs and behavior. Because the occupa-

---

16 Ira S. Rohter, "A Social-Learning Theory Approach to the Study of Political Socialization." My thanks to Prof. Kurt Steiner of Stanford University for calling my attention to this paper.
17 *Ibid.*, p. 3.   18 *Ibid.*, p. 4.

tional role is central in the adult life of a male, I decided to test the hypotheses by controlling for occupation on a few selected, but important, dimensions of political belief and behavior. As we saw previously, the types of occupations most frequently entered were the intellectual professions and business or government. In the light of the frequently asserted differences between these types of occupations (business and government being more bureaucratic, and in Japan more diffuse and particularistic), controlling for their effects can test whether adult roles do indeed bring about a change in orientations and activity. Needless to say, the full-time political activists will be excluded from the analysis.

To summarize, I am hypothesizing (1) that entrance into the professions on the one hand, or business and government occupations on the other, will have a greater effect on political behavior than on political belief, and (2) that because of the different prior socialization experiences of the activists and the less active, the effect of occupational role may vary with these two types of students.

ADULT ROLES AND POLITICAL BELIEFS

I first tested for the effects of occupation on selected dimensions of political belief: political orientation, belief in the influence of special interests on policy, change and maintenance of an attraction to Marxism. The results are given in tables 17, 18, and 19. We find that occupational role appears to have almost no effect on the beliefs of the activists. Although the activists in the professions seem to have maintained their beliefs slightly better than those in business and government, the differences between those who entered the two types of occupations do not exceed 10 percent on any level of the dependent variables. For example, in table 19, 73 percent of the activists who en-

TABLE 17. RELATIONSHIP BETWEEN POLITICAL ORIENTATION AND FORMER ACTIVITY IN THE STUDENT MOVEMENT, CONTROLLING FOR TYPE OF OCCUPATION (IN PERCENT)

Political orientation	LA		INA	
	Prof.	Bus.-Gov.	Prof.	Bus.-Gov.
Conservative	0	10	0	59
Progressive	50	50	100	29
Extremely progressive	50	40	0	12
	100%	100%	100%	100%
	(n = 14)	(n = 10)	(n = 7)	(n = 17) N = 48 [a]

[a] N does not equal 53 because 2 LA and 1 INA answered, "Don't know," and the 2 professional political activists were excluded from the analysis.

TABLE 18. RELATIONSHIP BETWEEN BELIEF THAT SPECIAL INTERESTS EXERT
UNDUE INFLUENCE ON POLICY-MAKING AND FORMER ACTIVITY IN
THE STUDENT MOVEMENT, CONTROLLING FOR TYPE
OF OCCUPATION (IN PERCENT)

Belief in undue influence	LA		INA		
	Prof.	Bus.-Gov.	Prof.	Bus.-Gov.	
High	80	90	100	71	
Low	20	10	0	29	
	100%	100%	100%	100%	
	(n = 15)	(n = 10)	(n = 7)	(n = 17)	N = 49 [a]

[a] N does not equal 53 because 1 LA and 1 INA answered, "Don't know," and the 2 professional political activists were excluded from the analysis.

TABLE 19. RELATIONSHIP BETWEEN CHANGES IN ATTRACTION TO MARXISM,
1962–1970, AND FORMER ACTIVITY IN THE STUDENT MOVEMENT,
CONTROLLING FOR TYPE OF OCCUPATION (IN PERCENT)

Attraction to Marxism	LA		INA		
	Prof.	Bus.-Gov.	Prof.	Bus.-Gov.	
Retained or acquired	73	64	57	6	
Continued nonattraction or lost attraction	27	36	43	94	
	100%	100%	100%	100%	
	(n = 15)	(n = 11)	(n = 7)	(n = 18)	N = 51 [a]

[a] N does not equal 53 because the 2 professional political activists were excluded from the analysis.

tered the intellectual professions were likely to maintain or acquire an attraction to Marxism, but so were 64 percent of the activists in business and government. There is little evidence, therefore, to suggest that occupational role has affected the maintenance of our activists' beliefs in adulthood.

It is interesting to note that these results confirm our previous analysis: the generational model is most appropriate to the development of our activists' political beliefs, and the weakening of belief in Marxism is attributable to changes in social conditions and earlier socialization rather than to entrance into new adult roles. But when we turn to the changes in belief of our less active students we find a very different picture: occupational role does seem to make a difference. In all the dimensions of belief tested, the less active students who went into the professions are more likely to have a sympathy for Marxism and a progressive orientation than the less active students who are in business and government roles. The data thus indicate that the less active students who enter a profession rather than business or government are likely to have a set of political beliefs resembling the activists'. The less active students who went into business or government careers, on the other hand, are more conservative, non-Marxist, and politically trusting than any type of student who enters the professions. Of particular significance may be our finding that somewhat over half of the former less active students in business and government positions refuse to identify themselves as "progressive" in orientation. Since most of these less active students were intermittent activists who participated in the 1960 antitreaty demonstrations, we may have some evidence of a definite decline in left-wing identification among those who enter business or government careers. Furthermore, since most college graduates in Japan, as did most of the less active in our sample, enter large business firms or government employment, this trend would be typical of most Japanese students.

We should note, however, that despite the tendency of those in business or government roles to refuse to identify themselves as "progressive" after graduation, one sign of continued political alienation remains among most of the less active students, whatever the occupation entered. The differences between the less active in the two types of professions on the political-trust variable are smaller than on the others. Whereas the differences between those in the professions and those in business and government were on the order of 40 percent or more on the Marxism and political-orientation measures, the difference on the question of special interests having too much influence on public policy is only 29 percent at most. Moreover, a large majority in both types of occupations still believe that government ignores the interests of the majority because it caters to special interests. In fact, almost the same percentage of less active in business or government believe this as do former activists who went into the professions! I was curious as to whether this sign of continued political alienation even among the less active in business or government would also be found on other measures of political trust or whether it would hold only for this one specific belief. I therefore controlled for occupational role on another measure of political trust—the belief that in the long run the government takes the desires of the average person into account. On this measure I found that the less active students in business or government were much more likely to be politically trusting (56 percent) than were the less active in the professions (14 percent), and once again the difference exceeded 40 percent. It therefore seems that despite the indications that they have become more conservative since their college days, this one belief which reflects low political trust—that special interests have an undue influence on policy—is quite widespread among the less active now in business and government careers.

The question will inevitably be raised as to whether the differences in adult political belief that we have found between our less active students in the two types of professions actually reflect the effects of occupational role or whether they reflect a self-selection process whereby the more leftist students entered the professions and the less leftist ones took business and government roles. One of the advantages of a longitudinal study is that it can provide us with some evidence to answer this type of question. As indicated by the discussion of occupational choice in chapter four, some of the less active students, along with most of the activists, who entered the professions seem indeed to have intentionally chosen their occupation in the hope of finding freer environments in which they could maintain and express their basic values, including political orientations. My evidence suggests, however, that occupational role *has* had some effect on the less active students' beliefs. One indication of this is that whereas all of our intermittent activists who entered business today identify themselves as conservative, a number of the nonactive students (and thus the more conservative of our less active students) who entered the professions have become more progressive in orientation. Although the number of nonactivists in the sample is quite small and therefore cannot be said necessarily to typify this type of student, it is noteworthy that three of the seven in the sample entered professions and all are politically progressive and alienated today. Two of the three have also become attracted to Marxism since graduating.

One example of the change that occupational role has brought to the nonactivists who entered the professions is the case of W, now a reporter for a top Japanese newspaper. His father was purged by the Occupation for his wartime role, and he told me that he grew up with strong anti-Communist beliefs, beliefs reflected in the 1962 survey. In 1962 he chose nationalism as a philosophical standpoint to which he felt close and said he wished to work to defend the capitalist system after graduation. Today he says he is not interested in what happens to the system and labels himself "ideologically free," but he also accepts the analysis of the contradictions in capitalism as correct, votes for the Communist Party, and admits to an increase of interest in, and agreement with, Marxism because of his deepening interest in social problems as a result of his experiences as a reporter.

Another example is that of U, who also became a reporter for a large and prestigious newspaper in Japan. Although he cannot bring himself to accept a philosophy such as Marxism, he has become interested in politics for the first time since graduation, and now identifies himself as "extremely progressive." Although he affirmed in 1962 that he wanted to defend the capitalist system, in 1970 he said that he wants to work to change it. When I asked him how his work and workplace environment had influenced his thinking, he acknowledged that their influence was great: "The job of a reporter is to see society well, especially, generally speaking, its contradictions. When I then thought to myself, "What must be done?" my humanism appeared. I think humanism is probably the judgment of what is necessary to live as a human being." U went on to say that his humanism was also mixed with anger: "When I saw many oppressed people, or people who lived a terrible life, I realized this has to be corrected, and to do this my interest in politics had to increase. Of course, half of it's my job. To give an example, while handling the problem of "public hazards" in my work I noticed that the people were in a weak position and that government policy is not sufficient. So my humanism and anger appeared simutaneously." [19] The reader will no doubt find U's words strangely familiar—they closely parallel the testimony our activists gave as to how they became politicized and acquired what I have called their "universalistic humanism" in middle school and high school. But for the nonactive students in the professions, their experiences in their adult occupational roles have brought about this concern for social and political problems. Consequently, they discern a gap between their perceptions of ideal democracy and equality and its actuality in Japan. U, for example, sees democracy as ideally being the "equality of each" and now believes that Japan "is *not* a sufficient democracy."

It would be foolish to argue on the basis of the few underrepresented nonactivists in our sample that this pattern is typical of the many nonactivist students in Japan. However, the evidence above, combined with the fact that the less active students who did join the anti-Ampo demonstrations in college and later entered business firms now consider themselves conservative, provides additional proof of the influence of occupational role on the less active students. Those nonactive and intermittently active students who enter the professions maintain or acquire beliefs more similar to those of the former activists. The intermittent activists who enter business or government seem to become somewhat more conservative than when they participated in the Ampo demonstrations.

We have so far presented evidence that occupational role does not seem to have a great effect on our activists' political beliefs but that it does make a difference in the type of political beliefs held by our less active students as adults. A partial explanation of this pattern is given

---

[19] Interview with U, April 16, 1970.

by our data on the political orientations of their close friends at work (*shokuba no nakama*). We asked our respondents if their peers at work were interested in politics and then, if they were, what political orientation these friends had. The response of 80 percent of the activists and 71 percent of the less active in the professions was that they had work-place peer groups with some progressive members, and in most cases the majority of these peers were progressive. In business or government occupations, 64 percent of the activists but only 23 percent of the less active had work-place peer groups that included some progressive friends. In other words, regardless of occupation entered the activists tended to have work-place peer groups containing close friends who were left-wing in their political beliefs. The less active who entered the professions also had left-wing friends in their peer groups at work, but those in business or government tended to have friends who were either uninterested in politics or more conservative in orientation.

These findings become particularly important when we look at the political-communication patterns of our former students. We asked our respondents how often they discussed politics when they were with their peers at the place of work, their friends other than those peers, and the people with whom they lived. The activists discussed politics most with their friends and work-place peers and least with the people they lived with, as is shown in these results:

FREQUENCY OF POLITICAL DISCUSSION (in percent)

	Often	Sometimes	Not much, hardly at all	Total (N = 28)
Peers at workplace	57	29	14	100%
Friends	57	36	7	100%
People lived with	32	43	25 [a]	100%

[a] Includes two activists who lived alone.

The political-communication patterns of our less active students show that they too discuss politics more with work-place peers and friends than with the people with whom they live, but in all cases less frequently than the activists:

FREQUENCY OF POLITICAL DISCUSSION (in percent)

	Often	Sometimes	Not much, hardly at all	Total (N = 25)
Peers at workplace	24	28	48	100%
Friends	32	20	48	100%
People lived with	12	32	56 [a]	100%

[a] Includes two less actives who lived alone.

Our former activists still discuss politics more than the former less active students, and, just as they discussed politics most with their age-mates in college, almost all still discuss politics most with their friends, at work and outside of work. Among our less active students, the frequency of political discussion is far less than we found during their college days and resembles the level of political communication that existed during their middle- and high-school years.

Significantly, the activists, who generally have work-place friends progressive in orientation, discuss politics with these friends. They also discuss politics with friends besides their work-place peers. Inasmuch as almost all these students said that their other friends were those from their student or student-movement days, they seem to have continued also to discuss politics with other former activists. Indeed, when we checked on the political orientation of their non-work-place friends, we found that all but two of the activists had groups of friends in which there were some progressive members, and almost all of these respondents had friendship groups in which most of the members were leftist. And the more progressive the friendship group, the more often they were likely to discuss politics with them. These results strongly indicate that one of the reasons the occupation entered has little effect on the political beliefs of our activists is that they have selected and maintained peer groups whose political beliefs are compatible with their left-wing orientations even when they have entered the world of business and government. Their friends both at work and from their school days are progressive in orientation, and it is with these friends that the former activists discuss politics most frequently; hence they receive continued reinforcement of their college beliefs.

The less active students who enter the professions also have work-place peer groups whose political beliefs are leftist. But those in business and government have work-place peer groups who are either apolitical or conservative. In the diffuse and particularist role-environment of the business or government work-place, they have little incentive to discuss politics with their colleagues. Neither do they seem to have made an attempt to maintain or seek out people with left-wing political beliefs for discussion of politics in their personal relationships outside the work-place. Without a reinforcing environment, many of the progressive beliefs they may have had in college decline. Consequently, the seeming conservative trend we found among those in business and government roles may well be related to a lack of reinforcement for leftist beliefs among their peers at the place of work and elsewhere.

OCCUPATIONAL ROLES AND POLITICAL BEHAVIOR

Occupational role seems to have little effect on our activists' beliefs but a greater effect on those of our less active. What effect does occupation have on political behavior? In order to test this relationship, I controlled for occupation on the most interesting dimension of political behavior for which I have data: participation in demonstrations in the two years preceding 1970. Our sample being composed of former activists and many less active students who participated in demonstrations at one time during their college years, we can determine whether selection of careers in the professions has allowed them to maintain their high rate of political activity. We may also learn whether our less active students' nonactive pattern of behavior is due to the nature of the work-place they entered.

Table 20 presents the data on type of occupation and participation in demonstrations as adults for both the active and the less active. We find here a difference both between the activists and the less active and between the professions and the world of business and government. The activists in the professions are more likely to have continued their active-protest behavior than the less active in the professions (but the difference is not large), and the activists in business and government are also more likely to be demonstrating than the less active in the same occupations, none of whom have participated in a demonstration during the two years in question. But it appears that occupational role seems to have a greater effect on behavior than on belief for both types of former students. The gap between the less active in the professions and those in business and government is particularly large, even larger than the gap we found earlier in terms of belief. What is surprising, however, in light of the previous discussion of orientations, is that almost twice as many activists in the professions

TABLE 20. RELATIONSHIP BETWEEN PARTICIPATION IN DEMONSTRATIONS AND FORMER ACTIVITY IN THE STUDENT MOVEMENT, CONTROLLING FOR TYPE OF OCCUPATION (IN PERCENT)

Participation in demonstrations	LA		INA		
	Prof.	Bus.-Gov.	Prof.	Bus.-Gov.	
Yes	87	45	71	0	
No	13	55	29	100	
	100%	100%	100%	100%	
	(n = 15)	(n = 11)	(n = 7)	(n = 18)	N = 51 [a]

[a] N does not equal 53 because the 2 professional political activists were excluded from the analysis.

as in business and government are demonstrating today. Although the continued activity of almost half the activists compared to none of the less active in the world of business and government shows that the effect of earlier socialization persists, the differences between activists in the two types of occupations argue strongly for the conditional effect of adult roles on behavior.

Can we attribute the difference due to occupation to the effect of work-place peer encouragement in the professions? Because I asked my respondents what attitude their work-place colleagues would take if they participated in a demonstration, I obtained some data on this point. I found that few of the respondents in either type of occupation said that even some of their work-place colleagues would give positive approval to such action. Most said they would be indifferent or oppose their participation; most in each type of occupation expected indifference.[20] Although we found that work-place-peer influence may be partly responsible for our results concerning the effect of occupation on political belief, attitudes of such peers toward participation in demonstrations cannot explain why occupation so greatly affects the political behavior of our sample. We must look elsewhere for an explanation.

This explanation may lie in the many reports of observers that organizational roles in Japan are diffuse, particularly in business firms, where great loyalty and dedication to the organization are expected and left-wing political activity is considered antithetical to organizational goals. We would thus expect that because of the diffuse occupational-role expectations, the norm of differentiating between the employee's "private" political behavior and his role expectations at work would be rare in Japanese private and public organizations. I had included in my 1970 survey a question designed to test just such a problem. Each respondent was asked: "If you participated in political activity, do you think it would have a harmful influence on your work life?" We found that the reports of observers are essentially correct: the failure to differentiate between specific occupational expectations and the exercise of the citizen's right to engage in political activity

---

[20] Among the less active there was a slight difference between the two occupations in the positive approval that colleagues would give to participation in demonstrations: 29 percent in the professions, compared with 11 percent in business and government, said that at least some colleagues would give positive approval. But among the activists, the percentage of those in business and government (45 percent) who had some colleagues who would approve was larger than that of those in the professions (36 percent), despite the fact that a greater percentage of activists in the professions are demonstrating today than those in business and government! Not only are the differences slight in both cases, but in the wrong direction in the case of the activists.

is prevalent. This attitude is much more common in business and government than in the professions:

If demonstrate, expect harmful influence	Occupation	
	Prof. (percent)	Bus.-Gov. (percent)
Yes	50	86
No	50	14
	100%	100%
N = 50 [a]	(n = 22)	(n = 28)

[a] N does not equal 53 because the two professional political activists were excluded and one respondent answered, "Don't know."

Many of the respondents in both types of occupation believe that under all or certain circumstances engaging in political activity would be detrimental to their work-life. However, whereas an equal number of respondents in the professions believe it would not be detrimental, six times as many in business and governmental roles believe such participation would have a harmful influence as believe it would not. Incidentally, almost all of those who thought political activity would be harmful under certain conditions but not under others specifically said that left-wing activity would definitely be harmful. For example, one respondent said, "I can't say unqualifiedly, but in the case of left-wing activity it would always have a bad influence." Another said, "It's harder on the new left," and also explained that if a right-winger were sought by the police for political activity, the company would cover for him, but if a left-winger were on the run, the company would not.

A more detailed scrutiny of the type of harmful influence antici-pated by the respondents found other differences between role-expecta-tions in the professions and those in business. In follow-up questions I asked either what type of harmful influence political activity would have, or why the respondent believed there would not be harmful effects. Taking the latter first, the answers indicated greater differentia-tion between occupational role and the political sphere in the profes-sions. Many of those in the professions who did not believe partici-pating in a demonstration would be detrimental to their careers cited either that political activity was their right, or, more frequently, that political activity was judged at their place of work as an individual ac-tivity separate from their occupational role, as in the case of a respon-dent in the professions who said, "If one has ability, it is not necessary to be careful about relations with superiors." More importantly, the reasons given by respondents for their belief that participation would influence their occupational life disclose differences between the professions and the business world in both the type and the strength of the diffuse role expectations. In the professions, all but a few of the respondents cited a specific sanction that would result: jeopardizing career advancement. "Slow promotion," "You couldn't advance," "Advancement—it [whether or not one is politically active] is one of the criteria for evaluation in the present academic world," are just a few such answers given by those in the professions.

During the depth interviews, I encountered graphic illustration of the subtle ways in which political activity could hinder career advancement in the professions. R, a former intermittent activist now a reporter, told me about his experiences before and after he was transferred to Tokyo to take a choice post as a correspondent covering one of the most powerful ministries in the Japanese government. In relating his story below, I have invented a name for the city he came from and omitted the name of the ministry in order to preserve R's anonymity:

> When I was the leader of the labor union [as a reporter for his organization in "Western Sea City"] I always insisted on my opinion in a loud voice. Although I insisted on it, I was a coward and always worried about its affecting my being transferred to Tokyo. . . . When I came to Tokyo one of my direct superiors told me that he was very pleased that I had come; moreover, I would be put in charge of X Ministry, which is a post rarely given to those who have just come to Tokyo and which is a very important one for a reporter of economics. Then he told me to do my job wholeheartedly and work as hard as I could. As I had expected when I was in "Western Sea City," they indirectly had "checked" my labor-union activity.[21]

There was no doubt in R's mind of the meaning of his superior's words: he was telling R subtly but effectively that keeping his new and important post was contingent on his stopping his labor-union activities.

J provided another example in the teaching profession. While answering questions on the fixed-format interview-survey, J, a college teacher at a well-known national university, had said that most of his work-place colleagues and superiors would approve (*mitomeru*) of his engaging in political activity. Later he said that such activity would have a harmful influence on his career. Wanting to find out more about this seeming contradiction, I asked him about it during the depth interviews:

> The word *"mitomeru"* in Japanese can have two meanings: the first, "to agree with," and the other, "to permit." Well, after all, universities have

---

21 Interview with R, May 26, 1970.

academic freedom, and even toward political activity they are very tolerant. Therefore, limitations in a formal sense don't come up very much. For example, there isn't any dismissal or firing. Still there are, of course, superiors with whose political views and opinions you differ. Even if he is tolerant, if your political opinions are different it becomes a matter of his not agreeing to let people like me be promoted. . . . It's not the Ministry of Education. The Ministry of Education is the highest superior, but for what we're talking about it's the department chairman (*gakubuchō*) who's the highest superior.[22]

These two cases and the reasons given by many of those in the professions for believing that engaging in political activity would be detrimental to their careers illustrate my previous point: in the professions the chief negative expectation of the consequences of political activity is the belief that one's career advancement may be subtly jeopardized. The indirect methods of R's superiors, and the distinction J made between formal and informal sanctions, are also intriguing because they imply that a gap may exist in the professions between the explicit and formal criteria governing role relations—universalistic and specific criteria—and the informal and actual criteria that are particularistic and diffuse.

When we turn to those in business who thought political activity would harm their occupational goals, we find a somewhat different picture. Two different consequences of diffuse role-expectations seem to be at issue here. One may be called the "general role demands" of the salary man: the dedication, loyalty, hard work, long hours, and interpersonal harmony within the organization that are demanded of the salary man are incompatible with engaging in political activity. Answers such as "It would take time and energy away from work," "It would worsen human relations," "I wouldn't be able to do my work," "If it causes trouble for the job, it would be a problem," and "The people around me would not think well of it," illustrate one way in which diffuse and particularist role relations in Japanese organizations, particularly large business, inhibit political activity. The other consequence is severe and formal sanctions by those in authority for engaging in left-wing political activity. In some cases, as in the professions, the expected sanction was the inhibiting of upward career mobility. One respondent in a large business firm said, "We are being marked as to whether we are engaging in political activity or not. It would influence advancement." But others in large business predicted much direr consequences: "I'd be fired," "Your post would be changed or you would be demoted," "There's the possibility of being fired," "Firing or ignominious transfer," were answers given by respondents in business, whereas none of the respondents in the professions ever

---

[22] Interview with J, April 25, 1970.

mentioned the possibility of discharge for political activities. Hence, although diffuse role criteria exist in the professions, they exist less frequently than in the business world, and more specific and universalistic formal criteria seem to force action taken against political activity to be confined to more subtle and limited means. In the world of business, on the other hand, particularistic relations at the place of work and the diffuse and total work demands on the salary man, as well as formal sanctions, can operate to limit participation in political activity. And when those formal sanctions are applied, they can be far more severe than the informal ones found in the professions.[23]

The question still remains, however, whether the diffuse nature of occupational roles in Japan has something to do with the impact that occupation seems to have on political behavior. When I cross-tabulated the belief that political activity would be harmful to one's work-life with participation in demonstrations during the two years prior to the 1970 interviews, an interesting relationship emerged. Such a belief does indeed seem to inhibit political activity for both the activists and the less active. Whereas 89 percent of the activists who thought demonstrating would not harm their work-life participated in demonstrations, no more than 62 percent of those who thought it would be harmful participated. Moreover, all but one of the activists who were not now engaging in political protest activity said such activity would be a detriment to their careers. Similarly, whereas only 15 percent of the less active who thought participation in demonstrations would be harmful participated anyway, participation by the less active who thought it would not be detrimental came to 40 percent. In other words, the activists are more likely to engage in political demonstrations than the less active in either case, but such a belief does seem to inhibit political activity by both types of former students. Although the diffuse role relationships in Japanese organizations cannot account for all the effect of occupation on political activity, they do account for a good part of it.

We have found a relationship between occupation and political activity on the one hand, and occupation and diffuse role expectations on the other. Linking them together, we saw that these diffuse role norms do tend to inhibit political activity, but that of the less active more than that of the activists. The tendency of the activists in the professions to continue demonstrating even in the face of sanctions at their place of work can be attributed, I believe, to the interaction

---

[23] Their severity is compounded, of course, by the life-long employment system. Transfer to the "provinces," demotion, or firing, and the anxiety in regard to them, therefore can be extremely potent in limiting political activity when they occur in the Japanese employment context.

of earlier socialization and the more specific criteria for role relations in the professions in Japan. Just as the activists insisted on self-expression and participation when in middle and in high school, even in the face of unresponsive authority, in many cases today they are willing to risk slower career advancement rather than give up their activity. Expression of their political beliefs through behavior still takes precedence. But a contributing factor is the more limited and informal sanctions that apply in the professions. The expectations that govern the occupational role relations of many of our activists in the professions include specificity of roles and the autonomous evaluation of job performance. Even where these criteria are legitimized as the formal norms but particularistic and diffuse criteria enter informally in actual role evaluations, sanctions are less severe and more subtly and indirectly applied than in the business world. As those who entered the professions expected, they have found a politically freer and more compatible occupational environment than they would have found in the business world, if not a completely tolerant one.

A SPECIAL CASE OF CHANGE

We have seen, as Rohter predicted, that behavior is more situationally determined than is belief and that occupational role determines whether political behavior such as participation in demonstrations is maintained after graduation more than it determines the change or maintenance of political beliefs. A special type of postgraduate change we should note is the direct result of this phenomenon: activists and intermittent activists now in large business firms who give up political activity but retain their strong left-wing beliefs. They may stop participating in demonstrations during their last year or two in college in order not to jeopardize their chances for employment, or they may continue their activity as long as possible. In either case, once in a company they no longer engage in political activity and usually hide their strong left-wing beliefs from their colleagues at work.[24]

I came across a number of such respondents during my depth interviews. H had been a leader of Zengakuren but stopped his participation in the student movement during college. He decided to join

24 This type of behavioral change without a corresponding change in belief in some respects resembles the *gisō tenkō* ("false," or "camouflaged," *tenkō*) of the prewar period: false recantations by Marxists to police authorities in order to be released from prison, often for the purpose of returning to society, once again to work for their original goals. See Patricia Golden Steinhoff, "Ideology and Societal Integration in Prewar Japan," pp. 239–240. The similarity between our post-war students and the *gisō tenkōsha* of the prewar period rests, of course, in their similar false outward conformity while really retaining leftist beliefs, not in similarity of motivation.

a large enterprise after graduation. After a sudden rejection by a company that had initially hired him, he finally got a job as an accountant, but left that job to start two very successful small companies with a college friend. He is still leftist in orientation and has sympathy for Marxism but feels that his work now takes precedence over politics. While in college, he never felt any restrictions on talking about politics, but when he entered his first job, things changed:

> After I entered that company, I was in a situation where if my previous record came to light, I might have been fired. So I tried not to talk about myself. Since I began my present job, I know everyone in the company and can talk freely with them. But once I get out of it, I come in contact with many different kinds of people, and because some of them are somewhat conservative I think of my own interests and don't touch upon those kinds of things. But even now when I meet old friends we discuss various things and they have invited me to reading circles. But since I don't have time to go, I ask them only to send me materials and I enjoy reading them.[25]

H's testimony illustrates a number of things I have touched upon—the diffuse role relations and expectations in many companies, the inhibition on behavior because of particularist role relations, and the maintenance of belief through continuing contact and communication with progressive friends. In one sense, however, H is luckier than most. Now that he is in his own company he can discuss politics freely with his colleagues at work. Others I met were not so fortunate, and their hidden frustrations were intense. K, an intermittent activist and now a clerk in a large banking conglomerate, says he has never learned to talk to his more conservative work colleagues about politics. Nor, he says, will he associate with any of his college friends whose left-wing thinking has changed. Nervous at first about revealing his real opinions, he gradually became more and more open as the interview progressed, and his leftist beliefs emerged more strongly. So did the hostility and frustration he felt as a result of the discrepancy between the ideals of democracy he believed in and the reality of his daily life in a bureaucratic organization:

> Most people are working in companies, and unless democracy is established in companies, a real democracy won't appear. Whatever freedom of speech or publishing there is in a political sense, if things don't change in each school, in each company, there isn't true democracy. For example, when it isn't like the military in China which doesn't have a hierarchy, it can't become a democracy. We don't have a democracy once we enter the company. Everything is decided by those at the top and handed down—it's just like a military system. I think the companies in the United States are

---

25 Interview with H, May 23, 1970.

the same. For example, when they choose superiors or decide on policy and it's not decided by everyone, the "brains" are gathered and they make the decisions and everyone else follows. As long as things like this don't change, democracy won't be established. In the same way, I don't think the Soviet Union is really socialistic.[26]

M was the best example of a former activist who has entered the world of business and who has hidden his left-wing beliefs from his bosses and colleagues at work in order to become a salary man. M, a former leader of Zengakuren now working as a salesman for a large company, had been cooperative during the fixed-format interview, if not terribly open, answering some questions with "Don't know." When I began the depth interview by starting the tape recorder he became nervous and, in effect, refused further cooperation, saying he was afraid to talk into a tape recorder. Instead he offered to go to a coffee shop where we could talk more freely without a tape recorder. Once there, occasionally glacing around to make sure no one was listening, he expressed his strong left-wing beliefs and discussed the problem of former student activists who enter large companies. On the basis of the notes I jotted down immediately after returning home, I can reconstruct the major points of the conversation. He said he felt a strong sympathy for the new left and their actions as well as for the younger generation, who he said were greatly dissatisfied because they want to be creative but cannot be in contemporary society where the organization takes precedence over the individual. Yet he was aware of the contradiction (*mujun*) that organizations may be necessary to resist organizations. Another contradiction he felt was that former activists who enter companies and large industry, while continuing to be alienated from society, simultaneously work diligently to advance their company's interests and Japan's GNP. He thought nevertheless that these former activists who enter large companies are really dissatisfied. They keep quiet and don't usually express their dissatisfaction through politics because they can't or because they are too busy. Although they feel dissatisfied "they repress it into their hearts." He saw this as characteristic of Japanese history and culture. Unlike the West, where people are more frank and express their frustrations, the Japanese repress them. But when a great event such as the 1960 Ampo crisis occurs, the former activists and others sympathize and support it. Their pent-up frustration and alienation emerge at those times. He didn't think 1970 Ampo was going to be one of those events, but he thought that if a "good leader" emerged, maybe they could do something about society.[27]

26 Interview with K, April 18, 1970.   27 Interview with M, May 23, 1970.

YOUTH AND ADULTHOOD RECONSIDERED

The two hypotheses I set out to test at the beginning of this chapter—that behavior may be more affected by adult roles than belief but that the effect of adult roles may vary with the prior socialization experiences of the individual—have been confirmed. The adult occupational role that is entered does seem to have a greater influence on the change or maintenance of former activists' political behavior than on their beliefs, which did not seem affected by the type of occupation entered by the respondent. Occupational role caused the former less active students either to revert back to their precollege nonactivity if they went into business or government, or to maintain their intermittent activity (or acquire such participatory behavior for the first time) if they entered the professions.

Less influence can be attributed to the effect of occupation on political beliefs. The extent of change, however, depends on whether the student was a former activist or less active, and on the prior socialization experiences associated with these two types of students. The activists' beliefs were almost totally unaffected by occupational role, partly because of their inclination to seek out and maintain interpersonal relationships supporting their political beliefs.

Thus no simple or direct generalization about the relative importance of youth versus adulthood can be made. The "generational" hypothesis seems generally valid in this study, especially for the activists, but the way in which adult roles interact with prior experience has important consequences for the change and maintenance of political belief and behavior. Our analysis brought out an added complexity: much depends on whether the individual does or does not attempt to select compatible role and personal environments in the transition to adulthood. The greater continuation of left-wing orientations and activity into adulthood on the part of the former activists and the less active students who entered the professions seems strongly related to their intentional choice of an occupation allowing them greater autonomy, an occupation where their beliefs could find reinforcement from sympathetic peers and where their behavior would be less subject to conflicting demands. In addition, maintaining friendships with college friends whose beliefs could reinforce theirs aided the continuity of their beliefs. On the other hand, the activists and the less active students who entered the world of the salary man have had to adapt their beliefs or their behavior, or both, to conflicting role demands. Yet the search for compatible environments itself seems largely dependent on the nature and intensity of prior socialization experience: the activists were more likely to select environments compatible with left-wing beliefs and activity than were the less active. We are dealing here not with a static process but with one involving a complex and dynamic interrelation of socialization stages.

In the concluding chapter I shall attempt to analyze the overall political-socialization process of our Japanese students and place it in its historical and cultural context, using a model of individual change that focuses on the continuities and discontinuities in the process. I shall then explore the implications of our findings for political-socialization research and for the Japanese political system.

7

POLITICAL SOCIALIZATION
AND THE JAPANESE
POLITICAL SYSTEM

A "DEVELOPMENTAL PROFILE" based on the findings in the preceding three chapters concerning the occupational and political world of my respondents since they were interviewed in 1962 would show that the typical student activist entered one of the professions, usually one of the "intellectual" professions such as teaching, publishing, or journalism. He chose his occupation in order to attempt to fulfill his need for autonomy, his concern for political and social problems, or his desire for political change. He has maintained his interest in politics and discusses it frequently, both with his work colleagues and with friends from his college days. His political orientation, like that of his friends, is leftist, usually extremely so.

Although he continues to believe in his own political efficacy, he is still alienated from the political system of which he is a member, believing that, in violation of his own ideals and the professed aims of the government itself, it is unresponsive to the people because of its close ties to special-interest groups. He believes that he can take action to try to oppose the government, but realizes that he must depend mainly upon mass protest, which is unlikely to succeed. Despite his pessimism, he continues to engage in all forms of political activity, including participation in demonstrations. His orientation toward politics and his manner of participation thus place him far to the expressive side of an expressive-instrumental continuum of political involvement and action. Unlike his college days, today he is likely to protest as an individual, or together with friends, rather than as a member of a formal political organization. He has taken to the streets again in 1970, as in 1960, to protest the U.S.-Japan mutual-security treaty, for although the treaty is not as salient an issue for him today as it was then, he still strongly believes that it should be terminated immediately. When the polls opened for the December 1969 general election, he was unlikely to be there casting his vote, having become disillusioned with the Socialist Party in the years since 1960.

Less sympathetic to Marxism now than ten years ago, he is likely to combine any belief in Marxism with other beliefs and is losing his faith in Marxism's predictions of revolutionary change and in the type of society that might result from such a revolution. Nonetheless, he still strongly maintains his "universalistic humanism" (i.e., his belief in equality, democracy, peace, and universal human solidarity), his belief in the basic correctness of Marxism's premises, and his desire to work for a change in the capitalist system in Japan.

Most less active students share with the former activists a belief that the legitimate ideals of postwar democracy in Japan are being betrayed by the government's close relations with special interests. Beyond this one point, however, much depends on whether the less active student entered a career in the professions or in business or government. Those who entered the professions, even those who were conservative or completely nonactive during their college days, tend to resemble the activists today in belief and behavior. But the more typical less active student who entered other occupations, particularly a career in business, experiences political life quite differently. He is less interested in politics than he was as a student, and is not likely to talk about it. Other than in the one belief about the undue influence of special interests on government policy, he is unlikely to be politically alienated today. He tends to identify himself as "conservative" and not to engage in political demonstrations. Although he may agree with certain of Marxism's premises, the ideology still does not have much appeal for him. He is quite sure that its predictions of revolutionary change are not applicable to Japanese society, and he does not particularly care to work for a change in the capitalist system. He tends rather to confine any leftist leanings he has to the ballot box, where, when he does vote, it will be for the Socialist Party or one of the other progressive parties.

Just as the activists and the less active developed differently in their precollege years, the typical activist and the typical less active student follow somewhat different paths after graduation. These differences allow us to understand more clearly the persistence of the conception, prevalent in Japan, that student activists enter large business firms and stop their protest activity. First of all, some student activists do indeed change in the manner expected. In my sample, about one-quarter of the activists entered a business profession, and about the same proportion have given up political-protest activity. Only a few have become professional political activists. During my depth interviews, when I asked the former activists if any of their friends had changed since graduation, most could cite examples who had. However, they also always mentioned some who had not. And as we have seen, the data from my sample indicate that activists have tended to enter the intellectual professions and to continue participating in active political protest. A second reason for the persistence of the belief in the "conversion" of the student activist may lie in the scholarly and journalistic "publicity" concerning the changes of a few of the more famous leaders of the 1960 movement. But as I have pointed out, some of these reports about Japanese activists have been based upon only a few examples, and some on case studies of only those who have changed, without any attempt to study a wider sample. At least some of these reports also seem to confuse assumption of a normal occupational role with political "conversion."

Whatever the two reasons mentioned above may have had to do with maintaining belief in the conversion of student political activists, or their correctness, a third reason seems to be central to the persistence of this popular misconception: the confusion of committed activist with intermittent activist. The number of students who actually hold leadership positions in the student movement or who belong to factions and are committed activists is quite small. Many more students, however, at one time or another during their college years, are stimulated by the university atmosphere, or by events, to protest, or are caught up in the mood of the demonstrations and spontaneously join in. To those aware of the course of student demonstrations during Ampo or later student protest activities as reported in the media—which in Japan means nearly everyone—it is no easy matter to differentiate between the small number of mobilizers and the larger number of mobilized, between the real student radical and the more typical student. All become "student activists" in the popular mind. When the intermittent activist graduates, enters the world of business, and devotes himself completely to his job rather than to political activity, the belief that Zengakuren leaders and activists experience a political conversion after graduation is reinforced.

Yet, as we have seen, the committed activist and the less active student, although they have a few characteristics in common, differ in many others. In Mannheim's terms,[1] the two types of students do indeed constitute a "generation in actuality," having been exposed at one time or another in their youth to the postwar universalistic ideas

---

[1] See Karl Mannheim, "The Problem of Generations," pp. 287–312 passim, and above, ch. 1, for the basis of the following analysis.

of democracy, equality, and peace. During their college years, and particularly during the 1960 Ampo crisis, they formed a generation-unit, their common ideas motivating them to "an identity of responses" and into the same concrete movement. After graduation, however, the differences in their prior experience, and in their adult environments, cause them to lose the "identity of responses" that characterize a generation-unit and they become separate units within the same generation, responding differently in a number of ways to the same historical and political situation. They share the same beliefs in democracy, governmental responsiveness, equality, and peace, but differ in the extent to which they believe these values are being violated and in their willingness to act to bring the political process more into conformity with their ideals. These similarities and differences, and the developmental process to which they are related, have particular significance for political-socialization theory and the operation of the Japanese political system.

CONTINUITIES AND DISCONTINUITIES IN THE POLITICAL-SOCIALIZATION PROCESS

In the preceding pages I have attempted to portray, by means of interview data and interpretation, the way fifty-three individuals experienced the growth of their political identities. In effect, I have presented the political biographies of these members of the 1960 Ampo generation of students. Attempting to improve upon the static cross-sectional analyses of political socialization so common in the literature, I used both longitudinal and retrospective methodologies to trace the political development of the sample through each of the stages of their lives—from the family, to the school and university, and finally into adult roles. The long time span of our study and the data it has provided now present us with an opportunity rarely found in the study of political socialization: the opportunity to go beyond the speculation of one-stage, cross-sectional studies to observe the over-all process of political socialization and to examine how its continuities and discontinuities help to explain its adult products.

As I mentioned in the first chapter, the most developed theory of discontinuities and the emergence of youth groups is that of S. N. Eisenstadt.[2] Eisenstadt sees youth groups emerging when a discontinuity arises between the particularistic norms of the family and the universalistic norms of adult institutions, as a result either of modernization or of cultural contact. These youth groups serve as a transitional stage between the family and eventual adjustment to the uni-

---

[2] Eisenstadt, *From Generation to Generation.*

versalistic public and occupational sphere in adulthood. Eisenstadt's emphasis on the eventual adjustment of youth to the norms of adult society is the result in great part of his functional approach, in which function is synonymous with the "integration" or continuity of the social system.[3] The work of Flacks and Pinner [4] on student activists in the United States and western Europe has underlined the importance of discontinuities as an explanatory variable in the political-socialization process of students. At the same time, they challenge Eisenstadt's two assumptions that these youths must necessarily adapt themselves to adult institutional norms after graduation and that they completely reject all apects of role relations learned in the family. Flacks and Pinner have convincingly demonstrated that youth may, to use Pinner's term, engage in "role-seeking"—reject the norms prevailing in the adult society and attempt to find or create new, alternative roles. The basis for these new roles they seek may even lie in their earlier experiences in the family, as in the case of Flacks's students who seem to be rejecting the bureaucratic roles of adult society in favor of the more egalitarian role relations they first experienced in their permissive families.

My findings, and those of Fendrich and his associates,[5] that student activists reject the prevalent bureaucratic occupational roles of adult society in favor of the professions and humanistic service occupations, maintain their political beliefs and liberal-radical behavior, and continue to work toward changing the existing political and social system, confirm that "role-seeking" may continue through adulthood. Although a discontinuity between family and adult norms may well explain the emergence of youth groups, this gap does not necessarily result in the individual's adaptation to adult roles different from those found in his family. I intend to evaluate the consequences of discontinuities in the political-socialization process of my sample without the limiting and conservative biases of Eisenstadt's particular functional approach. Discontinuities in the political-socialization process may have consequences for the system—an aspect that I shall examine in the next section—but they need not a priori be posited as integrative and functional.

One further modification of Eisenstadt's original theory of discontinuities is in order: a distinction implicitly contained in his work but never completely analyzed should be given emphasis. In examin-

[3] Ibid., p. 270.

[4] Richard Flacks, "The Revolt of the Advantaged: Exploration of the Roots of Student Protest"; Frank A. Pinner, "Student Trade Unionism in France, Belgium, and Holland: Anticipatory Socialization and Role-Seeking."

[5] Fendrich, Tarleau, and Simons, "Marching to a Different Drummer: The Occupational and Political Orientations of Former Student Activists."

ing cases of age groups in various societies, Eisenstadt occasionally distinguishes between the "sphere of role allocation and that of value orientation," [6] thus allowing for certain societies in which the legitimate values of the collectivity do not necessarily govern prevailing institutional-role processes. For example, Eisenstadt writes of the ambiguous status of the German family in a society where expectations for total community could not be realized in the institutional structure; in the Nupe state, ascriptive criteria in values coexisted with universalistic achievement criteria in role structure; amongst the Plains Indians, achievement dominates value orientations and symbolic processes, but ascription dominates the allocation of roles.[7] Allowing for such discrepancies between the realm of legitimate and ideal community values and the realm of actual role relations helps us to understand better the political-socialization process of our students in the context of postwar Japanese society. I believe we can explain this process and the differences in the development of our two types of students only by first understanding that a discrepancy exists in postwar Japanese culture between the universalistic values legitimized in the public (political) sphere and the norms that govern actual role relations, norms that still contain particularistic elements. This discrepancy is to a great extent the result of the historical process by which Japan has made the rapid transition from a traditional, agrarian, kinship-oriented society to a modern nation. Although a detailed elaboration of this transitional process is beyond the scope of this study, a brief analysis of the origins and nature of this discrepancy must be offered as background to the discussion of the political socialization of our students that follows.

The impact of the West and industrialization on Japan after the Meiji Restoration resulted in the creation of a tension in her value and social structure by now familiar to students of developing non-Western nations: the tension between the universalistic, achievement-oriented, individualistic values of the Western industrial society and the particularist, kinship and pseudokinship, collective, traditional order. The problems created by the tension between the new order and the old are common to all transitional non-Western societies, but the "reaction" to the tension may vary with the particular historical and cultural circumstances, and to a large extent, with the nature of the political leadership. The Meiji leaders attempted to resolve the problem by adopting modern technology and universalistic criteria where these were necessary for the creation of a modern nation, as in the abolition of feudal classes in favor of equality of citizenship, the adoption of achievement criteria in recruitment to the bu-

---

6 Eisenstadt, p. 196.   7 *Ibid.*, pp. 319, 196–198.

reaucracy, the introduction of universal male conscription, etc. But these changes were justified by the need to preserve the "traditional" values: not the "traditional" values as they had actually existed historically, but the old values as transformed by the requirements of defense, national integration, and modernization. The Emperor, who had rarely been the central authority symbol in actual historical fact, became the "traditional" symbol and myth in whose name the nation was to be built, and family loyalties were transformed into the basis for loyalty to the new state. Therefore, although universalistic elements were introduced, they continued to be subordinated to the ultimate and legitimate particularistic, pseudokinship values of the Emperor system in which the family was the main cellular unit of the nation and the nation and its citizens were considered a family writ large. The Emperor was the nation's patriarch, and the family's father was the Emperor's surrogate in daily life.[8]

This process, in which no attempt was made to replace completely particularistic values and relations by universalistic ones but wherein, rather, the former were actually reinforced and used in the modernization process as its ultimate rationale, has been called "reinforcing dualism" and "incorporative modernization."[9] However, not all of the dualism was reinforcing, and incorporative modernization was not without its costs. As continued cultural contact and industrialization increased the tension between the new values and the old, it became more and more necessary to prop up the particularistic values being eroded, as Thomas Smith has pointed out in an article concerned with this very problem:

> Rationalist thought, which an educational system dedicated to the advancement of science and technology could not but promote, increasingly called into question the Japanese political myth. Modern industry gave rise to new and harsher class antagonisms that made the familial ideal of society harder to cherish. The authority of the family and the power of its symbols declined as the family lost economic functions to the market and as the difference in outlook between generations widened with accelerating change. Nevertheless, the primary old values—throne and family—did not collapse, for they were continuously reinforced by stronger and more efficient measures of indoctrination and thought control by the state.[10]

The later nationalism and repression of the 1930s can thus be interpreted as an attempt to reassert the ultimate legitimacy of the par-

---

8 The predominance of particularist relations over universalistic ones in the prewar Emperor system is one of the main themes in Kazuko Tsurumi, *Social Change*, chs. 2 and 3.

9 Robert E. Ward and Dankwart A. Rustow, *Political Modernization in Japan and Turkey*, p. 445; Nobutaka Ike, *Japanese Politics: Patron-Client Democracy*, p. 4.

10 Thomas C. Smith, "Old Values and New Techniques in the Modernization of Japan," p. 356.

ticularistic order in the face of the continuing threat of modernization and Western values. Indeed, as one scholar has pointed out, the forced *tenkō* of Marxists in the 1930s may be seen as an attempt to integrate a nation suffering from the tension between modernization and the particularistic values used to justify it: "thought reform" was necessary because the universalistic ideals contained in Marxism threatened the particularistic ideals being used in attempting to integrate the society.[11]

In effect, until the defeat in World War II, although universalistic values were introduced and often combined with particularistic values, the latter not only predominated in role relations but were also the ultimate legitimate values of the society. With the defeat and Occupation, universalistic criteria replaced particularistic ones as the ultimate legitimate values, particularly in the political sphere: this, in brief, was the chief accomplishment of the Occupation. The Occupation did not create these values, but as the postwar catch phrase "peace and democracy" attests, it did sanctify them, diffuse them, and set up an institutional structure that held hope for allowing their fulfillment.

What the defeat, the Occupation, and the passage of time accomplished in the realm of ideal political values and structural arrangements, however, was less easily accomplished in the realm of actual patterns of interaction and institutional processes. Given the basic durability of cultural patterns, the rapidity of Japan's transitional process, the official sanction and reinforcement they were given under the Emperor system, and the imposition of the new values and arrangements from above, it is hardly surprising that actual role relations have continued to contain strong particularistic elements. One should, in fact, view contemporary Japanese politics and society as the result of an acculturation process whereby the prewar generation, socialized into a particularistic culture, had to adapt itself to the universalistic values, goals, and institutions introduced by the Occupation and by continued modernization. Democracy has been accepted as the postwar political ideal, but parties are coalitions of leader-follower factions, votes are mobilized through interpersonal networks, and personal and family ties play a large role in political recruitment. The politician's need for money to run for election in the postwar democratic political system and the businessman's need for political stability to pursue the ultramodern goal of economic growth have been attained through close personal ties between busi-

----

[11] Steinhoff, "Ideology and Societal Integration in Prewar Japan," p. 178. It is interesting to note that those *tenkōsha* who did not give up their belief in the universalistic ideals of Marxism but "recanted" only to the extent of admitting that they were not applicable to Japan often returned to the Communist Party after the war.

nessmen, LDP politicians, and bureaucrats. Villagers vote today to gain concrete benefits and interests, but on the basis of collective village solidarity rather than from a civic-participant orientation to government. Seniority advancement and recruitment from selected prestigious universities by big business is also a "rational" adaptation of an older generation that matured in a particularistic culture to one of the requirements of a modern economy—the need for skilled, educated, white-collar workers—in a time of economic expansion and labor shortage.

Achievement orientations have penetrated deeply into the postwar Japanese family, but these orientations have become mixed with the particularistic, collective, and strongly affective nature of Japanese family roles to produce the phenomenon of the *kyōiku mama* (education mama) who pushes and supports her male offspring in a drive for educational achievement in which he is perceived as a representative of the entire family. The prewar generation, which had internalized the particularistic values and norms of their youth, was faced with the task of adapting them to the new legitimate universalistic values and to the institutional forms based on them. The results are the present political, economic, and social systems which have destroyed the idea that democracy and modernization necessarily mean a repetition of the Western pattern: the acceptance of democratic and modern goals and structural forms in non-Western societies may still result in political and social processes quite different from those found in the West.[12]

If the prewar generation's adaptation to the "new," legitimate values has resulted in a relatively successful interpenetration of universalistic goals and structural forms on the one hand, and particularistic process on the other, the discrepancy between them continues. And the midwar and postwar generations in Japan may experience most acutely the discrepancy between "pure" legitimate universalistic values and actual process. Coming into contact with and internalizing the ideal values at a formative time in their youth, they must eventually confront adult role relations that do not completely conform to these values. Their parents' problem of acculturation becomes for them the reverse problem in socialization: whereas their parents faced an adult adjustment of their existing particularistic orientations to the new universalistic values and institutional forms, many postwar

---

[12] The manner in which the new values and particularistic interaction have combined is one of the themes present in most writings on postwar Japan. For some of these works that contain more detailed descriptions of the examples presented above, see Ike, *Japanese Politics;* Flanagan, "Voting Behavior in Japan"; Langdon, *Politics in Japan;* Thayer, *How the Conservatives Rule Japan;* Chitoshi Yanaga, *Big Business in Japanese Politics;* and Vogel, *Japan's New Middle Class.*

youths face the problem of adjusting to an adult world in which institutions do not operate and roles are not carried out completely in accord with the legitimate universalistic ideals they themselves have already accepted. That this discrepancy is perceived by Japanese youth to be especially large in the political sphere was shown by a recent survey in which "guarantee of individual freedoms" was one of the concepts seen as suffering the largest gap between ideal and actuality. It was also one of the few gaps whose origins the youth in the sample perceived as resting with society and not with the individual.[13] Whether postwar youth adjust themselves to the processes or seek to transform those processes to fit better with the ideals seems to depend on the way in which they experience the discontinuities in the socialization process resulting from this discrepancy.

Let us look more closely at the continuities and discontinuities—between the family, education, occupation, and politics—in the political-socialization process of our two types of students. Family relations in all societies are inherently particularistic, diffuse, ascriptive, and hierarchical. The anthropological and sociological literature tells us that family relations in postwar Japan are still particularly close, affective, and markedly different from relations with outsiders. The postwar family, however, seems to have been penetrated by strong achievement orientations, and the result is the collective-achievement orientations manifested in the kyōiku mama and "exam-hell" phenomena. Postwar reforms and social change also seem to have made the relations between parents and children less hierarchical than in the authoritarian and paternalistic prewar family. However, as we saw in the data from the family background of our activists and less active students, the extent to which more permissive and egalitarian elements have been introduced varies from family to family. Our activists tended to come from more permissive families than did our less active students. Role relations in the Japanese family seem to be particularistic, diffuse, and collective-achievement-oriented, the extent of hierarchy in roles varying with the family. As we have seen in chapter two, the postwar Japanese family also tends to be depoliticized.

Chapter four brought out that role relations in the world of business and government are often depoliticized, particularistic, diffuse, hierarchical, and pseudoascriptive. The pseudoascriptive ele-

---

13 Matsubara Haruo, " 'Youth Power' and the Problem of Identity," pp. 162–164. Miyajima Takeshi's assessment of the "generation gap" ("Kachi Ishiki ni okeru Sedaiteki Dansō" (The Generation Gap in Value Consciousness), p. 80, is similar to my argument here. He sees Japanese youth as accepting democratic principles and being alienated by a perception of a lack of content (tatemae) and fraudulence (gimansei) in the actual operation of the democratic system.

ments of the seniority system and recruitment from selective universities, from the point of view of the individual employee, are really collective-achievement criteria: he is assumed to be a representative of his collectivity—his university and his age group in the firm—and achievement and skill are assumed to adhere to his membership in these collectivities—the prestigious university or firm and the elder age groups. On all these criteria, then, much less discontinuity exists between the Japanese family and the prevailing occupational sphere of the salary man than in many "modern" societies. Kiefer [14] therefore can see the family, the educational process, and bureaucratic organizations in postwar Japan as closely articulated. The examination hell is a necessary puberty rite for the student primarily to transfer both affect from the family to age-mates (later office-mates) and collective-achievement drives from the family to larger institutions, eventually the company, without negating family roles:

> With the passing of high school and college entrance examinations, he is socialized into an increasingly elite and close-knit group of age-mates, and the emotional significance of his classmates for him continues to grow as the examinations extend his energies toward the classroom—*without,* I repeat, undermining family roles. His final transition from school to office is made with relatively little effort and with the help of both school and family since the relationship between these three institutions in Japan is much closer than is typically the case in America and since the mutual emotional dependence of age-mates functions to bind the office group together in exactly the same way it binds classmates together. Direct observation of many Japanese salary men and students has convinced me that this is the case, and the fact is further implicitly recognized in the Japanese notion that certain companies have their own "personality," and that they recruit students only from certain universities—appropriate to the company.[15]

Kiefer's analysis of the transition of Japanese youth from the family to the adult bureaucratic sphere via the puberty rite of the "exam hell" seems to me accurately to portray the continuities between family, school, and occupational sphere. The major deficiency in his analysis is that the socialization process is pictured as operating in a vacuum, devoid of any contact with wider social and political values and events. Such a portrayal cannot explain why some middle- and high-school students "transfer affect" to politicized peer groups and some do not, why some students do not choose to enter the world of the salary man, or why many of those who make the transition to large business firms do so with an important detour into political activity while in college. The answer to all these questions, I believe,

---

[14] Kiefer, "Psychological Interdependence of Family, School, and Bureaucracy in Japan."

[15] *Ibid.,* p. 73.

is that the universalistic political values of the postwar period do affect the socialization process and create serious and important discontinuities in it.

Many students experience a discontinuity in the socialization process when they encounter, and internalize, the ideal values legitimized in postwar Japan—democracy, participation of all citizens in the decision-making process, peace, equality, individual rights and autonomy, etc.—and realize the discrepancy between these newly acquired ideals and their institutionalization in adult political and social processes. At this point, as Eisenstadt predicts, a discontinuity results between these universalistic values and the particularistic, depoliticized relations of the Japanese family, which in turn gives rise to an increase in politicized relations between age-mates. These formal and informal youth groups are strongly oriented toward universalistic political values. It is important to note that contact with these values alone may not be sufficient to produce this discontinuity. All Japanese schoolchildren are taught these values in their civics classes but, as we have seen, explicit classroom teaching will not necessarily bring about real internalization. Rather, this internalization will usually come through direct contact with society or social and political events. The process by which many of our activists internalized these values through this type of contact occurred in middle school and high school. Their realization of the differences between rich and poor, the existence of war, the alienated political opposition in a democracy, and the other conditions that led to their politicization and acquisition of "universalistic humanism" during these years are manifestations of this process of internalization.

During this same period the politicized peer group became their most important political-socialization agency, and they participated frequently in peer-group activities. These universalistic values (eventually leading them to adopt Marxism), participatory orientations and behavior, and politicized peer group were to continue being important through their college years as they committed themselves to the student movement in order to work toward the achievement of these values. Our less active students did not experience the discontinuity between universalistic political values and particularistic family norms until they entered college, at which time the politicized atmosphere of the university and such events as the 1960 Ampo crisis created this discontinuity. Only then did the peer group supplant the family as the most important political-socialization agency.

A second discontinuity in the process occurs in the transition from the university, with its politicized environment dominated by postwar ideals and strongly egalitarian relationships among age-mates, to the occupational world. These students, having internalized the postwar ideals, must now face the problem of which I spoke earlier: adjusting the values to the institutional roles of adult Japanese society which contain large elements of particularism—the result of the Japanese modernization process—and hierarchy—common to all modern bureaucratic societies; or they may choose to seek out or create roles that better fit with their values. As we have seen, our activists tend to enter roles in the professions to maintain their beliefs and activity. The intellectual professions provide greater specificity between one's roles as citizen and as employee, and greater autonomy. In these professions universalistic values are more salient and more connected to the performance of tasks, and contact with the process of political and social change is closer. In their personal lives, too, the activists prefer friends who share their beliefs and commitments. Politically, they continue to act to express their values and to try to bring Japanese society more in line with those values. Our less active students, on the other hand, tend to enter business and government roles where they give up their activity and sometimes even their progressive identifications, if not all of their beliefs. The effect of their earlier socialization and contact with the postwar democratic values remains to the extent that they are still alienated by and cynical about what they perceive as the violation of these values through the close relations between business and other special interests and their government, and they still reject the LDP when they cast their ballots.

I believe the difference in the choices made by our two groups of students in resolving the second discontinuity is partly explainable by the timing and nature of the first discontinuity. The activists came into contact with the ideal universalistic political values of postwar Japan—which created the discontinuity between these values and the depoliticized particularistic norms of their family life—and made the transition to the politicized peer group at a younger age than did the less active. Consequently the values were internalized earlier and reinforced for a longer period, so that there was a greater commitment to them. The less active, on the other hand, did not experience the first discontinuity until they were already in college; hence the experience was less formative and of shorter duration. Their commitment to these ideals was generally shallower than that of the activists, and they required a major "crisis of democracy" to become mobilized to act in fulfillment of their newly acquired values. They not only do not necessarily seek environments in adulthood conducive to the fulfillment of the ideals, but, when confronted with work-place norms in business and government that make the cost of continuing political activity prohibitive, they more easily lose interest in politics and give up political participation.

Rejection of the bureaucratic world of business and government by the activists, and the relative ease with which the less active make the transition to this world,[16] are also related to differences in the family background of the two types of students. I wanted to see whether the extent of egalitarian relationships in the family might contribute to the acceptance or rejection of bureaucratic and hierarchical roles in adulthood. When I cross-tabulated father's attitude toward the respondent as a child with occupation entered in adulthood, I discovered that there was indeed a relationship: the students who came from families with strict fathers were more likely to enter bureaucratic roles in business and government (69 percent) than those who came from families with ordinary or permissive fathers (43 percent).[17] Entering the professions, with their greater autonomy, or the world of the salary man, with its stricter and more hierarchical control of the individual, is thus also related to the extent to which the family resembles one authority pattern or the other. Inasmuch as the less active students were more likely to come from families with strict fathers than were the activists, we have one further explanation of the adult choices of our two types of students. For the less active students, not only does the particularistic family remain the chief agency of political socialization until college, but authority relationships in their families more closely resemble those in the bureaucratic world of business and government than do the relationships in the activists' families. I believe this is a key factor in smoothing the transition from the college environment to the world of the salary man for this type of student.

Our activists, on the other hand, much as the student activists in Flacks's American sample, are rejecting the prevailing bureaucratic

---

16 Vogel, p. 274, found that although the attraction of the salary man's life had lost much of its luster by 1970, and the discontinuity between the free world of the university and disciplined company life is great, "even those youths who have weathered the stormy transition accept company discipline almost immediately." The explanation for this phenomenon is undoubtedly related to the basic continuities in role relations between the family and the Japanese company, which were examined above, and may also be related to the authority patterns within the families of those who enter business firms, described below.

17 This tendency and the percentage differences generally held true even when we controlled for former activity in the student movement, thus demonstrating that we are dealing with the effect of family background and not a spurious relationship owing only to activity in the student movement. However, as I point out below, the fact that more of the activists came from one type of family and more of the less active from the other can help to explain the adult occupational choices of our two types of students.

roles of adult society partly because of their experience with more egalitarian family relationships. Our activist students experience earlier and more intensely the first discontinuity between their depoliticized and particularistic families and the universalistic ideal political values of postwar Japan. They also experience more strongly the second discontinuity—at the time of entrance into adult occupational roles—because of the gap between the authority patterns in their family and peer group and those in the bureaucratic world of the salary man. The politicized, universalistic, and egalitarian orientations produced by this political-socialization process stimulate them to continue their "role-seeking" through adulthood.

Eisenstadt's theory of the origin of youth groups and their role in the transition from family to the adult world can now be seen to have a complex application to postwar Japanese students. Politicized peer groups both before and during college do indeed bridge the gap between the family and universalistic values in adulthood. This bridge, however, is primarily to the new public (political) values legitimized in postwar Japan. The Japanese modernization process has created added complexities in the criteria governing roles. The persistence of particularistic values in the bureaucratic occupational world, the maintenance of hierarchical and particularistic relations in many families, and the penetration of both family and work-place by collective-achievement criteria have decreased the gap we would expect to find between the family and adult roles. For most Japanese college students who become white-collar workers, participation in politicized and universalistically oriented youth groups is a temporary and age-related phenomenon, and entering the adult world results in the maintenance of some of their earlier political values but readjustment to particularistic and hierarchical roles. In a sense, the discrepancy between the ideal postwar political values and the actual nature of social relationships in postwar Japan has become a part of their lives. The possible tension inherent in this incongruity is lessened in many cases by the decreasing importance of politics in their personal and occupational environments. Such tension is less easily managed by the "deviant cases"—the former activists and intermittent activists who enter jobs in business but whose commitment to political values remains strong. The fruits of this tension are the bitterness and repressed hostility that they feel, as was strongly demonstrated in the interviews presented in the last chapter.

For the typical committed activist who enters the professions (a minority of all college students), youthful participation in political movements has also served as a bridge to the new public values. But their commitment to these values has not resulted in their adjusting to the role relationship prevalent in adult society. Rather, they have continued to attempt to remake those relationships and bring them more into line with their and the system's stated values.

The inevitable question may be raised: how long-lasting are the results of the political-socialization process I have described? We may well ask whether the adult patterns I found will be as true when our former students are 45 or 55 years old. It is possible to argue that not enough time has elapsed in the first five or ten years since graduation from college to allow for the full impact of adult roles and the passage of time to change the effect of earlier socialization. Will our activists tire of receiving only symbolic rewards from their noneffectual protest? Will those in business and government who retain strong leftist values eventually resolve the tension inherent in their situation by giving up their leftist beliefs or their behavioral adjustment? Will our less active students become even more conservative as they advance up the ladder of seniority to higher administrative career positions? Will changes now occurring in the occupational and political climate in Japan bring about far different belief and behavior patterns than those we have found exist today? Such questions cannot be answered by this study, but must merely serve as a final caveat as to its limitations. Nevertheless, if my preceding analysis of the continuities and the discontinuities in the Japanese political-socialization process adequately explains my findings, it has a number of important implications for political-socialization theory and for our understanding of certain aspects of the political system in postwar Japan.

IMPLICATIONS: POLITICAL SOCIALIZATION AND THE JAPANESE POLITICAL SYSTEM

Most political-socialization studies have ascertained the political orientations of children at one point in their lives, have studied the origins of these orientations in family and school environments, have projected the results to forecast adult beliefs, and from these beliefs have assumed what adult behavior will be.

This study has shown the theoretical and methodological shortcomings of such an approach. We need longitudinal designs that follow a sample over long periods, tracing the changes that occur during the life cycle to ascertain empirically which childhood beliefs are indeed persistent and which are not. Political scientists must pay greater attention to the peer group and the effect of the child's direct interaction with society and political events as socialization agents. Moreover, my analysis has shown that no one-to-one relationship can be assumed between beliefs and behavior. The two must be considered as separate dependent variables whose relationship must be tested empirically. Further empirical testing may well find that in all cultures behavior is more situationally determined than are beliefs. Or we may find that the extent of congruence between the two varies with the culture. Perhaps of even more importance is the fact that we need more dynamic models of the political-socialization process, models that consider relations between stages as independent variables in their own right. Studying the discontinuities and continuities in the process may yield greater understanding of the development of the political self through the life cycle than can studying the content of separate stages. Nor can we assume that the discontinuities in the process will always be found at the same point in different cultures. Discontinuities in the process, and therefore what constitutes a "stage" of the process, must also be empirically determined. We need, in effect, to find the political equivalents of the periods of "cultural compression" that anthropologists have studied cross-nationally: "They are the points in his (the individual's) development as a creature of culture when the norms of his group and society bear in upon him with the greatest intensity and where, as a consequence, he undergoes a change in social identity." [18] At what point in different cultures does the individual confront new political values and roles, and with what results? Not until we can identify the timing, nature, source, and consequences of these periods of political discontinuity in many different cultures shall we be able to build a viable comparative theory of political socialization.

We cannot assume that the political-socialization process inevitably results in the individual's induction into the prevailing adult political culture. Political culture becomes quite complex in transitional and modern societies and may contain a number of subcultures. The existence of these subcultures often indicates latent tensions in values arising from the modernization process. We need to study the political socialization process by which these subcultures originate, are maintained, and change as much as we have studied the process by which individuals are inducted into the assumed "majority" political culture. The individuals who compose these "deviant" subcultures, by their very rejection of the existing values and norms of the society, are often important agents of change whose beliefs and actions have significant consequences for the operation of political systems.

I believe that my study of Japanese students has implications for understanding some of the roots of stability and instability in the postwar political system in Japan. Postwar Japanese democracy has been basically stable, but disturbing elements of real and potential instability exist. On the one hand, Japan has had basic stability in that

---

[18] George D. Spindler, "The Transmission of American Culture," p. 165.

one political party, the LDP, has remained in power for most of the postwar period. The chief opposition party, the Socialists, has been unable to gather enough support either to capture power or stalemate the policy-making process. Nor does violent change in the system appear likely. In 1960, many in Japan (as well as elsewhere) had truly believed, or feared, that the Ampo crisis would be the first step to revolution. These hopes or fears have proved illusory. The events of 1960 Ampo may have been one of Japan's greatest political crises, and the legitimacy of the regime may indeed have been challenged, but, in retrospect, there was really little threat of successful violent revolution. Not only did the antitreaty forces lack the strength to accomplish such action, but many of the protestors, as we have seen, were not challenging the "rules of the game" in the system so much as the failure of the regime to act in accordance with those rules. Since 1960 Ampo, the likelihood of success of a revolution has decreased rather than increased, as even the most ideologically left-wing of our respondents admit.

On the other hand, the system holds many elements of actual and potential instability. The intensity of the 1960 Ampo crisis and the persistently recurring student uprisings of increasing violence since 1960—such as the widespread campus disputes of 1968–1969 in which many campuses were closed down—[19] are but two examples. The alienation and cynicism of many urban Japanese toward their government and politics in general, the rise of citizen-action groups and the new left in the late 1960s demanding greater governmental responsiveness to urban citizens' needs,[20] and the failure of the LDP or the Socialist Party to attain a mass organizational base and deep-rooted popular support make fears of potential instability in the system seem far from naive.

Because many of these sources of stability and instability involve the beliefs and behavior of students and of urban, educated Japanese, the findings of this study can help us to understand these problems, most directly and obviously in its description of the origins of student rebellion. The continuities and discontinuities described above will, it is hoped, have broadened our understanding both of why some students become student activists and why others are susceptible to mobilization by activists while in college and of some of the sources of student rebellion. It is interesting to note that surveys of Japanese students of the late 1960s disclose many of the same patterns of sociali-

---

[19] In 1968 alone, 117 campuses were affected. Stuart Griffin, "Losers in the Long Run?," p. 165.

[20] Taketsugu Tsurutani, "A New Era of Japanese Politics: Tokyo's Gubernatorial Election," pp. 432–443; Fukashiro Junrō, "The New Left."

zation as those that characterized the Ampo generation. Japanese student activists surveyed by Takahashi and Suzuki tended to come from higher-status, relatively permissive families.[21] Freshmen of a Tokyo University sample discussed politics and social problems more with their peers than with their teachers and families.[22] And a survey at three Japanese universities showed that many students first had become politicized and acquired their political views in high school and college through the stimulus of domestic and international political events, particularly the 1960 Ampo crisis (when they were about 12 years old, on the average), which had led them to critical views of authority and a belief in the necessity of political participation. An overwhelming majority agreed to a statement quite similar to the one used in this study concerning the large influence of special interests on government and the consequent lack of government responsiveness to the interests of the majority. The three standards of political evaluation most often chosen by the sample involved such values as expecting impartiality and concern for the public interest in the policy and behavior of those in power, permitting the widest possible political participation by the people and governance by their will, and making primary the goal of bettering the people's life. Demonstrations, strikes, and mass action were their most favored means of political protest.[23] Much of the political-socialization process described in our study appears to have become a long-term feature of the political socialization of many postwar, educated Japanese youths, the Ampo students being a transitional generation and the forerunners of the type of new-left students who shook Japanese society and politics in the campus struggles of 1968–1969.

The widespread alienation and cynicism among the urban, white-collar, and professional classes, an alienation and cynicism shared by our respondents, can also to some extent be explained by our findings. There has yet to be a thorough study of political cynicism and political socialization in Japan. Nor do we thoroughly understand whether or how the traditional belief that governmental authority should be fair and impartial has been transmitted and incorporated into universalistic values diffused in Japan by the Occupation, or how this belief con-

---

[21] Takahashi Akira, "Nihon Gakusei Undō no Shisō to Kōdō" (Thought and Behavior of the Japanese Student Movement), *Chūō Kōron* (The Central Review). June 1968, p. 168; Suzuki Hirō, *Gakusei Undō* (The Student Movement), pp. 233–234.

[22] "Nyūgakuji no Sugao o Saguru: Honsha Mensetsu Chōsa" (Searching for the True Face of the College Entrance Period: Our Interview Survey), *Asahi Shimbun*, April 1, 1970, p. 8.

[23] Asanuma Kazunori, "Seijiteki Shakaika ni tsuite no Ippōkoku: Daigakusei no Seiji Ishiki Chōsa Kara" (A Report Concerning Political Socialization: From a Survey of the Political Consciousness of University Students), pp. 10–17.

tributes to impossibly high expectations of governmental performance that eventually breed cynicism.[24] Certainly, cynicism towards politics is not confined to the postwar generation. But if my analysis of the discrepancy between ideal postwar political values and role relationships in postwar Japan is valid, this discrepancy and its effect on the political-socialization process may be one major source of political cynicism and alienation among the younger, urban, educated middle class in Japan. The close personal ties between special-interest groups and LDP politicians, the factional and bitter personal infighting within political parties, the difficulty of access to decision-makers in a system where personal connections are primary, are all consciously or unconsciously contrasted with the postwar ideals of popular and responsive government, equality, and the expectation that the individual *should* be able to influence his government.

This political cynicism and alienation, however, is a two-edged sword, for it hurts the opposition Socialists as well as the LDP government. At the beginning of the 1960s, the Socialist Party commanded the support of about one-third of the electorate and was expected greatly to increase their percentage of the vote during the 1960s. Not only has this *not* occurred, but their percentage of the vote has declined greatly. This decline was reflected in microcosm in our sample's changes in party preference during the decade: many of the Party's youthful former supporters have become disillusioned with it and do not bother to vote. Factional infighting within the Party has shown it to be ineffective in attaining progressive goals and subject to the same discrepancy between universalistic goals and particularistic processes as the rest of the political system. For young, urban professionals or white-collar workers not tied into the *kankei* network within the blue-collar and government-employee labor unions that make up so much of the Party's grass-roots organization, the Party fails to provide an institutionalized channel to attain the legitimate goals of the postwar political system. The rise of the new left and citizen-action groups in recent years must be seen in this context: their greatest appeal is to those urban professional workers (and housewives) in their thirties who are disillusioned with, or lack access to, the *kankei* networks of the institutionalized political process, and who seek to bridge the gap be-

24 The "Japanese people have continued, in the postwar period, to maintain their faith that government authority is, by definition, to be fair and impartial. ... To the people who look to government authority for complete impartiality, the way in which Japan's postwar parliamentary politics have operated has been a source of great disappointment and moral indignation. The prestige of politicians has inevitably declined because they have behaved in partisan ways and have been frequently involved in corruption." Jun-ichi Kyōgoku, "Changes in Political Image and Behavior," p. 122. See also Nobutaka Ike, "An Experiment in Political Forecasting: Japan, 1965–75," pp. 24–25.

tween universalistic political goals and political process by grass-roots democracy and direct action.[25]

Robert Merton's analysis of social "deviance" thus can be said to have political implications. Merton argues that such deviance occurs when there is a "dissociation between culturally prescribed aspirations and socially structured avenues for realizing these aspirations." [26] Although some "dissociation" between cultural goals and institution-alized means may characterize all societies, "societies do differ in the degree to which the folkways, mores, and institutional controls are effectively integrated with the goals which stand high in the hierarchy of cultural values." [27] I have argued that as a result of the Japanese modernization process, an especially large gap between goals and process exists in Japan and that this discrepancy has created a discontinuity in the political-socialization process of our students. In adulthood also, the activists' perception of the dissociation between sanctioned political goals and institutional processes helps maintain alienation and cynicism and the tendency to choose mass, expressive forms of political action.

Relating the political-socialization process to the above-described discrepancy between goals and means can also help to explain one of the most important sources of stability in the political system. Large numbers of Japanese college students in the postwar period have been involved in demonstrations at one time or another.[28] Had all or even most of these individuals continued their protest activity after graduation, the instability in the Japanese political system would certainly be greater than it is today. But for the majority of educated Japanese youth, political protest is an age-related phenomenon. Many college students, even those who intermittently participated in student political activity, have entered the world of business, become less politicized, and given up left-wing political activity. This has helped prevent constant and widespread urban protest which might otherwise have

---

25 Tsurutani, "A New Era of Japanese Politics," pp. 433–434. Tsurutani sees the citizen movement as a "long-overdue systemic response to the structural deficiency of Japan's democratic system." Fukashiro, "The New Left," p. 31, cites Beiheiren's emphasis on civic consciousness and states that the movement "seeks to perform the transitional function of stimulating social change and does not itself yearn for political power."

26 Robert K. Merton, *Social Theory and Social Structure*, p. 128. I am indebted to Prof. Kurt Steiner of Stanford University for the insight that Merton's analysis had implications for the study of political socialization.

27 *Ibid.*, p. 128.

28 For example, Minoru Kiyota, "Recent Japanese Student Movement (1968–1969): Its Impact on Educational Reform," p. 12, cites an *Asahi* report that in 1968 over 66 percent of the students of Kyūshū University, 50 percent of those at Todai, and 20 percent of those at Nihon University had participated in demonstrations at one time or another.

immobilized the political process. The norms of Japanese institutional processes which by their violation of the legitimate democratic values of the system have helped to create alienation, protest, and instability also have helped to limit it.

In conclusion, I should like to add a personal coda to this study. Many of the anonymous men whose beliefs, behavior, and memories have been analyzed here are among the most articulate, intelligent, concerned individuals whom I have ever met. Certainly some may have questionable motivations, as did the professional activist who seemed overly concerned with politics as personal power, or the timid white-collar worker whose political bravado and hostility could be attributed even by one untrained in psychotherapy to personal problems resulting from an overbearing family. But by and large, these men, former activist and less active alike, impressed me as sincere, intelligent individuals. Their tragedy is not that many are politically alienated and express deep opposition to their government. Such alienation and opposition may serve a "functional" purpose in a democratic political system where even many of the more politically allegiant believe their government unresponsive to the desires and needs of the people. Rather, their tragedy, and Japan's potential danger, is that such talented and concerned men cannot find institutionalized channels to translate their opposition effectively into constructive reform. Only when and if they succeed in doing so will the gap close between their perception of the democratic political ideals of postwar Japan and their perception of the implementation of those ideals.

METHODOLOGICAL NOTE

THIS NOTE is designed to supplement the information concerning methodology presented in chapter 1 of the text. The details presented below should be of interest chiefly to fellow scholarly toilers in the Japanese vineyards and to students of political socialization.

The Follow-up: Finding the sample eight years after the Tsurumi interviews proved somewhat more difficult than I had anticipated. Students are inevitably transients, and the addresses of their student days were of little help in tracing the respondents. In addition, of the mediums through which respondents have been successfully traced for follow-up studies in the United States (see Bruce K. Eckland, "Retrieving Mobile Cases in Longitudinal Surveys," *POQ*, XXXII, 1, Spring 1968)—postal services, telephone services, public records, parents, college-alumni files, and personal contacts—only the last two proved really useful in the Japanese context. Public records were deemed too time-consuming to be used, because in Tokyo alone this would have required going to twenty-three different ward-offices (*kuyakusho*). Letters sent to addresses from which the respondents had moved almost invariably were returned with no forwarding address. The telephone directory was not particularly useful because of the common practice of *yobidashi* (using the telephone of a neighbor or landlord) in Japan. Parents were not always terribly cooperative in revealing their son's whereabouts to a complete stranger who wished to interview their offspring for some unknown purpose. The best means of tracing respondents proved to be through the alumni offices of the universities they attended. However, as I indicated in the text, the extent to which these records were complete and up to date varied greatly with the university. The best information obtained from these offices was the job the student took after graduation: once I had found the name of the employer I usually could find the respondent. Another means by which a number of respondents were located was to ask a respondent at the end of an interview if he knew the whereabouts of some of his classmates. In Japan, where university, workplace, and friendship ties form the main nexus of social interaction for many individuals, these channels proved valuable.

The Sample: My decision to limit the follow-up sample only to males known or thought to be living in major urban areas was based not only on the theoretical complexity that would have been introduced into the analysis by the problem of sex-roles, but also on very real practical considerations. There were only six women in the original Tsurumi sample and the difficulty of locating female respondents whose names were likely to have changed through marriage made the costs of their inclusion in the sample greater than the potential benefits. I concentrated on urban residents primarily because I lacked the time and money to travel to outlying areas in order to interview individual respondents. As it was, even some respondents who were in urban areas outside of Tokyo could not be interviewed because of the same problems. Also eliminated were five original respondents who were abroad at the time of the research and three who had "evaporated" (*jōhatsu shita*), completely disappeared, or were missing persons even to their families and closest friends. I was told later that one or two of these three had gone underground because they were wanted by the police for radical activities.

I was successful in finding 79 percent of those being sought from Tokyo University's Hongo campus, 73 percent from the Komaba campus, 78 percent from Keiō University, 40 percent from Chūō University, and 60 percent from the few other universities in the Tsurumi sample. The average member of my sample was slightly more than thirty years of age and had graduated a little over six and one-half years before the 1970 follow-up. The leaders of Zengakuren were older than the sample average (average age, thirty-five) and had graduated earlier (nine and one-half years, on average, since graduation). This difference reflects the inclusion in the original sample of some Zengakuren chairmen and other high officers who had held office (and in a few cases had graduated) before the 1960 crisis.

Questionnaires and Interviews: The standard questionnaire administered to all respondents consisted of about 117 items, many with subparts. A goodly number of questions were drawn from surveys of political socialization and political culture, including the Almond and Verba study cited frequently in the text, as well as from survey questionnaires developed by Yasumasa Kuroda, Robert E. Ward and Akira Kubota, Douglas Johnson, and J. A. Massey and generously provided me by the authors.

Although most of the questions were of the fixed-format, multiple-choice variety, many of these were followed by one or more sub-parts of open-ended questions to examine more fully the respondent's beliefs. In the cases of the twenty-three respondents who received the depth-interview, the administration of the standard questionnaire was usually followed by my asking further questions to probe points raised by the interviewee's responses and then by the open-ended questions—put by my assistant or by me—that I had drawn up for the depth interview. The depth-interview schedule was quite flexible and I frequently pursued a line of questioning with the respondent far beyond the original question. The aim of this approach was to engage the respondent in discussion that would draw out franker, more spontaneous, and more detailed answers than a rigidly structured interview could elicit.

The settings of the interviews varied considerably. Although every effort was made to administer the questionnaire and conduct the depth interviews in the respondent's home or in the office at Sophia University provided me for that purpose by Professor Tsurumi, this was not always possible. Japanese professional and white-collar workers are extremely busy and spend a tremendous amount of time at their workplace or away from home. I was sometimes faced, therefore, with the alternative of no interview or an interview conducted at the respondent's place of work or in a *kissaten* (coffee shop) or restaurant near it. Whatever the place of interview, efforts were made to obtain privacy and to ensure that no friend, coworker, or relation was present. Indeed, probably because coffee shops and restaurants are often places where Japanese conduct their own personal and intimate conversations, I found that respondents interviewed in these places were frequently as candid and voluble as the respondents (the majority) interviewed in Professor Tsurumi's private office or in their own homes, and sometimes more so.

Once located, the respondents were extremely cooperative. Only one, a nonactive student in 1962, refused an interview, on the grounds that his employment in a court of law made it professionally impossible for him to be interviewed for a "political" study. Except for the one other respondent who was uncooperative during the interview, the respondents patiently answered my questions. Before a respondent was approached, a letter introducing me and requesting his help was sent to him by Professor Tsurumi. This letter undoubtedly helped in eliciting the great cooperation I received.

BIBLIOGRAPHY

Aberbach, Joel D. "Alienation and Political Behavior," *American Political Science Review*, LXIII, 1, March 1969.

Adler, Norman, and Charles Harrington (eds.). *The Learning of Political Behavior*. Glenview, Illinois: Scott, Foresman and Company, 1970.

Agger, Robert, Marshall N. Goldstein, and Stanley A. Pearl. "Political Cynicism: Measurement and Meaning," *Journal of Politics*, XXIII, August 1961.

Aiken, Henry David. "The Revolt Against Ideology," *The Political Imagination*, ed. Edgar Litt. Glenview, Illinois: Scott, Foresman and Company, 1966. Originally published in *Commentary*, April 1964.

Almond, Gabriel A., and G. Bingham Powell, Jr. *Comparative Politics: A Developmental Approach*. Boston: Little, Brown and Company, 1966.

——— and Sidney Verba. *The Civic Culture*. Princeton: Princeton University Press, 1963.

——— and James S. Coleman (eds.). *The Politics of the Developing Areas*. Princeton: Princeton University Press, 1960.

Altbach, Philip. "Japanese Students and Japanese Politics," *Comparative Education Review*, VII, 2, October 1963.

Anderson, Ross. "Missing Marchers: Still Concerned But No Longer Active in Demonstrations," *The Seattle Times*, December 12, 1971.

Asahi Evening News, February 11, 1969.

Asahi Shimbun, October 1, 8, 13, December 29, 1969; March 23, April 7, June 11, 15, 16, 17, 22, 23, 24, 1970.

Asanuma Kazunori. "Seijiteki Shakaika ni tsuite no Ippōkoku: Daigakusei no Seiji Ishiki Chōsa Kara" (A Report Concerning Political Socialization: From a Survey of the Political Consciousness of University Students), *Takushoku Daigaku Ronshū* (Takushoku University Review) No. 62.

Azumi, Koya. *Higher Education and Business Recruitment in Japan*. New York: Teachers College Press, Columbia University, 1969.

Baber, Roy E. *Youth Looks at Marriage and the Family*. Tokyo: International Christian University, 1958.

Beck, Paul Allen. "Panel Models of Attitude Change: Analysis and Application." Unpublished paper, 1969.

Becker, Howard S., and Anselm L. Strauss. "Careers, Personality, and Adult Socialization," *The American Journal of Sociology*, LXII, 3, November 1956.

Befu, Harumi. *Japan: An Anthropological Introduction*. San Francisco: Chandler Publishing Co., 1971.

Bell, Daniel. *The End of Ideology*. 2d. revised edition. New York: Collier Books, 1962.

———— and Henry David Aiken. "Ideology—A Debate," *The Political Imagination*, ed. Edgar Litt. Glenview, Illinois: Scott, Foresman and Company, 1966. Originally published in *Commentary*, October 1964.

Bernstein, Gail. "Kawakami Hajime: A Japanese Marxist in Search of the Way." Paper read at the Duke University Conference on Taishō Japan, January 1969.

Breer, Paul E., and Edwin A. Locke. *Task Experience as a Source of Attitudes*. Homewood, Illinois: Dorsey Press, 1965.

Brim, Orville G., Jr. "Adult Socialization," *Socialization and Society*, ed. John A. Clausen. Boston: Little, Brown and Company, 1968.

————. "Socialization Through the Life Cycle," *Socialization After Childhood*, ed. Orville G. Brim, Jr. and Stanton Wheeler. New York: John Wiley & Sons, 1966.

Bruner, Edward M. "Cultural Transmission and Cultural Change," *Personality and Social Systems*. 2d. edition. Neil J. Smelser and William T. Smelser (eds.). New York: John Wiley & Sons, 1970.

Campbell, Angus, Gerald Gurin, and Warren E. Miller. "Sense of Political Efficacy and Political Participation," *Political Behavior: A Reader in Theory and Research*, ed. Heinz Eulau, Samuel J. Eldersveld, and Morris Janowitz. New York: The Free Press, 1956.

Coladarci, Arthur P. "The Professional Attitudes of Japanese Teachers," *Journal of Educational Research*, LII, 9, May 1959.

————. "Measurement of Authoritarianism in Japanese Education," *California Journal of Educational Research*, X, 3, May 1959.

Cole, Robert E. "Japanese Workers, Unions, and the Marxist Appeal," *The Japan Interpreter*, VI, 2, Summer 1970.

Connell, R. W. "Political Socialization in the American Family: The Evidence Re-examined," *Public Opinion Quarterly*, XXXVI, 3, Fall 1972.

Crittenden, John. "Aging and Party Affiliation," *Public Opinion Quarterly*, XXVI, 4, Winter 1962.

Cutler, Neal E. "Generation, Maturation, and Party Affiliation: A Cohort Analysis," *Public Opinion Quarterly*, XXXIII, Winter 1969–70.

Dawson, Richard E. "Political Socialization," *Political Science Annual: Volume One*, ed. James A. Robinson. Indianapolis: Bobbs-Merrill Company, 1966.

———— and Kenneth Prewitt. *Political Socialization*. Boston: Little, Brown and Company, 1969.

Dore, Ronald. *City Life in Japan*. Berkeley and Los Angeles: University of California Press, 1958.

Douglas, Stephen A. *Political Socialization and Student Activism in Indonesia.* Urbana: University of Illinois Press, 1970.

Duke, Ben C. "Amercan Education Reforms in Japan Twelve Years Later," *Harvard Educational Review*, XXXIV, 4, Fall 1964.

Easton, David, and Robert D. Hess. "The Child's Political World," *The Learning of Political Behavior*, ed. Norman Adler and Charles Harrington. Glenview, Illinois: Scott, Foresman and Company, 1970.

———— and Jack Dennis. *Children in the Political System.* New York: McGraw-Hill Book Company, 1969.

———— and Jack Dennis. "The Child's Acquisition of Regime Norms: Political Efficacy," *American Political Science Review*, LXI, 2, March 1967.

Eckland, Bruce K. "Retrieving Mobile Cases in Longitudinal Surveys," *Public Opinion Quarterly*, XXXII, 1, Spring 1968.

Eckstein, Harry. "A Theory of Stable Democrocy." Research monograph No. 10, Center of International Studies, Woodrow Wilson School of Public and International Affairs, Princeton University, 1961.

Eisenstadt, S. N. *From Generation to Generation.* New York: The Free Press, 1956.

Erickson, Erick H. *Gandhi's Truth.* New York: W. W. Norton & Company, 1969.

————. *Identity: Youth and Crisis.* New York: W. W. Norton & Company, 1968.

————. *Young Man Luther.* New York: W. W. Norton & Company, 1958.

Eulau, Heinz. *Micro-Macro Political Analysis.* Chicago: Aldine Publishing Co., 1969.

Fagen, Richard R. *The Transformation of Political Culture in Cuba.* Stanford: Stanford University Press, 1969.

Fendrich, James M., Alison T. Tarleau, and Ronald L. Simons. "Marching to a Different Drummer: The Occupational and Political Orientations of Former Student Activists." Paper presented at the Southern Sociological Society Conference, 1972, New Orleans, La.

Feuer, Lewis S. *The Conflict of Generations.* New York: Basic Books, Inc., 1969.

Fjermedal, Grant. "The Movement . . . On the Wane, But Not Forgotten," *The Seattle Times*, December 12, 1971.

Flacks, Richard. "The Revolt of the Advantaged: Exploration of the Roots of Student Protest," *Learning About Politics*, ed. Roberta S. Sigel. New York: Random House, 1970. Excerpted from *The Journal of Social Issues*, XXIII, 3, 1967.

Flanagan, Scott C. "The Japanese Party System in Transition," *Comparative Politics*, III, 2, January 1971.

————. "Voting Behavior in Japan," *Comparative Political Studies*, I, 3, October 1968.

————. "Zengakuren and the Postwar Japanese Student Movement." Unpublished Master's thesis, University of California, no date.

Friedman, Lucy N., Alice R. Gold, and Richard Christie, "Dissecting the Generation Gap: Intergenerational and Intrafamilial Similarities and Differences," *Public Opinion Quarterly*, XXXVI, 3, Fall 1972.

Fujita, Wakao. "The Life and Political Consciousness of the New Middle Class," *Journal of Social and Political Ideas in Japan*, II, 3, December 1964.

Fukashiro Junrō. "The New Left," *Japan Quarterly*, XVII, 1, January–March 1970.

"Gakusei Kaikyū, Sono Konnichiteki Kōzō: Katsudōka no Kiseki" (The Student Class, Its Present Structure: The Tracks of the Activists), *Asahi Jānaru*, XIII, 16, April 23, 1971; 17, April 30, 1971; 19, May 14, 1971; 20, May 23, 1971.

Glenn, Norval D., and Ted Hefner. "Further Evidence on Aging and Party Identification," *Public Opinion Quarterly*, XXXVI, Spring 1972.

Glock, Charles R. "Some Applications of the Panel Method to the Study of Change," *The Language of Social Research*, ed. Paul F. Lazarsfeld and Morris Rosenberg. Glencoe, Illinois: The Free Press, 1955.

Goertzel, Ted. "Generational Conflict and Social Change," *Youth and Society*, III, 3, March 1972.

Greenberg, Edward S. (ed.). *Political Socialization*. New York: Atherton Press, 1970.

Greene, Daniel St. Albin. "Chicago Epilog: What the Kids Think, Three Years Later," *The National Observer*, August 30, 1971.

Greene, Wade. "Where Are the Savios of Yesteryear?," *New York Times Magazine*, July 12, 1970.

Greenstein, Fred I. "A Note on the Ambiguity of 'Political Socialization': Definitions, Criticisms, and Strategies of Inquiry," *Journal of Politics*, XXXII, 4, November 1970.

———. "The Benevolent Leader: Children's Images of Political Authority," *The Learning of Political Behavior*, ed. Norman Adler and Charles Harrington. Glenview, Illinois: Scott, Foresman and Company, 1970.

———. *Children and Politics*. New Haven: Yale University Press, 1965.

——— and Raymond E. Wolfinger. "The Suburbs and Shifting Party Loyalties," *Public Opinion Quarterly*, XXII, Winter, 1958–59.

Griffin, Stuart. "Losers in the Long Run?," *Far Eastern Economic Review*, 65, July 17, 1969.

Harada Hisato. "The Anti-Ampo Struggle," *Zengakuren: Japan's Revolutionary Students*, ed. Stuart Dowsey. Berkeley: The Ishi Press, 1970.

Hess, Robert. "The Socializaton of Attitudes Toward Political Authority: Some Cross-National Comparisons," *International Social Science Journal*, XV, 4, 1963.

——— and Judith V. Torney. *The Development of Political Attitudes in Children*. New York: Oxford Universty Press, 1969.

Hyman, Herbert. *Political Socialization*. New York: The Fress Press, 1959.

Ike, Nobutaka. *Japanese Politics: Patron-Client Democracy*. 2d. edition. New York: Alfred A. Knopf, 1972.

———. "An Experiment in Political Forecasting: Japan, 1965–75." Stanford: Institute of Political Studies, Stanford University, 1966.

————. *Japanese Politics: An Introductory Survey.* New York: Alfred A. Knopf, 1957.

————. "The Political Role of Japanese Intellectuals," *Transactions of the Asiatic Society of Japan,* V, 3, December 1957.

Inglehart, Ronald. "The Silent Revolution in Europe: Intergenerational Change in Post-Industrial Societies," *American Political Science Review,* LXV, 4, December 1971.

Ino Kenji. *Zengakuren.* Tokyo: Futabasha, 1968.

Ishida Takeshi. "Katei to Seiji" (The Family and Politics), *(Gekkan) Rōdō Mondai* (Labor Problems Monthly), January 1968.

Ishimoto, Arata. "Radical Intellectuals and the End of Ideology," *Journal of Social and Political Ideas in Japan,* II, 1, April 1964.

Japan Statistical Yearbook. Tokyo: Bureau of Statistics, Office of the Prime Minister, 1970.

The Japan Times, April 26, June 23, 24, 1970.

Jennings, M. Kent, and Richard G. Niemi. "The Transmission of Political Values from Parent to Child," *American Political Science Review,* LXII, 1, March 1968.

Johnson, Chalmers. *Conspiracy at Matsukawa.* Berkeley and Los Angeles: University of California Press, 1972.

Journal of Social and Political Ideas in Japan, I, 2, August 1963; II, 1, April 1964; V, 2–3, December 1967.

Kawai, Kazuo. *Japan's American Interlude.* Chicago: University of Chicago Press, 1960.

Kelman, Herbert C. "Processes of Opinion Change," *Public Opinion Quarterly,* XXV, 1, Spring 1961.

Keniston, Kenneth. *Young Radicals: Notes on Committed Youth.* New York: Harcourt Brace & World, 1968.

Kiefer, Christie W. "Psychological Interdependence of Family, School, and Bureaucracy in Japan," *American Anthropologist,* 72, 1, February 1970.

————. "Social Change and Personality in a White Collar Danchi." Paper presented at the Colloquium of the Center for Japanese and Korean Studies, November 15, 1967, University of California at Berkeley.

Kiyota, Minoru. "Recent Japanese Student Movement (1968–1969): Its Impact on Educational Reform." Paper presented at the Midwest Conference on Asian Affairs, October 29–31, 1971, Madison, Wisconsin.

Koyama, Kenichi. "The Zengakuren," *The New Politics,* I, 2, Winter 1962.

Krauss, Ellis S., "Ideology in Transition: A Study of Marxism in Postwar Japan." Unpublished Paper, 1972.

Kublin, Hyman. *Asian Revolutionary: The Life of Sen Katayama.* Princeton: Princeton University Press, 1964.

Kubota, Akira, and Robert E. Ward. "Family Influence and Political Socialization in Japan: Some Preliminary Findings in Comparative Perspective," *Comparative Political Studies,* III, 2, July 1970.

Kuroda, Yasumasa. "Agencies of Political Socialization and Political Change: Political Orientation of Japanese Law Students," *Human Organization,* XXIV, 4, Winter 1965.

Kuroda, Alice and Yasumasa. "Aspects of Community Political Participation in Japan," *Journal of Asian Studies,* XXVII, 2, February 1968.

Kyōgoku Jun-ichi. *Gendai Minshusei To Seijigaku* (Contemporary Democracy and Political Science). Tokyo: Iwanami Shoten, 1969.

———. "Changes in Political Image and Behavior," *Journal of Social and Political Ideas in Japan,* II, 3, December 1964.

Lane, Robert E. *Political Ideology.* New York: The Free Press, 1962.

Langdon, Frank. *Politics in Japan.* Boston: Little, Brown and Company, 1967.

Langton, Kenneth P. *Political Socialization.* New York: Oxford Unixersity Press, 1969.

LaPalombara, Joseph. "Decline of Ideology: A Dissent and an Interpretation," *American Political Science Review,* LX, 1, March 1966.

Leites, Nathan. "Psycho-Cultural Hypotheses About Political Acts," *World Politics,* I, 1, October 1948.

Levin, Martin L. "Social Climates and Political Socialization," *Public Opinion Quarterly,* XXIV, 1961.

Lifton, Robert. "Youth and History: Individual Change in Postwar Japan," *The Challenge of Youth,* ed. Erik H. Erikson. Garden City, New York: Anchor Books, 1965. Originally published in *Daedalus,* Winter 1962.

Lipset, Seymour Martin. *Student Politics.* New York: Basic Books, 1967.

———. "Some Further Comments on 'The End of Ideology,' " *American Political Science Review,* LX, 1, March 1966.

———. *Political Man.* Garden City, New York: Anchor Books, 1963.

——— and Everett Carll Ladd, Jr. "The Political Future of Activist Generations," *The New Pilgrims: Youth Protest in Transition,* ed. Philip G. Altbach and Robert S. Laufer. New York: David McKay Company, 1972.

Litt, Edgar. "Political Cynicism and Political Futility," *Journal of Politics,* XXV, 2, May 1963.

McClosky, Herbert. *Political Inquiry: The Nature and Uses of Survey Research.* Toronto: The Macmillan Company, 1969.

Mainichi Shimbunsha (ed.). *Suchūdento Pawā* (Student Power). Tokyo: Mainichi Shimbunsha, 1968.

Mainichi Shimbun Shakaibu (Ampo Gakusei Han) (ed.). *Ampo: Gekidō no Kono Jūnen* (The Security Treaty: These Ten Years of Upheaval). Tokyo: Bungei Shunjū, 1969.

Manis, Jerome G., and Leo C. Stine. "Suburban Residence and Political Behavior," *Public Opinion Quarterly,* XXII, Winter 1958–59.

Mannheim, Karl. "The Problem of Generations," *Essays On the Sociology of Knowledge.* London: Routledge and Kegan Paul, 1952.

Matsubara Haruo. " 'Youth Power' and the Problem of Identity," *The Japan Interpreter,* VII, 2, Spring 1971.

Merelman, Richard M. "The Development of Political Ideology: A Framework for the Analysis of Political Socialization," *American Political Science Review,* LXIII, 3, September 1969.

Merton, Robert K. *Social Theory and Social Structure.* Glencoe, Illinois: The Free Press, 1949.

Milbrath, Lester W. *Political Participation*. Chicago: Rand McNally & Company, 1965.

Miyajima Takeshi. "Kachi Ishiki ni okeru Sedaiteki Dansō" (The Generation Gap in Value Consciousness), (*Gekkan*) *Rōdō Mondai* (Labor Problems Monthly), December 1969.

Miyata Mitsuo. *Gendai Nihon no Minshushugi*. Tokyo: Iwanami Shinsho, 1969.

Moore, Wilbert E. *Order and Change: Essays in Comparative Sociology*. New York: John Wiley & Sons, 1967.

Nakane, Chie. *Japanese Society*. Berkeley and Los Angeles: University of California Press, 1970.

Newcomb, Theodore. "The Persistence and Regression of Changed Attitudes," *Journal of Social Issues*, XIX, 4, October 1963.

New York Times, June 16, 1970.

Nihon Shakai Minzoku Jiten (Dictionary of Japanese Social Customs). Vol. IV. Seimondō Shinkōsha, 1960.

Nishihara, Shigeki. "Are Young People Becoming More Conservative?," *Journal of Social and Political Ideas in Japan*, II, 3, December 1964.

Oda, Makoto. "The Meaning of Meaningless Death," *Journal of Social and Political Ideas in Japan*, IV, 2, August 1966.

Odaka Kunio. *Nihon no Keiei* (Japanese Management). Tokyo: Chūō Kōronsha, 1965.

Okamura, Tadao. "The Child's Changing Image of the Prime Minister," *The Developing Economies*, VI, 4, December 1968.

Olson, Lawrence. *Dimensions of Japan*. New York: American Universities Field Staff, 1963.

Ōmori Shigeo. "June, 1970," *Japan Quarterly*, XVII, 4, October–December 1970.

Ōno Tsutomu. *Demo ni Uzu-maku Seishun* (Youth in a Whirlpool of Demonstrations). Tokyo, 1968.

————. "Student Protest in Japan—What It Means to Society," *Journal of Social and Political Ideas in Japan*, V, 2–3, December 1967.

Packard, George R. *Protest in Tokyo*. Princeton: Princeton University Press, 1966.

Parsons, Talcott. "Youth in the Context of American Society," *The Challenge of Youth*, ed. Erik H. Erikson. Garden City, New York: Anchor Books, 1965.

Passin, Herbert. *Society and Education in Japan*. New York: Teachers College, Columbia University, 1965.

————. "The Sources of Protest in Japan," *American Political Science Review*, XVI, 2, June 1962.

Pinner, Frank A. "Student Trade Unionism in France, Belgium, and Holland: Anticipatory Socialization and Role-Seeking," *Sociology of Education*, XXXVII, 3, Spring 1964.

Plath, David W. *The After Hours: Modern Japan and the Search for Enjoyment*. Berkeley and Los Angeles: University of California Press, 1964.

"Results of the 1971 Survey on Labor Force Announced," *Japan Report*, XVIII, 10, May 16, 1972.

Rohter, Ira S. "A Social-Learning Theory Approach to the Study of Political Socialization." Paper presented at the annual meeting of the American Political Science Association, September 8–12, 1970, Los Angeles, California.

Rokeach, Milton. "Attitude Change and Behavioral Change," *Public Opinion Quarterly*, XXX, 4, Winter 1966–67.

Rose, Arnold. "Incomplete Socialization," *Sociology and Social Research*, XLIV, 1960.

Rōyama Masamichi. *Yomigaeru Nihon* (Japan Revived). Nihon no Rekishi, XXVI. Tokyo: Chūō Kōronsha, 1967.

Scalapino, Robert A., and Junnosuke Masumi. *Parties and Politics in Contemporary Japan*. Berkeley: University of California Press, 1962.

Schonfeld, William R. "The Focus of Political Socialization Research: An Evaluation," *World Politics*, XXIII, 3, April 1971.

Sekai Daihyakka Jiten (World Encyclopedia). Vol. XXXI. Tokyo: Heibonsha.

Sewell, William H. "Some Recent Developments in Socialization Theory and Research," *Annals of the American Academy of Political and Social Science*, 349, September 1963.

Shakai Mondai Kenkyūkai (ed.). *Zengakuren Kakuha: Gakusei Undō Jiten* (Zengakuren Factions: A Dictionary of the Student Movement). Tokyo: Futabasha, 1969.

Shannon, Donald H. "The Student Revolution in Japan," *Almanac* of the Stanford Alumni Association, November 1969.

Shimizu, Ikutarō. "Ideology in an Age of No Ideology," *Journal of Social and Political Ideas in Japan*, II, 1, April 1964.

Shinohara Hajime. *Nihon no Seiji Fūdo* (The Political Climate of Japan). Tokyo: Iwanami Shinsho, 1968.

Shisō no Kagaku Kenkyūkai. *Tenkō* (Ideological Transformation). 3 vol. Tokyo: Heibonsha, 1959.

Sigel, Roberta S. (ed.). *Learning About Politics*. New York: Random House, 1970.

Sissons, D. C. S. "The Dispute Over Japan's Police Law," *Pacific Affairs*, XXXII, 1, March 1959.

Smith, Thomas C. "Old Values and New Techniques in the Modernization of Japan," *Far Eastern Quarterly*, XIV, 3, May 1955.

Sobol, Marion Gross. "Panel Mortality and Panel Bias," *Journal of the American Statistical Association*, LIV, 285, March 1959.

Spindler, George D. "The Transmission of American Culture," *Education and Culture*, ed. George D. Spindler. New York: Holt, Rinehart and Winston, 1963.

Steiner, Kurt. "Popular Political Participation and Political Development in Japan: The Rural Level," *Political Development in Modern Japan*, ed. Robert E. Ward. Princeton: Princeton University Press, 1968.

Steinhoff, Patricia Golden. "Ideology and Societal Integration in Prewar

Japan." Unpublished Doctor's dissertation, Harvard University, 1969.

Stockwin, J. A. A. "Foreign Policy Perspectives of the Japanese Left: Confrontation or Consensus?," *Pacific Affairs*, XLII, 4, Winter 1969–70.

———. "Is Japan a Post-Marxist Society?," *Pacific Affairs*, XLI, 2, Summer 1968.

Stoetzel, Jean. *Without the Chrysanthemum and the Sword*. New York: Columbia University Press, 1955.

Sumiya Mikio. "The Function and Social Structure of Education: Schools and Japanese Society," *Journal of Social and Political Ideas in Japan*, V, 2–3, December 1967.

Suzuki Hirō. *Gakusei Undō: Daigaku no Kaikaku ka, Shakai no Henkaku ka* (The Student Movement: University Reform or Social Revolution?). Tokyo: Fukumura Shuppan, 1969.

Tachibana Takashi. "Rokujūnen Ampo Eiyū no Eikō to Hisan" (The Glory and the Tragedy of the 1960 Ampo Heroes), *Bungei Shunjū* (Spring and Autumn Culture), XLVII, 2, February 1969.

Takahashi Akira. "Nihon Gakusei Undō no Shisō to Kōdō" (Thought and Behavior of the Japanese Student Movement), *Chūō Kōron* (The Central Review), May, June, August, September 1968.

Takane, Masaaki. "Economic Growth and the 'End of Ideology' in Japan," *Asian Survey*, V, 6, June 1965.

Thayer, Nathaniel B. *How the Conservatives Rule Japan*. Princeton: Princeton University Press, 1969.

Todai Zengaku Kyōtō Kaigi (ed.). *Toride no Ue ni Warera no Sekai o* (Our World on Top of the Fortress). Tokyo, 1969.

Tsurumi, Kazuko. *Social Change and the Individual*. Princeton: Princeton University Press, 1970.

———. "The Japanese Student Movement: (2) Group Portraits," *Japan Quarterly*, XVI, 1, January–March, 1969.

———. "Jiko Kyōiku no ba toshite no Gakusei Undō" (The Student Movement as a Place of Self-Education), *Shisō no Kagaku* (The Science of Thought), 1–2 April, May 1968.

———. "The Japanese Student Movement: (1) Its Milieu," *Japan Quarterly*, XV, 4, October–December, 1968.

———. "Student Movements in 1960 and 1969: Continuity and Change." Research paper, Series A-5, Institute of International Relations, Sophia University, Tokyo, no date.

Tsurumi, Shunsuke. "Cooperative Research on Ideological Transformation," *Journal of Social and Political Ideas in Japan*, II, 1, April, 1964.

Tsurutani, Taketsugu. "A New Era of Japanese Politics: Tokyo's Gubernatorial Election," *Asian Survey*, XII, 5, May 1972.

———. "The Japan Socialist Party in Transition." Paper presented at the annual meeting of the Western Political Science Association, April 8–10, 1971, Albuquerque, New Mexico.

Ukai, Nobushige. "Whither Students of Today," *Contemporary Japan*, XXVI, November 1960.

Verba, Sidney. "Comparative Political Culture," *Political Culture and Political Development*, ed. Lucian W. Pye and Sidney Verba. Princeton: Princeton University Press, 1965.

―――. "Germany: The Remaking of Political Culture," *Political Culture and Political Development*, ed. Lucian W. Pye and Sidney Verba. Princeton: Princeton University Press, 1965.

―――. "The Comparative Study of Political Socialization." Prepared for delivery at the annual meeting of the American Political Science Association, September 9–12, 1964, Chicago.

Vogel, Ezra F. *Japan's New Middle Class*. 2d. edition. Berkeley and Los Angeles: University of California Press, 1971.

―――. "Entrance Examinations and Emotional Disturbances in Japan's 'New Middle Class,'" *Japanese Culture: Its Development and Characteristics*, ed. Robert J. Smith and Richard K. Beardsley. Chicago: Aldine Publishing Company, 1962.

Ward, Robert E. "Reflections on the Allied Occupation and Planned Political Change in Japan," *Political Development in Modern Japan*, ed. Robert E. Ward. Princeton: Princeton University Press, 1968.

―――. "Japan: The Continuity of Modernization," *Political Culture and Political Development*, ed. Lucian W. Pye and Sidney Verba. Princeton: Princeton University Press, 1965.

――― and Dankwart A. Rustow. *Political Modernization in Japan and Turkey*. Princeton: Princeton University Press, 1964.

Watanuki Joji. *Gendai Seiji To Shakai Hendō* (Contemporary Politics and Social Change). 2d ed. Tokyo: Tokyo Daigaku Shuppankai, 1967.

―――. "Patterns of Politics in Present-Day Japan," *Party Systems and Voter Alignments: Cross-National Perspectives*, ed. Seymour M. Lipset and Stein Rokkan. New York: The Free Press, 1967.

Yabe, Teiji. "Background of Recent Mass Demonstrations," *Contemporary Japan*, XXVI, November 1960.

Yanaga, Chitoshi. *Big Business in Japanese Politics*. New Haven: Yale University Press, 1968.

Yasuda Saburō (ed.). *Shakai Chōsa Handobukko* (Social Survey Handbook). Tokyo, 1969.

Yoshino, M. Y. *Japan's Managerial System*. Cambridge, Massachusetts: The MIT Press, 1968.

Zeisel, Hans. "The Panel," *Sociological Methods: A Sourcebook*, ed. Norman K. Denzin. Chicago: Aldine Publishing Company, 1970.

"Zengakuren: Where Are They Now?," *The Japan Times*, November 16, 1967.

INDEX